DATE DUE

MAY 27 2010			
OCT 24 2010			

Demco, Inc. 38-293

MAR 1 6 2010

Women, Advertising and Representation

Beyond Familiar Paradigms

Women, Advertising and Representation

Beyond Familiar Paradigms

Edited by

Sue Abel

Marjan deBruin

Anita Nowak

HAMPTON PRESS, INC.
CRESSKILL, NJ 07626

Printed in the United States of America

Library of Congress Cataloging-in-Publication Data

Women, advertising and representation : beyond familiar paradigms / edited by Sue
Abel, Marjan deBruin, Anita Nowak.
     p. cm. — (The Hampton Press communication series)
    Includes bibliographical references and index.
    ISBN 978-1-57273-927-7 (hardbound) — ISBN 978-1-57273-928-4 (paperbound)
    1. Women.   2. Mass media and women.   3. Feminism and mass media.   I. Abel,
Sue.   II. Bruin, Marjan de.   III. Nowak, Anita.
    HQ1180.W6516 2009
    302.23082—dc22   2009028104

Hampton Press, Inc.
23 Broadway
Cresskill, NJ 07626

Contents

Acknowledgments

The editors would like to express their appreciation to all the authors who have contributed to this book. The process has been lengthy and at times difficult, and we are grateful for their good-humoured patience.

Introduction

Sue Abel, Marjan de Bruin, and Anita Nowak

With the exception of pornography and violence in children's programming, no other form of mass communication has received as much condemnation as advertising—so much so that "the list of sins committed by advertising is limited only by the creativity of its critics" (Kirkpatrick, 1990, p. 508). Sarcasm aside, an exhaustive review of work criticizing advertising shows that the industry has been upbraided on many counts, including the role it plays in cultivating a materialist society based on the ethos of consumption at the expense of social and spiritual pursuits and beliefs; creating cynicism in people by idealizing the "good life" and promising it is easily attainable through the continuous purchase of commodities; hypnotizing individuals into patterns of irrational behavior, most significantly the compulsion to consume unneeded products; promoting greed, envy, false pride and selfishness; reinforcing stereotypes through simplistic conventions and representations; and leaving the greater population perpetually dissatisfied, with feelings of inadequacy, insecurity, and anxiety (Hovland & Wilcox, 1990).

In the same way that a general discussion about the effects of advertising is fraught with contentious accusations, so, too, is the specific discussion concerning the implications of women's portrayal in advertising (Bignell, 1997; Budgeon, 1994; LaTour & Ford, 1993; Lin, 1999; Maynard & Taylor, 1999). In fact, after decades of research and theorizing, this topic remains. The aim of this volume, therefore, is to contribute to this ongoing scholarly dialogue.

Studies into the portrayal of women in advertising have tended to fall into one of three categories—content analysis, audience-centered media effects research, and critical and cultural studies—each with their respective strengths and weaknesses.

Content Analysis

Since the 1960s, the findings of many large-scale content analyses have concluded that women are portrayed as passive, self-subordinating, and less competent and intellectual than are men. Women are seemingly obsessed with their physical appearance, and are often portrayed as sex objects (Brittain McKee, & Pardun, 1999; Walsh-Childers, 1995). Indeed, sexually explicit imagery of women is three times more common that sexually explicit imagery of men (Reichert, Lambiase, Morgan, Carstaphen, & Zavoina, 1999). Women are also depicted as being dependent on men, their place is seen to be in the home, and they do not make important decisions (Lin, 1999). As a whole, then, women are depicted in highly gendered roles and are often stereotyped (Belknap & Leonard, 1991; Demarest & Garner, 1992), despite the recent introduction of the "egalitarian woman" who shares household responsibilities with her mate (Jaffe & Berger, 1994) or the "superwoman" (i.e., working mothers who can "do it all").

As a whole, then, content analyses have been extremely important in providing quantifiable evidence of problematic representations of women in advertising. Yet, as a research method, it is limited on several counts. First, it has little to say about the social, cultural, and discursive construction of women within representational systems (Jhally, 1994). Second, it fails to discuss the implications of the media's portrayal of women. As such, both effects studies and cultural studies have tried to compensate for these limitations.

Effects Studies

As O'Sullivan, Hartley, Saunders, Montgomery, and Fiske (1994) explained, "Effects is a heavily loaded term, traditionally and still commonly used to refer to the supposed direct consequences and impact of media messages on individuals" (p. 100). In terms of addressing the portrayal of women in advertising, effects research has attempted to establish a causal relationship between exposure to idealised images of women and body dissatisfaction, lowered self-esteem/body image, and/or an increase in the incidence of eating-disordered behaviors (Botta, 1999; Gustafson, Popovich, & Thomsen, 1999; Martin & Gentry, 1997). Effects research has also tried to confirm social comparison and cultivation theory (Hitchon & Reaves, 1999).

Although research findings first appeared to be rather conclusive with respect to some of the detrimental effects of advertising on women, including raised comparison standards for attractiveness and lowered satisfaction with one's own appearance (Richins, 1991), several subsequent studies have rejected this negative effects hypothesis. Instead, scholars purport that media images do not similarly affect all women's body esteem (Henderson-King & Henderson-King, 1997). Furthermore, it has been shown that women are now accustomed to seeing ultra-thin models

(Gustafson et al., 1999) and, therefore, give them little regard. Despite these claims, plenty of research studies continue to confirm that the media do indeed have an impact on body-image disturbance (Botta, 1999).

Although these studies have made important statements about the effects of advertising's portrayal of women, they are problematic owing to their reliance on statistical evidence stemming from tests of immediate impacts within artificially controlled environments. This is a significant weakness because results and conclusions fail to take into account important factors such as social, historical, and cultural contexts. Furthermore, the effects model, too, makes no attempt to understand the social construction of meaning, nor is it grounded in theory.

Cultural Studies

The last category of research into the media's portrayal of women is that of cultural studies. Broadly speaking, cultural studies focuses on how "social divisions are made meaningful" by investigating how class, gender, race, and other inequalities are represented and naturalised (O'Sullivan et al., 1994). Cultural studies is also concerned with the personal and societal implications of advertising (Duffy, 1994) and problematizes the portrayal of women within the context of ideology, hegemony, power, patriarchy, and class structures (McGuigan, 1997; Storey, 1993).

In the early stages of feminist cultural and communication studies—that is, the 1960–1970s—research was overwhelmingly concerned with the underrepresentation of women working in the media industries (King, 1992; Meyers, 1999; van Zoonen, 1994). Thus, one practical aim of research was to call attention to the scant number of women employed in advertising agencies to help theorize why "negative" and "detrimental" gender stereotypes were so prevalent. There was little concern at that time about the nature of representation *per se*, nor the social construction of gendered identities.

With the advent of semiotics, however, or the "science of signs" as introduced by Peirce and de Saussure, and later popularized by Barthes, came the "systematic analysis of symbolic systems" (Manning & Cullum-Swan, 1998). This included studying the representation of women in advertising, and it was through such analysis that the female body was shown to possess powerful cultural signs and political connotations (Balsamo, 1997; van Zoonen, 1994). There was a move away from the documentation of negative and stereotyped portrayals of women toward an examination of the multiplicities of meanings and interpretive possibilities (Danuta Walters, 1999).

By the late 1980s and early 1990s, textual analyses (variously informed by semiotics, structuralism, psychoanalytic and poststructuralist theories) came under increasing scrutiny and criticism. Semiotics, in particular, came under attack for assuming a correct or true reading of media texts that laypeople were unable to elicit without the help of a trained scholar because they were "in the grip of ideology" (Bignell, 1997). This era was, therefore, marked by a paradigm shift toward perspectives in which meaning was understood to be constructed out of historically and socially situated positionalities (van Zoonen, 1994). Contemporaneously, feminist cultural and communication studies are concerned with how ideology continues to be produced and circulated through the mass media, and how audiences negotiate with various forms of media products and texts to become constructors of meaning.

This Volume

As the title of this book suggests, one of its aims is to go beyond the familiar paradigms of writing about women in advertising. To this end, we have selected works that offer a unique approach to analyzing individual ads or entire advertising campaigns, studies that look at advertising audiences in both the Western and non-Western world (including Indonesia, Japan, Turkey, Singapore, and rural India), and research that focuses on less traditional forms of advertising (i.e., promotional flyers and merchandise). To provide context to this volume, in Chapter 1, Anita Nowak, Sue Abel, and Marjan de Bruin delineate a useful framework in which to consider the topic of women/representation/advertising.

In Chapter 2, Isabelle Wallace explores issues of the representation of women and cloning in her close textual analysis of a Versace advertising campaign shot by the often controversial fashion photographer Steven Meisel. Previous writing about Meisel's images has centered on issues of ethics and censorship (as in, e.g., the Opium ad featuring Sophie Dahl, in 1999), or on the leaky boundary between advertising and art (exemplified in this instance when the Versace campaign Wallace discusses was exhibited in a prestigious London Art Gallery). Wallace, on the other hand, is more interested in the idea of "sameness" encoded into the Versace images through the choice of models, their poses, and the general styling and composition of the photographs. She argues that these ads function "as a meditation on ideas of sex and gender at a moment when these concepts are being radically renegotiated by the possibility of cloning and genetic engineering." She also explores the implications of cloning, and how these play out in ideas of sex and gender in Meisel's campaign.

Taking as her definition for pornography "the sexually explicit subordination of women," Jane Caputi (Chap. 3) argues from a radical feminist perspective that many of the advertising images we regularly see around us are, as her title suggests, "everyday pornography." In a wide-ranging account of social practices and ideologies as well as their visual manifestation on magazine covers and in posters and advertising images, Caputi discusses the pursuit of hypermasculinity in contemporary society, that is, a form of masculinity that endorses male violence. She argues: "Whenever there is a strong woman, there is a weak and castrated man—male potency veritably requires female impotence." To her, the advertising representations she discusses are another form of violence, akin to the emotional abuse in interpersonal relationships that "feeds the sense of omnipotence of the dominators."

In Chapter 4, Birgit Pretzsch narrows her focus to the figure of Lara Croft, the star of action-adventure computer games and movies. Croft, as with other action heroines in popular culture, has been the center of debates about whether she is "a liberating feminist icon" or "a reactionary object of male desire." Pretzsch explores this question by analyzing the advertising and marketing of Lara Croft in television and Internet ads and posters, and the merchandise associated with the Tomb Raider franchise. She then expands the debate to consider the representation of Lara Croft in terms of postmodern notions of the body, identity, and reality itself. Pretzsch argues that while challenging some traditional social codes of femininity, Lara also reinforces others. Therefore, although she does have the potential to be a feminist icon, advertising and marketing construct her more as an object of male desire, thus limiting her capacity to act as a liberatory source of identity. Nevertheless, like Caputi, Pretzsch concludes that there are cracks that allow for subversive readings.

In Chapter 5, Todd Holden elaborates on Goffman's classic "genderisms" by identifying "an associative set" of confluent signs in the thousands of Japanese television ads he collected and analysed over more than a decade. He contends: "Women are depicted as efficacious—and therefore most powerful—in watery environments, whereas men are presented as most potent in landed contexts." Holden's semiotic approach indicates strategies in gender representation in Japanese ads that are "more than merely a stylized way of selling a product." Rather, they clearly adhere to certain rules of encoding rooted in cultural mythology. His analysis of a sample exceeding 5,000 ads convincingly illustrates how contemporary Japanese TV advertising "wraps men and women in a discourse of power, one that revolves around—and in large part is defined by—the physical spaces which they inhabit."

While living in Japan, Fabienne Darling-Wolf was fascinated by the presence of Western images and even language in Japanese advertisements and the obvious question of how Japanese viewers and readers negotiate these imported Western representations and artifacts. Her study (Chap. 6), which acknowledges the possible biases inherent to her as a White Western scholar, brings to the foreground the voices of rural Japanese women and shows how "these women negotiated their gendered, cultural and racial identity through their consumption of Western-influenced Japanese popular cultural texts." Based on her 8 months of in-depth interviews and participant observation, she shares "the complexity of the relationship between producer and audiences and the multi-faceted nature of identity formation." Her female subjects, who live in southern, rural Japan and belong to the relatively lower echelons of the Japanese socioeconomic order, reflect on advertising imagery found in popular women's magazine and television programs. Their comments make it clear how rich and sometimes contradictory and ambiguous the range of audience interpretations can be, and how this very ambiguity seems to exert influence on negotiated identity formation.

A different process of exoticizing is the red thread in Damla Isik's study of a selection of Internet sites that romanticize the Turkish village carpet industry by displaying "carpets and women to the Western gaze." In Chapter 7, Isik describes how "the stereotypical and inaccurate representation of village women as happy and content contributors to both family income and national heritage is used as a tool to sell a traditional image of Turkey to the Western consumer." Using a detailed analysis of Web sites, she demonstrates how this "magical" layer of meaning, suggesting authenticity and original, traditional craftsmanship creates stereotypical and ahistorical representations of rural Turkish women—driven by an ideology of mediation and control. Referring to Barthes, and comparing the images of this industry with facts and figures reflecting the Turkish reality, Isik reminds us of what has been erased or is hidden from the portrayals we see.

In Chapter 8, Wiwik Sushartami explores the complex process of gender-identity formation in contemporary Indonesian society through an analysis of representations of single women in Indonesian advertisements in the period from 1996 to 1998, a time of political upheaval that culminated in the downfall of the long-running New Order regime in Indonesia. She sets out the intersecting trajectories of a gender ideology, which clearly differentiates between single and married women, leading to the marginalization of single women, and then explores advertising's use of single women in narratives that work to sexualize and/or trivialize important political issues, while reconstructing them as benevolent. Her case study is of three ads that are skillfully connected by advertisers to three historical and tragic events (a food shortage crisis, the mass rape of Chinese Indonesian women, and the struggle for independence of East Timor). She concludes that the use of single women in the ads helped to "reconstruct them as politically 'neutral' signifiers. The meaning of reform as equated with freedom of expression has thus been replaced with freedom to consume."

Given that television advertising in India is mostly designed for the urban middle and upper class—"an elitist urban audience with purchasing power"—the advertising industry has not yet developed an effective strategy to reach rural audiences. Therefore, it is fascinating to read a study on television reception among rural (agrarian) women in Baruraj, a small village in India. In Chapter 9, Ila Patel uses a combination of qualitative methods (i.e., focus groups, in-depth interviews, participant observation, and rapid rural appraisal methods) to understand the reception behavior of this particular audience. Her findings illustrate how contextual variables of rural women's access to television, such as the broader context of the village and the gendered context of their households, mediate their television viewing habits. Studies such as Patel's are essential for building a reliable body of reflection and new insights, necessary to lead to sound theory formation.

Too many of our accepted theories are based on evidence gathered in a selection of Western societies, relevant to narrow social and economic contexts. Too rarely have we tried to challenge some of the standard notions used in reception studies by investigating non-Western audiences in their unique social, cultural, political, and economical situations. As with that of Darling-Wolf, Patel's study is a valuable step toward redressing the balance.

In Chapter 10, Anita Nowak explores the representation of "plus-size" women in *Mode* magazine advertisements placing emphasis on the reception of these ads by women in two different cultural contexts: Canada and Singapore. Based on the results of 30 interviews that involved using a metaphor-elicitation technique, Nowak's study reveals that women from these two distinct countries, of various ethnic origins, ages, professions, and educational backgrounds, have a tendency to read advertisements featuring plus-size women rather consistently. That is, women in *Mode* are in line with age-old stereotypes of femininity and maternity. Interestingly, however, the same results also support the notion of "polysemic" reading, but only in terms of individual advertisements, and not for the group of ads as a whole. This finding suggests an interplay, rather than dichotomy, between the power of the text and the power of the audience. Thus, Nowak posits that audience meaning-making activities are simultaneously—albeit to varying degrees—dependent on three things: the openness of the text, the positionality of the reader, and the relevant social discourses to which each reader is privy.

Advertisements in *Mode* magazine appear again in Chapter 11 by Vickie Shields and Dawn Heinecken. Together, they examine the increasingly prevalent advertising strategy that advertisers use to reach a modern female audience, namely feminist rhetoric and signifiers of gender equality. A common mechanism to do this, the authors argue, is by incorporating a "wink" into ads—whereby the wider political challenge of feminism is ignored. As Shields and Heinecken point out, many contemporary ads seemingly promote women's empowerment, but they nonetheless still promote traditional notions of female beauty and often "actually work to reconfirm the status quo by co-opting signifiers and reattaching them to regressive, patriarchal codes." Shields and Heinecken demonstrate the wink strategy in action through an analysis of *Special K* ads as well as those found in *Mode* magazine, while also acknowledging the more recent complexity of ads that portray body sizes outside the slender ideal. As a point of departure, they then move on to discuss an advertising campaign produced for the National Abortion and Reproductive Rights Action League (NARAL) in the United States which flips the coin in that it co-opts the traditional American ideology of individualism, freedom, choice, and nurturing motherhood to put forward an argument in favor of abortion. The authors contend that the "PSA [public service announcement] by NARAL can stand alone as counter-hegemonic, because in the end the social political agenda is the product and in all other advertising conditions the profit motive inherent in ads must water down the progressive political potential of those ads."

The final chapter, Chapter 12, returns again to a nontraditional form of advertising, and also to issues of pornography. In metropolitan Montreal, Canada, Aurélie Lebrun collected and analyzed 1,000 flyers for "Ladies Nights" and argues that these leaflets advertise much more than a time and place for nocturnal events. Rather, she contends that they serve as "technology that produces both a heteronormative night landscape—where going out equates with having sex—and heteronormative identities." In so doing, "Ladies Nights," which were originally claimed by feminists, have "been usurped and re-appropriated by heteronormative culture." Using distinct categories of representation, Lebrun describes how the flyers seem to suggest, at first glance, the sexual empowerment of women, but ultimately turn out to merely reaffirm men's dominance of night spaces through an exploitative powerful male gaze, contributing to the overall "pornophication of public space."

References

Balsamo, A. (1997). *Technologies of the gendered bodies: Reading cyborg women*. Durham, NC: Duke University Press.

Belknap, P., & Leonard, W. M. (1991). A conceptual replication and extension of Erving Goffman's study of gender advertisements. *Sex Roles, 25*(3/4), 103–118.

Bignell, J. (1997). *Media semiotics: An introduction*. New York: Manchester University Press.

Botta, R. A. (1999). Television images and adolescent girls' body image disturbance. *Journal of Communication, 49*(2), 22–41.

Brittain McKee, K., & Pardun, C. J. (1999). Face-ism reconsidered: Facial prominence and body emphasis of males and females in magazine advertising. In M. G. Carstaphen & S. C. Zavoina (Eds.), *Sexual rhetoric: Media perspectives on sexuality, gender and identity* (pp. 109–121). Westport, CT: Greenwood Press.

Budgeon, S. (1994). Fashion magazine advertising: Constructing femininity in the "post-feminist" era. In A. Manca & L. Manca (Eds.), *Gender utopias in advertising: A critical reader* (pp. 55–70). Syracuse, NY: Procopian Press.

Danuta Walters, S. (1999). Sex, text and context: (In) between feminism and cultural studies. In M. M. Ferree, J. Lorber, & B. B. Hess (Eds.), *Revisioning gender* (pp. 222–257). Thousand Oaks, CA: Sage.

Demarest, J., & Garner, J. (1992). The representation of women's roles in women's magazines over the past 30 years. *The Journal of Psychology, 126*(4), 357–368.

Gustafson, R., Popovich, M., & Thomsen, S. (1999). The "thin ideal." *Marketing News, 33*(6), 22–24.

Henderson-King, E., & Henderson-King, D. (1997). Media effects on women's body esteem: Social and individual difference factors. *Journal of Applied Social Psychology, 27*(5), 399–417.

Hitchon, J., & Reaves, S. (1999). Media mirage: The thin ideal as digital manipulation. In M. G. Carstaphen & S. C. Zavoina (Eds.), *Sexual rhetoric: Media perspectives on sexuality, gender, and identity* (pp. 65–76). Westport, CT: Greenwood Press.

Hovland, R., & Wilcox, G. B. (1990). *Advertising in society: Classic and contemporary readings on advertising's role in society.* Lincolnwood, IL: NTC Business Books.

Jaffe, L. J., & Berger, P. D. (1994, July/August). The effect of modern female sex role portrayals on advertising effectiveness. *Journal of Advertising Research*, *34*(4), 32–42.

Jhally, S. (1994). Intersections of discourse: MTV, sexual politics and dreamworlds. In J. Cruz & J. Lewis (Eds.), *Viewing, reading, listening: Audiences and cultural reception* (pp. 151–168). Boulder, CO: Westview Press.

King, C. (1992). The politics of representation: A democracy of the gaze. In F. Bonner, L. Goodman, R. Allen, L. Janes, & C. King (Eds.), *Imagining women: Cultural representations and gender* (pp. 131–139). Cambridge: The Open University Press.

Kirkpatrick, J. (1990). Philosophic defence of advertising. In R. Hovland & G. B. Wilcox (Eds.), *Advertising in society: Classic and contemporary readings on advertising's role in society* (pp. 508–520). Lincolnwood, IL: NTC Business Books.

LaTour, M. S., & Ford, J. B. (1993). Differing reactions to female role portrayals in advertising. *Journal of Advertising Research*, *33*(3), 43–52.

Lin, C. (1999). The portrayal of women in television advertising. In M. Meyers (Ed.), *Mediated women: Representation in popular culture* (pp. 253–276). Cresskill, NJ: Hampton Press.

Manning, P. K., & Cullum-Swan, B. (1998). Narrative, content and semiotic analysis. In N. K. Denzin & Y. S. Lincoln (Eds.), *Collecting and interpreting qualitative materials* (pp. 246–273). Thousand Oaks, CA: Sage.

Martin, M. C., & Gentry, J. W. (1997). Stuck in the model trap: The effects of beautiful models in ads on female pre-adolescents and adolescents. *Journal of Advertising*, *26*(2), 19–33.

Maynard, M. L., & Taylor, C. R. (1999). Girlish images across cultures: Analysing Japanese versus U.S *Seventeen* magazine ads. *Journal of Advertising*, *28*(1), 39–48.

McGuigan, J. (Ed.). (1997). *Cultural methodologies.* London: Sage.

Meyers, M. (Ed.). (1999). *Mediated women: Representation in popular culture.* Cresskill, NJ: Hampton Press.

O'Sullivan, T., Hartley, J., Saunders, D., Montgomery, M., & Fiske, J. (1994). *Key concepts in communication and cultural studies.* London: Routledge.

Reichart, T., Lambiase, J., Morgan, S., Carstaphen, M., & Zavoina, S. (1999). Cheesecake and beefcake: No matter how you slice it, sexual explicitness in advertising continues to increase. *Journalism and Mass Communication Quarterly*, *76*(1), 7–20.

Richins, M. L. (1991). Social comparison and the idealized images of advertising. *Journal of Consumer Research*, *18*, 71–83.

Storey, J. (1993). *An introductory guide to cultural theory and popular culture.* Athens: University of Georgia Press.

van Zoonen, L. (1994). *Feminist media studies.* London: Sage.

Walsh-Childers, K. (1995). Women as sex partners. In P. M. Lester (Ed.), *Images that injure: Pictorial stereotypes in the media* (pp. 81–85). Westport: Praeger.

1

Contextualizing Women/ Advertising/Representation

Anita Nowak, Sue Abel and Marjan de Bruin

The last four decades have generated a significant amount of research about the representation of women in the media, mostly from feminists and poststructuralists who challenge the idea that true and/or essential gender identities exist. Much of this theorizing was set in motion by the Foucauldian project (Bailey, 1993; Ramazanoglu, 1993). Most feminists and poststructuralists argue that markers of identity such as gender are merely "culturally constructed" (Lorber & Farrell, 1991) because, unlike sex, which is predicated on biological criteria, gender refers to the socially prescribed roles, behaviors, preferences, and the like, attributed to men and women in a given culture (Baron & Byrne, 1997; Mackie, 1987; Yanagisako & Delaney, 1995). One notable exception is Judith Butler (1990) who does not view sex differently from gender.

This means that the characteristics traditionally associated with masculinity (i.e., being active and rational) and femininity (i.e., being passive and emotional), and assumed to be natural and biologically founded are, in fact, culturally constructed and variable. Thus, every woman is "the site of a multiplicity of subject positions proposed to her by the discourses with which she is confronted; her identity is the precarious and contradictory result of the specific set of subject positions she inhabits at any moment in history" (Ang, 1990, p. 84).

For many years, a significant body of research has asserted that the mass media are important tools of gender socialization. For example, it is often said that women's preoccupation with appearance is rooted in their experience with the mass media (Halprin, 1995). The overarching argument is that media texts work as "forms of pedagogy" (Kellner, 1995b), teaching and influencing the attitudes, behaviors, worldviews, values, and self-image of readers and viewers (Belknap & Leonard, 1991; Merskin, 1999; Pearson, West, & Turner, 1995), especially those of young people (Barrie, 1995; Buerkel-Rothfuss, 1993; Buijzen & Valkenburg, 2003). Moreover, because it is believed that the images seen in the mass media play a central role in structuring social subjectivity (Schwoch, White, & Reilly, 1992), as well as defining individuals and who they strive to be (Carstaphen & Zavoina, 1999), the media are seen not simply to reflect or represent gender differences, but rather, to help constitute them (Budgeon, 1994; Schwoch et al., 1992). In other words, gender is both a central perceptual filter and a social organizer (Rutledge Shields, 1990).

Advertising in particular, is considered a creator of dominant attitudes, values, ideology, social norms, and myths by which most people govern their behavior. Although gender representations in advertising have potential negative implications for both males and females, feminist scholars argue that advertising is part of a system that consolidates gender inequality by being "the most visible and most constant evidence of social and sexist mythologies [and] the clearest evidence of patriarchal ideology" (Humm, 1989, p. 4). Many feminists have therefore been waging what MacDonald (1995) called "a guerrilla war against advertising" (p. 87). Notably, the study of men's portrayal in advertising, and the media more generally, has begun to flourish in recent years, exposing how sexist mythologies work to define and bind men into socially sanctioned "male" roles as well (e.g., Clare, 2000; Lambiase et al., 1999; Lester, 1995; Manca & Manca, 1994).

Women/Advertising/Representation

The representation of women in advertising is condemned for a host of reasons including:

1. The role it plays in stereotyping, trivializing and symbolically annihilating women (Barrie, 1995; Belknap & Leonard, 1991; Demarest & Garner, 1992; Meyers, 1999).

2. Gratuitously emphasizing and objectifying women's bodies and their sexuality (Brittain McKee & Pardun, 1999; Reichert, Lambiase, Morgan, Carstaphen, & Zavoina, 1999; Whipple, 1992).

3. Symbolically dismembering women's bodies and the disembodiment of their identities (Caputi, 1999; Lin, 1999).

4. Creating a "cult of thin" and holding women hostage to deliberately unattainable beauty ideals (Botta, 1999; Faludi, 1991; Gustafson, Popovich, & Thomsen, 1999; Halprin, 1995; Hitchon & Reaves, 1999; Lazier & Gagnard Kendrick, 1993; Wolf, 1990).

5. Glamorizing violence against women and perpetuating the rape myth (Caputi, 1999; Kilbourne, 1999; Sarabia, 1995); eroticizing young girls (Walsh-Childers, 1995).

6. Exploiting "lesbian-chic" (Reichert, Maly, & Zavoina, 1999; Rutledge Shields, 1990).

7. Appropriating feminist discourse for the sale of commodities, thereby depoliticizing the feminist project (Dines & Humez, 1995; Goldman, Heath, & Smith, 1991), and so on.

In addition, research conducted around the world has shown that such problematic portrayals of women are remarkably consistent (Barrie, 1995; The International Women's Media Foundation, 1998; Suzuki, 1995; Zacharias, 1994). It is even argued that research itself on gender portrayals is replete with masculine bias owing to male-oriented conventions of writing and data collection (Duffy, 1994). In summary, then, advertising is seen as a significant and pervasive cultural institution that represents, exploits, and oppresses women in unacceptable ways (Kates & Shaw-Garlock, 1999).

What makes these findings so significant, however, as many scholars have pointed out, are the implications these depictions have on the manifest lives of women (Balsamo, 1997; Barthel, 1988; Budgeon, 1994; Humm, 1989). French philosopher Simone de Beauvoir articulated as early as 1949, how "woman" is "defined and differentiated with reference to man and not he with reference to her; she is the incidental, the inessential as opposed to the essential. He is the Subject, he is the Absolute—she is the Other" (1993, p. xxxix). Since the publication of de Beauvoir's classic text, *The Second Sex*, the notion of woman as "Other" has been widely used by feminists to explain the overall devaluation of women in society and the subsequent inequitable distribution of resources, power, opportunities, and rights between the sexes.

Hence, "when we ask 'What is a woman,' we are really asking questions about ideology: about how discourse has contoured the category of 'woman' and about what is at stake—politically, economically and socially—in maintaining or dismissing that category" (Conboy, Medina, & Stanbury, 1997, p. 1). Moreover, when feminist scholars analyze and theorize the female body under a political lens, known as "doing body politics,"[1] they do so to demonstrate how it is a crucial site on which culture and ideology are inscribed (Darling-Wolf, 2000), and to argue how its social constructedness serves to delimit the real lives of women.

For example, McCracken (1993) explained that fashion magazines and advertising constitute a wide-reaching cultural force that socialize women throughout several decades of their lives into becoming dependable consumers by juxtaposing beauty ideals and their female inadequacies. Disch (1997) concurred: "Few women believe they have acceptable bodies, and the media nurture this insecurity and self-hatred, pounding away at the expectation of perfection, leading people to see themselves as imperfect objects" (p. 132). Notably, these "images of female bodily perfection and messages of perfectibility exercise control over women's lives by constructing a self that is distorted and divided against itself, self-policing and self-destructive" (Valentine, 1994, p. 113). Bartky (1998) took this one step further: "In contemporary patriarchal culture, a panoptical male connoisseur resides within the consciousness of most women: they stand perpetually before his gaze and under his judgment" (p. 34).

This is why Bordo (1997) asserted, "the discipline and normalization of the female body . . . has to be acknowledged as an amazingly durable and flexible strategy of social control," with both political and psychological consequences for women (Saltzberg & Chrisler, 1997). Indeed, "the current scenario makes women morally accountable for making their bodies comply with an idealized image trumpeted and managed by the mass media . . . [and] failure to exercise appropriate self-restraint becomes internalized as a character flaw" (Goldman, 1992, p. 111). Additionally, it is argued that this social emphasis on appearance distracts women from achieving other important goals and developing an intrinsic self-worth (Greer, 1999; Wolf, 1990), especially because as girls/women construct a self-concept, they assimilate cultural ideals that inferiorize the feminine (Callaghan, 1994). Finally, women are seen by some to be accomplices in their own repression (Bordo, 1993), which is why feminists have been staunch about the connection between patriarchal images of female beauty and women's oppression and have identified it as an obstacle to women's full and complete liberation (Callaghan, 1994). Without a doubt, beauty, appearance, and representation have become politically charged issues for feminists, to such an extent that Humm (1989) contended that theories about the social, political, and metaphysical control of women's bodies by patriarchy are central to the feminist project and it is through feminist theory that work about the body has become legitimized and entrenched into critical thinking (Orbach, 1978; Probyn, 1992), arguably transforming Western intellectual paradigms (Bordo, 1993).

Women/**Advertising**/Representation

Advertising is a gargantuan industry that continues to grow: in 1993, annual sales were reported to be $150 billion in America alone (Lazier & Gagnard Kendrick, 1993) and by 2005, the Association of National Advertisers (ANA) estimated that advertising spending by businesses in the United States would reach approximately $278 billion (http://www.ana.net/). Advertising, however, had a much more humble beginning.

The word *advertising* is a Latin derivative of *adverto* and *advertere*, meaning to turn, the implication being, to call attention to something (Barnard, 1995). Advertising today, is defined as "the promotion of goods or services for sale through impersonal media" (Cook, 1992, p. xiv), and its sole purpose is to sell something. In fact, "*everything* that is in [an] advertisement, is subordinated to this purpose" (McAllister, 1996, p. 57; italics added). Williams (1993) noted in his classic paper, *Advertising: The Magic System*, originally published in 1961, that from the end of the 15th century until the early 1900s, advertising was essentially informative in nature, or of the classified kind. By the 1920s, a qualitative shift in advertising had taken place and from that point forward, it no longer merely informed the public about the availability, price, location, and qualities of products and services. Instead, it began to entice consumers to buy products based on their "symbolic significance" (Barnard, 1995). Furthermore, it had evolved to the point whereby it was involved in "the teaching of social and personal values" (Williams, 1993). An elaboration of these ideas follows, but first, a brief description of advertising as a form of communication is warranted.

As alluded to earlier, the main objective of contemporary advertising is to encode a message about a product/service in a way that will inform and persuade potential consumers of its existence and benefits, with the primary aim of increasing sales of that product/service. Simultaneously, advertisers hope their message will be decoded accurately and positively by the target market. Put simply, "an advertiser's aim is to capture our attention and favourably dispose us to a product or service" (Dyer, 1988, p. 96). Although this may sound rather straightforward, marketers and advertisers adamantly insist that the successful transmission of advertising messages is challenging at best. First, there is environmental noise to contend with, referred to as ad clutter, whereby the ubiquity of advertising, within an already over-saturated media environment, hampers communication effectiveness as marketers compete for consumers' attention (Jhally, 1995; Stewart & Ward, 1994). Second, even if consumers see/hear/read their advertisements, advertisers argue they have no control over the reception and decoding of them (Stewart & Ward, 1994).

Advertisers also see their work in simple economic terms and defend their industry by arguing that advertising is integral to postindustrial market economies. They do not view their industry as a creator of needs, but rather as one that merely communicates how consumer needs may be met in the marketplace. Yet, others retort: "To think that the effects of advertising . . . could be limited to economics, is as absurd as assuming that the effects of a hot climate upon a culture could be limited to tropical diseases" (Kuhns, 1970, cited in Hovland & Wilcox, 1990, p. 447). We know the goal of advertising is to strengthen the uniqueness of products/ services by focusing on something more compelling than the commodity itself. Even standard advertising textbooks emphasize the importance of understanding consumer motives, needs, self-concepts, and so on, in order to design effective advertising campaigns (Wells, Burnett, & Moriarty, 1995). As such, the notion that advertising merely informs consumers about products, then, seems to hold little weight and explains why critical scholars have long contended that advertising plays a much greater social role than advertisers are willing to admit.

According to critical theorists, one of the media's most pervasive ideological messages is that of consumption as a way of life (Dines & Humez, 1995; Kellner, 1995a; Manca & Manca, 1994; McAllister, 1996). Advertising, in particular, is criticized because it is believed to encourage people to view consumption under a positive light, while ultimately serving the interests of the powerful and ruling class (Bignell, 1997). And, as Kellner (1995a) explained, ironically, consumers end up paying for "the entire corporate infrastructure . . . actually subsidizing the very industries that indoctrinate and exploit [them]" (p. 348). Critics further posit that the ensuing commodity fetishism and capitalist hegemony that characterizes contemporary postindustrial society, comes at the expense of other more socially productive activities and pursuits, such as spirituality and a sense of community.

Advertising is also seen as fixated on selling "utopian visions of the 'here-after' " (MacCurdy, 1994, p. 32), by promising consumers that money spent on goods will buy happiness, love, security, peace of mind, peer acceptance, and hip-ness (McAllister, 1996). Consumer culture sells "antidotes to sadness, happiness in edible form, soul-numbing comfort" (Greer, 1999, p. 218) and advertising offers "ever-new possibilities, no longer via hard work but via the purchase of the right products" (Kilbourne, 1999, p. 132). Kilbourne added that advertising transforms statements about objects into statements about human kinship, to the point where relationships are "trivialized and we are encouraged to connect via consumption" (p. 112). And as Berger (1972) sees it, not only does advertising alienate people from one another; it alienates consumers from themselves. In his benchmark work, *Ways of Seeing*, he explained that the purpose of advertising is:

> [To] make the spectator marginally dissatisfied with [her] present way of life . . . so that she [will] . . . imagine herself transformed by the product into an object of envy for others, an envy which will then justify her loving herself. [Thus], the publicity image steals her love of herself as she is, and offers it back to her for the price of the product. (pp. 132, 134)

Thus, as advertisers project images, the more likely it becomes that readers will see themselves in the advertisements, "creating a feedback loop in which readers strive to produce a self-concept (identity) that confirms the images" (Maynard & Taylor, 1999, p. 40). Subsequently, because consumers' sense of selves are increasingly modeled on the logic of images (Lumby, 1997), a commodity self emerges, in which different products allow individuals to communicate different aspects of their personalities by using the right products (Kellner, 1995a). Put simply, individuals construct their identities out of consumption choices (Goldman & Rapson, 1996).

This has an especially important implication for women, in that self-determination is reduced to an apolitical lifestyle defined through the consumption of fashion and beauty commodities (Budgeon, 1994). Ads propagate the myth that women are to seek self-esteem, success, and social worth through physical attractive-ness, and in turn, women continue to learn that self-empowerment is contingent on self-objectification and the approving gaze of others. Significantly, however, consumers rarely, if at all, attain the status, beauty, youth, glamour, power, love, and so on, promised by advertisers. Accordingly, modern advertising promotes not so much self-indulgence as it does self-doubt: "It seeks to create needs, not to fulfill them; to generate new anxieties instead of allaying old ones" (Hovland & Wilcox, 1990, p. 454).

Advertising can therefore be seen as a political economy of sign values (Goldman, 1992) and a system of differences and oppositions which are crucial in the transfer of meaning (Dyer, 1988). This is because advertisements tap into meaning systems that already have social and cultural weight, providing an arena in which to exchange and rearrange meanings, which Goldman and Rapson (1996) say is "the heart of the commodity sign machine" (p. 5). Any and all products for sale can be endowed with this so-called mythic meaning (Bignell, 1997), and over time, this process is naturalized, when in fact, it exists only by virtue of the inherent structure of advertisements. McCracken (1993) explained: "Beneath the pleasurable and ostensibly innocent appearance of purchased ads are subtexts and codes that articulate ideology, [and] beyond their overt role of selling products, ads present selected value systems as merely 'common sense' " (p. 96). Jhally (1995) noted that advertising is especially efficient at absorbing and fusing together social discourses that are appropriated and distilled from an unbounded range of cultural references. This, of course, is because the media must continually react to ever-changing ideas and social norms to stay relevant (Shoemaker & Reese, 1995). Thus, as Goldman (1992) put it: "Advertising has become a form of internal cultural colonialism that mercilessly hunts out and appropriates those meaningful elements of our cultural lives that have value" (p. 8).

Women/Advertising/**Representation**

King (1992) explained that " 'represents,' in its widest sense, can mean 'stands for,' 'states,' 'announces,' 'symbolizes,' as well as 'suggests illusionistically' or 'gives a snapshot impression of' " (p. 131). Although these terms vary slightly, they each describe the process of putting ideological concepts into concrete forms. Significantly, however, nothing can be a representation without simultaneously being a construction because representations are not just a matter of mirrors, reflections, and keyholes. By virtue of being stand-ins for what they represent, they are constructions that carry ideological meanings as well. Indeed, when something is represented, there is a real and physical dimension to it—it can be heard, read, seen, and so on—but the meaning of the representation is created only by its context and conventions (Allen, 1992). This is because "all our understanding and all our new seeing is formed by what we have seen before" (Allen, 1992, p. 24), or as Hall (1996) put it, representation, like every social practice, "is constituted within the interplay of meaning and representation" (p. 23). Finally, since representations are "always produced within cultural limits and theoretical borders . . . [they] are necessarily implicated in particular economies of truth, value and power" (Giroux & McLaren, 1992, p. xxiv). Parker and Pollock (1987) summarized all of the above:

> . . . meanings depend on the relationships between a single image and its total cultural environment of images and social belief systems . . . For any viewer to understand any image she must carry a whole baggage of social knowledges, assumptions, values . . . What secures which connotations prevail as a preferred meaning is ideology, understood as a complex set of meanings and practices which form the dominant order of sense, a regime of truth for a particular culture or social group. (pp. 125–126, cited in Allen, 1992, p. 34)

The implications of this is that representations require someone to unleash their meanings. And the process by which readers/viewers give meaning to representations or texts inherently involves their situated perspective, or what is called "positionality." Positionality refers to an individual's viewpoint—something that changes over time because of shifting cultural contexts, personal circumstances, and political contingencies, and is influenced by such factors as gender, age, race, class, and sexual orientation (Bonner, Goodman, Allen, Janes, & King, 1992). Hart (1991) said:

> Texts need audiences in order to realize their potential for meaning. So a text does not have a single meaning but rather a range of possibilities which are defined by both the text and by its audiences. The meaning is not in the text but in the reading. It is only through the interaction of audiences with texts that any meaning is produced at all. Personal experiences and individual identities are diverse and texts therefore have potential for multiple meanings. What audiences bring to texts affects the meaning they take away. (p. 60)

This process of audience interactivity and of readers bringing and taking something from media texts based on their own positionality or socially located meaning systems and cultural experiences, has been coined *negotiation*. The term *negotiation*, then, implies that a text does not *have* meaning, but rather delimits a range of potential meanings. This is akin to literary reader-response theory, which emphasises that the meaning of any work depends on the subjective contributions of the reader (Bullock, Stallybrass, & Trombley, 1988).

Overall, the analysis of cultural representations involves investigating "the encounters between constructed images and constructing eyes" (King, 1992, p. 132). The goal of a feminist reading, however, is to "pull the symbolic enactments of popular fictions into frameworks which interpret the psychic, emotional and social forces at work in women's lives" (Gledhill, 1992, p. 208) so that critiques offer the possibility for meanings to be challenged and ultimately changed (Cameron, 1991, cited in King, 1992). It is no wonder, then, that the investigation of cultural representations was one of the first areas taken up by women's studies and that studying the social construction of women continues to be a priority for feminist cultural studies (Schwichtenberg, 1994, p. 170).

The remainder of this section is devoted to an overview of four seminal scholarly contributions that have explored the representation of women in advertising and the media, and have greatly contributed to an understanding of the socially constructed woman. They are the works of Frieden, Goffman, Williamson, and Mulvey.

In 1963, Betty Frieden's classic, *The Feminine Mystique*, was published and ignited the second wave of feminism. Essentially, through an analysis of advertisements and interviews with women, Frieden describes how the advertising imagery of post-World War II depicted middle-class American women as perfectly happy and fulfilled by their roles as housewives and mothers, when in fact, these portrayals were in direct conflict with the real feelings of women living in that era—that of intense boredom and depression. This is why her book's principal argument is that advertising, in its depiction of "this mystique of feminine fulfillment" (p. 16), contributed to "the problem that has no name" (p. 17).

A decade later, Erving Goffman's (1979) *Gender Advertisements* was published, offering insight into the nonverbal messages that advertisements communicate, such as the relative power and subordination between men and women. In his book, Goffman argued that "gender displays," "ritualized behavioral practices," and "hyperitualization" in advertising inform and educate audiences and readers about acceptable gender behavior and role positions. More specifically, in his analysis of hundreds of print advertisements, he found six significant themes, including: (a) the small size of women relative to men; (b) the frequency of a "feminine touch," whereby women touch themselves or products in shy, bashful ways; (c) a hierarchy and ranking between men and women (through gestures such as "head and body tilting" and "canting postures"); (d) family scenes, whereby women are seen only in maternal roles; (e) "ritualized subordination," in which women display a lack of seriousness (e.g., through bashful "knee bends"); and (f) "licensed withdrawal," whereby, as Goffman put it: "Women more than men . . . are pictured engaged in involvements which remove them psychologically from the social situation at large leaving them unoriented in it and to it, and, presumably, therefore, dependent on the protectiveness and good will of others who are (or might come to be) present" (p. 100). Notably, almost two decades later, a follow-up study by Belknap and Leonard (1991), which analyzed 1,000 magazine advertisements, concluded that the feminine touch and ritualization of subordination continued to be prevalent in advertising.

Published one year earlier, Judith Williamson's (1978) *Decoding Advertisements* argues that ideological "structures of meanings" are encoded in advertising. Through her seminal analysis of more than 100 advertisements, she sought to identify the deeper relationships or patterns embedded in the ads and theorized that consumers partake in a symbolic exchange with advertisers in order fulfill their love, security, popularity, status, needs. She explained how advertising connects human feelings, moods, or attributes with tangible objects, such that, for example, "a diamond comes to 'mean' love and endurance for us . . . and the two do become interchangeable" (p. 12). The tacit message is that if one buys the product(s) being advertised, one will effortlessly attain the youth, status and/or beauty depicted in the advertisement, giving advertising its currency. In this sense, "advertisements are selling us something else besides consumer goods: in providing us with a structure in which we, and those goods, are interchangeable, they are selling us ourselves" (p. 13).

Finally, in the same era as Goffman and Williamson, as the fields of semiotics and psychoanalysis were flourishing, Laura Mulvey (1975) published her critically acclaimed, *Visual Pleasure and Narrative Cinema*. Although it does not discuss advertising specifically, its analysis of the representation of women in cinema is nonetheless significant, and therefore, worth highlighting. Her work focused on how Hollywood cinematic experiences and conditions construct spectatorship as male, with men objectifying female characters through acts of voyeurism and fetishism, and that "this objectification of women is not an 'added-on' attraction, but rather endemic to the very structure of image-making" (Danuta Walters, 1999, p. 235). Notably, the idea that women, and images of women, are constructed so as to be *looked at* by men is consistent with theories in art history, especially related to the female nude, and therefore, is congruent with Berger's (1972) notion of "ways of seeing." He explained:

> . . . *men act* and *women appear*. Men look at women. Women watch themselves being looked at. This determines not only most relations between men and women but also the relation of women to themselves. The surveyor of woman in herself is male: the surveyed female. Thus she turns herself into an object—and most particularly an object of vision: a sight. (p. 47)

In her essay, Mulvey also described how the pleasure of looking divides into the active/male and the passive/female. To challenge what she referred to as popular cinema's "manipulation of visual pleasure," she called for the "destruction of pleasure as a radical weapon" (Storey, 1993). Consequently, although her claims have received very favorable response from feminists "for their power to explain the alternative misogyny and idealization of cinema's female representations . . . [they also] offer largely negative accounts of female spectatorship, suggesting colonized, alienated or masochistic positions of identification" (Gledhill, 1992, p. 194). Thus, over the last decade, several feminist scholars have challenged her assertions and reappropriated the gaze, insisting that her analysis "denies the experiences of women as spectators and forestalls the examination and development of female pleasure" (van Zoonen, 1994, p. 103). Despite these criticisms, Mulvey's work remains significant to feminist media and communication studies.

Conclusion

Every day, additional images of the female form are introduced into the public sphere and many argue that these representations play a significant role in determining and affecting the symbolic, material and psychological lives of women. van Zoonen (1994) explained:

> representation is a social practice in which current beliefs and myths about women and sexuality are (re)constructed, and that the act of consuming these representations is more than a private pleasure, but also embedded in gendered social and cultural formations that have defined women's bodies as sexual objects. (p. 21)

The problem, according to Storey (1993), is that images of women are "always constructed around a mythical individual woman" (p. 148). Advertisements do not depict how women actually are, but how society thinks women should be (Gornick, 1979). Women are expected to be sexy, powerful, beautiful, feminine, and so on, and to adopt attitudes and behaviors similar to those of the idealized women presented in the mass media. Yet the mythical feminine norms depicted in those very representations are not representative of reality.

The ensuing issue, however, as becomes evident in the chapters that follow, is that feminists are deeply divided over what constitutes positive or ideal representation of women. In fact, questions about "fair," "empowering," or "realistic" representations of women are fraught with intense debate, especially because this "assumes there is a norm against which images can be judged" (Gallagher, 1995, p. 13). Furthermore, "arguing for more realistic images is always an argument for the representation of 'your' version of reality" (Brundson, 1988, cited in van Zoonen, 1994, p. 31). Also, as Stevenson (1995) said: "To claim that there is one truth . . . is to capitulate to the dominant regime of truth, and deny the potentially liberatory pleasure of the text" (p. 93). Nonetheless, there remains a call for representations that work with a greater degree of fluidity and contradiction (Gledhill, 1992), and as King (1992) asserted, if a woman is "represented as an individual with will, with autonomous desires and powers, with a specific personality and with rights and human dignity, [that representation] would perhaps be regarded as acceptable" (p. 137).

Do such representations exist? Could they in advertising? These are some the questions being asked in the chapters that follow.

Notes

1. "The 'politics of the body' refers to the material site of political struggle" (Bordo, 1993, p. 16), since the body is a politicized and culturally constructed entity and bearer of cultural signs and meanings (Balsamo, 1997). It also refers to gendered power relations

especially in terms of all forms of direct and indirect violence against women and their bodies (Humm, 1989). Social theories about the body have become exceedingly hot topics (Chancer, 1998, p. 100) within a "remarkably short period of time" (Grosz, 1995, p. 1), whereby, in many academic fields, the body is "generating the most exciting new research and most interdisciplinary theoretical inquiry" (Conboy, Medina, & Stanbury, 1997, p. 7).

References

Allen, R. (1992). Analysing representations. In F. Bonner, L. Goodman, R. Allen, L. Janes, & C. King (Eds.), *Imagining women: Cultural representations and gender* (pp. 21–41). Cambridge: The Open University Press.

Ang, I. (1990). Melodramatic identifications: Television fiction and women's fantasy. In M. E. Brown (Ed.), *Television and women's culture: The politics of the popular* (pp. 75–88). London: Sage.

Bailey, M. E. (1993). Foucauldian feminism: Contesting bodies, sexuality and identity. In C. Ramazanoglu (Ed.), *Up against Foucault: Explorations of some tensions between Foucault and feminism* (pp. 99–122). London: Routledge.

Balsamo, A. (1997). *Technologies of the gendered bodies: Reading cyborg women.* Durham, NC: Duke University Press.

Barnard, M. (1995). Advertising: The rhetorical imperative. In C. Jenks (Ed.), *Visual culture* (pp. 26–41). London: Routledge.

Baron, D., & Byrne, R. A. (1997). *Social psychology.* Needham Heights, MA: Allyn & Bacon.

Barrie, G. (1995). *Television and gender representation.* London: John Libbey.

Barthel, D. (1988). *Putting on appearances: Gender and advertising.* Philadelphia: Temple University Press.

Bartky, S. L. (1998). Foucault, femininity, and the modernization of patriarchal power. In R. Weitz (Ed.), *The politics of women's bodies: Sexuality, appearance and behavior* (pp. 25–45). New York: Oxford University Press.

Belknap, P., & Leonard, W. M., III. (1991). A conceptual replication and extension of Erving Goffman's study of gender advertisements. *Sex Roles, 25*(3/4), 103–118.

Berger, J. (1972). *Ways of seeing.* London: British Broadcasting Corporation and Penguin Books.

Bignell, J. (1997). *Media semiotics: An introduction.* New York: Manchester University Press.

Bonner, F., Goodman, L., Allen, R., Janes, L., & King, C. (Eds.). (1992). *Imagining women: Cultural representations and gender.* Cambridge: The Open University Press.

Bordo, S. (1993). Feminism, Foucault and the politics of the body. In C. Ramazanoglu (Ed.), *Up against Foucault: Explorations of some tensions between Foucault and feminism* (pp. 179–202). London: Routledge.

Bordo, S. (1997). The body and reproduction of femininity. In K. Conboy, N. Medina, & S. Stanbury (Eds.), *Writing on the body: Female embodiment and feminist theory* (pp. 90–110). New York: Columbia University Press.

Botta, R. A. (1999). Television images and adolescent girls' body image disturbance. *Journal of Communication, 49*(2), 22–41.

Brittain McKee, K., & Pardun, C. J. (1999). Face-ism reconsidered: Facial prominence and body emphasis of males and females in magazine advertising. In M. G. Carstaphen & S. C. Zavoina (Eds.), *Sexual rhetoric: Media perspectives on sexuality, gender and identity* (pp. 109–121). Westport, CT: Greenwood Press.

Budgeon, S. (1994). Fashion magazine advertising: Constructing femininity in the "post-feminist" era. In A. Manca & L. Manca (Eds.), *Gender utopias in advertising: A critical reader* (pp. 55–70). Syracuse, NY: Procopian Press.

Buerkel-Rothfuss, N. L. (1993). Background: What prior research shows. In B. S. Greenberg, J. D. Brown, & N. Buerkel-Rothfuss (Eds.), *Media, sex and the adolescent* (pp. 5–24). Cresskill, NJ: Hampton Press.

Buijzen, M., & Valkenburg, P. M. (2003). The unintended effects of television advertising— A parent–child survey. *Communication Research, 30*(5), 483–503.

Bullock, A., Stallybrass, O., & Trombley, S. (Eds.). (1988). *The Fontana dictionary of modern thought.* London: HarperCollins.

Butler, J. (1990). *Gender trouble: Feminism and the subversion of identity.* New York: Routledge.

Callaghan, K. A. (Ed.). (1994). *Ideals of feminine beauty: Philosophical, social and cultural dimensions.* Westport, CT: Greenwood Press.

Caputi, J. (1999). The pornography of everyday life. In M. Meyers (Ed.), *Mediated women: Representation in popular culture* (pp. 57–79). Cresskill, NJ: Hampton Press.

Carstaphen, M. G., & Zavoina, S. C. (Eds.). (1999). *Sexual rhetoric: Media perspectives on sexuality, gender and identity.* Westport, CT: Greenwood Press.

Chancer, L. S. (1998). *Reconcilable differences: Confronting beauty, pornography, and the future of feminism.* Berkeley: University of California Press.

Clare, A. (2000). A semiotic analysis of magazine ads for men's fragrances. Retrieved September 8, 2000, from www.aber.ac.uk/ednwww/Undgrad/ED30610/awc401.html.

Conboy, K., Medina, N., & Stanbury, S. (Eds.). (1997). *Writing on the body: Female embodiment and feminist theory.* New York: Columbia University Press.

Cook, G. (1992). *The discourse of advertising.* London: Routledge.

Danuta Walters, S. (1999). Sex, text and context: (In) between feminism and cultural studies. In M. M. Ferree, J. Lorber, & B. B. Hess (Eds.), *Revisioning gender* (pp. 222–257). Thousand Oaks: Sage.

Darling-Wolf, F. (2000). From airbrushing to liposuction: The technological reconstruction of the female body. In B. Miedema, J. Stoppard, & V. Anderson (Eds.), *Women's bodies/women's lives: Health, well-being and body image* (pp. 277–293). Toronto: Sumach Press.

de Beauvoir, S. (1993). *The second sex.* New York: Alfred A. Knopf.

Demarest, J., & Garner, J. (1992). The representation of women's roles in women's magazines over the past 30 years. *The Journal of Psychology, 126*(4), 357–368.

Dines, G., & Humez, J. M. (Eds.) (1995). *Gender, race and class in media: A text-reader.* Thousand Oaks, CA: Sage.

Disch, E. (Ed.). (1997). *Reconstructing gender: A multicultural anthology.* Mountain View, CA: Mayfield.

Duffy, M. (1994). Body of evidence: Studying women in advertising. In A. Manca & L. Manca (Eds.), *Gender utopias in advertising: A critical reader* (pp. 5–30). Syracuse, NY: Procopian Press.

Dyer, G. (1988). *Advertising as communication*. London: Routledge.

Faludi, S. (1991). *Backlash: The undeclared war against American women*. New York: Anchor Books.

Frieden, B. (1963). *The feminine mystique*. Middlesex: Penguin Books.

Gallagher, M. (1995). *Lipstick imperialism and the new world order: Women and media at the close of the twentieth century*. Paper prepared at the Division for the Advancement of Women, Department for Policy Coordination and Sustainable Development, United Nations.

Giroux, H. A., & McLaren, P. L. (1992). Media hegemony: Towards a critical pedagogy of representation. In J. Schwoch, M. White, & S. Reilly (Eds.), *Media knowledge: Readings in popular culture, pedagogy, and critical citizenship* (pp. xv–xxxiv). Albany: State University of New York Press.

Gledhill, C. (1992). Pleasurable negotiations. In F. Bonner, L. Goodman, R. Allen, L. Janes, & C. King (Eds.), *Imagining women: Cultural representations and gender* (pp. 193–209). Cambridge: The Open University Press.

Goffman, E. (1979). *Gender advertisements*. Cambridge, MA: Harvard University Press.

Goldman, R. (1992). *Reading ads socially*. London: Routledge.

Goldman, R., Heath, D., & Smith, S. L. (1991). Commodity feminism. *Critical Studies in Mass Communication, 8*, 333–351.

Goldman, R., & Rapson, S. (1996). *Sign wars: The cluttered landscape of advertising*. New York: Guilford.

Gornick, V. (1979). Introduction. In E. Goffman, *Gender advertisements*. Cambridge, MA: Harvard University Press.

Greer, G. (1999). *The whole woman*. London: Anchor.

Grosz, E. (1995). *Space, time and perversion: Essays on the politics of bodies*. New York: Routledge.

Gustafson, R., Popovich, M., & Thomsen, S. (1999). The "thin ideal." *Marketing News*, 22–24.

Hall, S. (1996). Signification, representation, ideology: Althusser and the post-structuralist debates. In J. Curran, D. Morley, & V. Walkerdine (Eds.), *Cultural studies and communications* (p. 11–34). London: Edward Arnold.

Halprin, S. (1995). *"Look at my ugly face!": Myths and musings on beauty and other perilous obsessions with women's appearance*. New York: Penguin Books.

Hart, A. (1991). *Understanding the media: A practical guide*. New York: Routledge.

Hitchon, J. C., & Reaves, S. (1999). Media mirage: The thin ideal as digital manipulation. In M. G. Carstaphen & S. C. Zavoina (Eds.), *Sexual rhetoric: Media perspectives on sexuality, gender and identity* (pp. 65–76). Westport, CT: Greenwood Press.

Hovland, R., & Wilcox, G. B. (1990). *Advertising in society: Classic and contemporary readings on advertising's role in society*. Lincolnwood: NTC Business Books.

Humm, M. (1989). *The dictionary of feminist theory*. Hertfordshire: Prentice Hall/Harvester.

The International Women's Media Foundation. (1998). *Empowering women in the Asian media*. Washington, DC: Author.

Jhally, S. (1995). Image-based culture: Advertising and popular culture. In G. Dines & J. M. Humez (Eds.), *Gender, race and class in media: A text-reader* (pp. 77–87). Thousand Oaks, CA: Sage.

Kates, S. M., & Shaw-Garlock, G. (1999). The ever entangling web: A study of ideologies and discourses in advertising to women. *Journal of Advertising*, *28*(2), 33–49.

Kellner, D. (1995a). Advertising and consumer culture. In J. Downing, A. Mohammadi, & A. Sreberny-Mohammadi (Eds.), *Questioning the media: A critical introduction* (pp. 329–344). Thousand Oaks, CA: Sage.

Kellner, D. (1995b). Reading images critically: Toward a postmodern pedagogy. In G. Dines & J. M. Humez (Eds.), *Gender, race and class in media: A text-reader* (pp. 126–132). Thousand Oaks, CA: Sage.

Kilbourne, J. (1999). *Deadly persuasion: Why women and girls must fight the addictive power of advertising*. New York: The Free Press.

King, C. (1992). The politics of representation: A democracy of the gaze. In F. Bonner, L. Goodman, R. Allen, L. Janes, & C. King (Eds.), *Imagining women: Cultural representations and gender* (pp. 131–139). Cambridge: The Open University Press.

Lambiase, J. J., Reichert, T., Morgan, S. E., Carstaphen, M. G., Zavoina, S. C., & Callister, M. (1999). Gendered bodies still thrive in (post)modern magazineland. In M. G. Carstaphen & S. C. Zavoina (Eds.), *Sexual rhetoric: Media perspectives on sexuality, gender and identity* (pp. 147–158). Westport, CT: Greenwood Press.

Lazier, L., & Gagnard Kendrick, A. (1993). Women in advertisements: Sizing up the images, roles and functions. In P. Creedon (Ed.), *Women in mass communication* (pp. 199–221). Newbury Park, CA: Sage.

Lester, P. M. (Ed.). (1995). *Images that injure: Pictorial stereotypes in the media*. Westport, CT: Praeger.

Lorber, J., & Farrell, S. A. (Eds.). (1991). *The social construction of gender*. Newbury Park, CA: Sage.

Lumby, C. (1997). *Bad girls: The media, sex and feminism in the '90's*. New South Wales: Allen & Unwin Pty. Ltd.

MacCurdy, M. (1994). The four women of the apocalypse: Polarized feminine images in magazine advertisements. In A. Manca & L. Manca (Eds.), *Gender utopias in advertising: A critical reader* (pp. 31–48). Syracuse, NY: Procopian Press.

MacDonald, M. (1995). *Representing women: Myths of femininity in the popular media*. New York: Arnold, St. Martin's Press.

Mackie, M. (1987). *Constructing women & men: Gender socialization*. Toronto: Holt, Rinehart and Winston of Canada Ltd.

Manca, A., & Manca, L. (Eds.). (1994). *Gender utopias in advertising: A critical reader*. Syracuse, NY: Procopian Press.

Maynard, M. L., & Taylor, C. R. (1999). Girlish images across cultures: Analysing Japanese versus U.S *Seventeen* magazine ads. *Journal of Advertising*, *28*(1), 39–48.

McAllister, M. P. (1996). *The commercialization of American culture: New advertising, control and democracy*. Thousand Oaks, CA: Sage.

McCracken, E. (1993). *Decoding women's magazines: From "Mademoiselle" to "Ms."* New York: MacMillan Press.

Merskin, D. (1999). That time of month: Adolescence, advertising, and menstruation. In M. G. Carstaphen & S. C. Zavoina (Eds.). *Sexual rhetoric: Media perspectives on sexuality, gender and identity* (pp. 93–107). Westport, CT: Greenwood Press.

Meyers, M. (Ed.). (1999). *Mediated women: Representation in popular culture*. Cresskill, NJ: Hampton Press.

Mulvey, L. (1975). Visual pleasure and narrative cinema. *Screen, 16*(3), 6–18.

Orbach, S. (1978). *Fat is a feminist issue.* New York: Paddington Press.

Parker, R., & Pollock, G. (1987). *Framing feminism art and the women's movement 1970–1985.* London: Pandora.

Pearson, J. C., West, R. L., & Turner, L. H. (1995). *Gender and communication.* Boston: McGraw Hill.

Probyn, E. (1992). Theorising through the body. In L. Rakow (Ed.), *Women making meaning* (pp. 83–99). New York: Routledge.

Ramazanoglu, C. (Ed.). (1993). *Up against Foucault: Explorations of some tensions between Foucault and feminism.* London: Routledge.

Reichert, T., Lambiase, J., Morgan, S., Carstaphen, M., & Zavoina, S. (1999). Cheesecake and beefcake: No matter how you slice it, sexual explicitness in advertising continues to increase. *J&MC Quarterly, 76*(1), 7–20.

Rutledge Shields, V. (1990). Advertising visual images: Gendered ways of seeing and looking. *Journal of Communication Inquiry 14*(2), 25–39.

Saltzberg, E. A., & Chrisler, J. C. (1997). Beauty and the beast: Psychological effects of the pursuit of the perfect female body. In E. Disch (Ed.), *Reconstructing gender: A multicultural anthology* (pp. 134–145). Mountain View, CA: Mayfield.

Sarabia, A. L. (1995). Notes for a framework for the analysis of women, media and violence. In B. Tankha (Ed.), *Communication and democracy: Ensuring plurality* (pp. 119–129). Penang: Southbound Sdn. Bhd.

Schwichtenberg, C. (1994). In J. Cruz & J. Lewis (Eds.), *Viewing, reading, listening: Audiences and cultural reception* (pp. 169–180). Boulder, CO: Westview Press, Inc.

Schwoch, J., White M., & Reilly, S. (1992). *Media knowledge: Readings in popular culture, pedagogy, and critical citizenship.* Albany: State University of New York Press.

Shoemaker, P., J., & Reese, S. D. (1995). The influence of ideology. In *Mediating the message: theories of influences on mass media content* (pp. 183–207). New York: Longman.

Stewart, D. W., & Ward, S. (1994). Media effects on advertising. In J. Bryant & D. Zillmann (Eds.), *Media effects: Advances in theory and research* (pp. 315–363). Hillsdale, NJ: Erlbaum.

Storey, J. (1993). *An introductory guide to cultural theory and popular culture.* Athens: University of Georgia Press.

Suzuki, M. F. (1995). Women and television: Portrayal of women in the mass media. In K. Fujimura-Fanselow & A. Kameda (Eds.), *Japanese women: New feminist perspectives on the past, present and future* (pp. 75–90). New York: Feminist Press at the City University of New York.

Valentine, C. G. (1994). Female bodily perfection and the divided self. In K. A. Callaghan (Ed.), *Ideals of feminine beauty: philosophical, social and cultural dimensions* (pp. 111–123). Westport, CT: Greenwood Press.

van Zoonen, L. (1994). *Feminist media studies.* London: Sage.

Walsh-Childers, K. (1995). Women as sex partners. In P. M. Lester (Ed.), *Images that injure: Pictorial stereotypes in the media* (pp. 81–85). Westport, CT: Praeger.

Wells, W., Burnett, J., & Moriarty, S. (1995). *Advertising: Principles and practice.* Englewood Cliffs, NJ: Prentice-Hall.

Whipple, T. W. (1992). The existence and effectiveness of sexual content in advertising. In S. R. Danna (Ed.), *Advertising and popular culture: Studies in variety and versatility* (pp. 134–140). Bowling Green, OH: Bowling Green State University Popular Press.

Williams, R. (1993). Advertising: The magic system. In S. During (Ed.), *The cultural studies reader* (pp. 320–336). London: Routledge.

Williamson, J. (1978). *Decoding advertisements.* London: Marion Boyars.

Wolf, N. (1990). *The beauty myth.* Toronto: Vantage Canada.

Yanagisako, S., & Delaney, C. (Eds.). (1995). *Naturalizing power: Essays in feminist cultural analysis.* New York: Routledge.

Zacharias, U. (1994). The Sita myth and Hindu fundamentalism: Masculine signs and feminine beauty. In K. A. Callaghan (Ed.), *Ideals of feminine beauty: Philosophical, social and cultural dimensions* (pp. 37–52). Westport, CT: Greenwood Press.

2

Sex, Sameness and Desire
Thoughts on Versace and the Clone

Isabelle Loring Wallace

In the year 2000, Steven Meisel captured the West's attention yet again. Already known in Europe and America as the inventor of heroin and kiddie-porn "chic," Meisel was, by 2000, routinely linked with images that pack a titillating, yet uncomfortable punch, and as such, the prospect of a millennial media coup was merely consistent with everything one might expect of America's most notorious fashion photographer.[1] Indeed, given a decade that moved from the publication of Madonna's *Sex* in 1992 to the banning of an Opium advertisement in 1999, which is to say, given a decade already framed by scandals born of Meisel's camera, there was every reason to suspect that Meisel would close both the decade and millennium with a comparably scandalous bang.[2]

Enter here, the subject of this chapter. In the final months of 2000, Meisel did indeed provide something to talk about, yet these photographs would hold little interest for censors and ethical watchdogs. More perplexing than prurient, Meisel's advertising campaign for Versace's Fall 2000 line won the attention of Western art journalists and cultural critics instead, and although many of these columnists were quick to note the uncanny appeal of a campaign focused on two credibly adult females in lavish Los Angeles interiors, little more than that was ultimately said about the content of Meisel's descriptively named campaign *Four Days in L.A.*[3]

Comprised of roughly 30 photographs, most of which situate the campaign's female models together in imposing domestic settings, Meisel's campaign initially appeared both in the context of major fashion magazines in Europe and America and in the shop windows of Versace's own boutiques (providing what may have been its only non-Western exposure). Coinciding with the availability of Versace's Fall/Winter collection, the campaign was, like most campaigns, destined to disappear after only 6 months, and yet, for reasons that are, in part, the subject of this chapter, this campaign would not fade so quickly from view.

Enlarged and framed behind glass, a selection of Meisel's advertisements managed to elude certain death by undergoing a kind a metamorphosis, after which they reappeared *as art* at the prestigious White Cube gallery in London—a phenomenon that can be in large part be credited to Jay Jopling, gallery director and loyal Versace client.[4] On exhibit between July 19 and September 1, 2001, the transubstantiated 4 × 5 1/4-ft. photographs, available in sets of nine, did, by all accounts, sell quickly, despite both an original un-ownability (as advertisements, everyone and no one can claim to possess Meisel's photographs) and their impressive, art-based price range ($20,000–25,000).[5]

Emblematic of the campaign's enduring (but still untheorized) appeal, Meisel's debut at White Cube predictably generated a second wave of columns and essays about the campaign. Focused largely on the issue of the work's legitimacy as art—a focus that includes within it the issue of the campaign's impressive reference to earlier art historical sources, Bronzino and Ingres chief among them—this second wave of articles certainly evidenced continued interest in the campaign, but more importantly, it also demonstrated an enduring reluctance to engage the issue of the campaign's contents. As a quick examination of the reviews reveals, descriptions of the campaign abounded, but genuine analysis was hard to come by. Of course, this is, in part, a function of who wrote and where; yet I am tempted to say that the tendency of reviewers to avoid analyzing (even determining) their subject is a trend that reflects more than circumstance—indeed, as I see it, this silence, is, in some sense, a testament to fact that Meisel's ads *were* being engaged at this level, such that it is precisely an awareness of their difficult subject that kept its audience both interested and anxiously silent.[6]

In Excess of Excess

Asked to comment on *Four Days in L.A.*, Meisel suggested that the series is all about "extravagance" and "L.A.-excess," yet, given the decadent interiors and over-size sunglasses, the tranquilized poodles and turquoise eye shadow, the rhinestone lighters and 4-inch heels, Meisel's observation hardly qualifies as an insight, even if it does help us to understand what the ads look like.[7] Certainly, no one doubts that "the look" is terribly important in advertising—especially when the thing to be sold is *haute couture*—and yet I think it is possible to talk about Meisel's series in a different way, one that begins to account for aspects of the campaign not covered (in any straightforward sense) by the proffered, and much repeated rhetoric of excess. Indeed, it is aspects of the campaign *not* addressed by Meisel's superficial description, which will, in the end, reveal a much more ambitious and problematic subject. I start by reviewing these curiously unanalyzed characteristics, and then discuss the issues they seem to suggest.

First and foremost, there is the campaign's considerable investment in the idea of sameness. Not only are the primary models (Amber Valetta and Georgina

Grenville) virtually indistinguishable from one another in terms of physiognomy, body type, and aesthetic, they are also, lest one still not get the point, often positioned in ways that make one the mirror image of the other. In one of the campaign's most visible images, for example, we see Valetta and Grenville on a veranda on either side of a circular table perched atop identical chairs, each echoing the other with the crossing of her couture-clad legs. Wearing matching shiny pants and matching gold necklaces with matching, diamond-shaped pendants, both models sport 1970's styled hair, makeup, and nails, all the while betraying through their stiff, matching mirror-reversed poses and expressions little interest in their matching, and prominently displayed cups of espresso. Other ads in the series work along similar lines, using both the models and their context to get across the idea of sameness. One, seemingly ubiquitous image from the campaign, features Valetta and Grenville in matching yellow pantsuit separates, and again, sameness dominates. Matching handbags, matching posture, matching hairstyles, matching chairs, matching make up, matching manicures, and matching (and outrageous) diamonds are only the most obvious means by which Meisel's photograph insists on sameness. A close look at the ad's background reveals among other things, matching oil paintings of women in profile, themselves a frame for the model at left, and, playing a similar role *vis-à-vis* the model at right, a pair of matching, white-shaded lamps. Suffice it to say that here as elsewhere, there is nothing in the ad that doesn't somehow contribute to the idea of sameness and twinning.

If the sameness of the campaign's female models is the most striking and manipulated aspect of the campaign's interest in sameness, it is worth noting that the theme finds expression even when one or both models is absent from the frame. One photograph, for example, features one of the female models (who could say which one) dressed in black in the center of an eclectic, but essentially modern white room. As with any of these images, there's a great deal one could say, but for our purposes here, what is interesting is the fact that the model is dramatically flanked by two identically sized and styled white poodles. Moreover, if matching white poodles flank her in the foreground, matching black lamps atop matching end-tables flank her in the background—a fact that establishes well not only the interest of the campaign in symmetry, but also (and more importantly) its profound commitment to articulating the idea of sameness under necessarily varied circumstance.

Photographs centered around the campaign's lone, male model (Lucas Babin) are (and were) harder to come by—indeed, they were entirely absent from the exhibition at White Cube. Nevertheless, when they *do* appear they also express a commitment to the idea of twinning in the absence of twins. One photograph, for example, features Babin in a canary yellow suit, standing erect between two identical twin beds which are themselves flanked by identical end tables topped with, you guessed it, identical lamps. That the accents in this room each have an Asian sensibility—most notably the red silk bedspreads, and lacquered Asian screen—is a fact I touch on shortly. Here, suffice it to say that this aspect of the ad, when combined with the photograph's attention to men's fashion as modeled by Babin, makes it very much like another photograph in Meisel's series in which Babin trades in his yellow pantsuit for a more subdued ensemble in black. Leaving the bedroom for a less personal space within the same home, Asian motifs (two porcelain cranes and two ornamental scrolls) continue to suggest Babin's "otherness" within a campaign dominated by women, while at the same time returning our attention to the issue of twinning and sameness. Indeed, if these motifs can be said to feminize this interior and its inhabitant at the same time they mark him as "different," they also expose as relentless the focus of Meisel on the double.[8]

Although I have already touched on this point indirectly, here, I note explicitly a second aspect of the campaign ignored by columnists and reviewers: namely, the rigorous segregation of women from men. As strange as it seems in a context obsessively focused on relations *between* opposite sexes (and here I am thinking not only of fashion photography and advertisements, but also of Western television, movies, and politics), Meisel's refusal to represent heterosocial contact of any kind is absolute: In this series, men are never shown in the company of women, and women are never shown in the company of men.

Because the temptation to rely on simple, but culturally prevalent, narratives is great (wealthy suburban women stay home while their hypersuccessful husbands work together outside the home's confines), let me note expressly that all of the campaign's scenarios, whether centered on men or on women, are situated in the home during the day. As such, the segregation between men and women, neither of whom seem to work, is one we are asked to interpret without recourse to these kinds of clichés.[9] Seen in this light, the separation of women from men must be understood as meaningful rather than circumstantial, and as such we are pushed toward a difficult but compelling possibility: In the imaginary, pastiched world of L.A., in some unspecified and unspecifiable time, men and women lead distinct lives as a matter of choice.

A related and equally important issue is the campaign's indifference to the idea of men's and women's spaces within the home. Indeed, a quick review of the series shows women in the mahogany-paneled study, men in the airy yellow bedroom, and both men and women in the neutral spaces we might call living rooms or dens. Of course, this is not to say that the spaces and accessories are not gendered; they are, and it would escape no one's attention that the darkened study is a masculine counterpart to the campaign's floral, feminized bedroom. As such, what is interesting and perhaps productive within Meisel's campaign is that the photographs manage to level an assumed difference between politically charged terms like *masculine* by which we might mean dark, solid, rich, and so on, and an aesthetic term like *art deco* by which we might mean decorative, elongated, and curvilinear.[10] Reduced by these ads to transparent stylistic category, gendered and engendering terms lose much of their potential to damage and police. In other words, in this context, it may be possible to speak of a "feminine space," but in the world constructed by Meisel, the signifier is utterly liberated from its biological referent, if indeed that referent can be said to persist.

Working to destabilize this very possibility—the possibility that "male" and "female" persist as meaningful and essential categories—is the remarkable androgyny of Meisel's models.[11] Again, although little was said about this in the popular press, there is an uncanny indeterminacy at work here, one we might attribute to physiognomy and context in equal measure. Consider by way of description, two more images from Meisel's campaign, each of which features a tall, flat-chested model with shoulder-length hair in androgynous attire. The first features the campaign's male model in the airy yellow bedroom, reclining, fully dressed on the bed wearing black jeans, a black cardigan, and a white dress shirt, cufflinks, and tie. The second, features one of the campaign's female models—although here it might be said that her femaleness is no way certain, an ambiguity nicely underscored by a name like Georgina—sitting in a living room wearing a spectacular red pantsuit, complete with a red, fur-cuffed overcoat that rests regally atop her shoulders.

Given the visual evidence, one would be hard-pressed to identify either of these figures as male or female, let alone, masculine or feminine. If anything, advertisements like these can be seen to subvert essentialist notions of gender through savvy reference to established codes of visual culture; here, it is the male model who takes up the recumbent pose of the female nude, while his erect female counterpart adopts the established codes of male portraiture, more specifically in this case, codes already deployed by David and Ingres in their neo-classical portraits of Napoleon, a reference secured here by Meisel's canny inclusion in the ad of two pillows each embroidered with France's signature motif, the *fleur de lis*. Existing as hybrids somewhere between the poles of masculine and feminine, the characters that populate Meisel's world refer openly to the codes of both, even if they conform, in the end, to neither.

All that said, the questions that remain are these: Where can the above observations take us, and what, if anything, do my remarks about gender and sex have to do with the idea and image of sameness? In other words, if the above observations reveal the limits of Meisel's much repeated "interpretation," do they also help us to establish an alternative framework for thinking about this campaign? In short, is it possible, and moreover, how is it possible to link the campaign's interest in twinning and sameness to its indifference toward traditional conceptions of heterosocial and perhaps, heterosexual behavior?

In the section that follows, I suggest that it is possible to link these untheorized aspects of the campaign, and that it is contemporaneous scientific developments, specifically the phenomenon of cloning, which will allow us to make the connection between sameness and sex. Indeed, as I argue in the chapter's remaining pages, these advertisements can be seen to function (whatever Meisel's intention) as a meditation on the ideas of sex and gender at a moment when those concepts are being radically renegotiated by the possibility of cloning and genetic engineering.

The Hell of the Same

Writing in the year 2000, the French theorist, Jean Baudrillard observed, "There is something occulted inside us . . . lying in wait for us within each of our cells: the forgetting of death" (5).[12] What Baudrillard was talking about here is the connection each of us has to an earlier state of being in which we were neither mortal nor sexed. Reminding us of this, our universal pre-history, Baudrillard noted that this primordial era came to an end with what he called the original sexual revolution, the one in which organisms evolved from a-sexual subdivision—a state of guaranteed immortality—to a state of being that entails both sexual difference and death. Given that this evolution is our shared history, Baudrillard concluded that all of us somehow maintain, whether as cellular memory or intellectual fantasy, the idea of an un-sexed and immortal state of existence.[13]

With this in mind, Baudrillard read the current interest in cloning as regression, rather than progress, for what cloning aims, nostalgically, to achieve is a return to this primordial moment in which immortality is once again assured through the infinite, and moreover, the clinical reproduction of the same.[14] Thus, having replaced a-sexual reproduction with the sexual act of procreation, which is also to say, having replaced reproduction of the same, with creation of the different, the recent invention of cloning suggests that we now long to *reverse* evolutionary history by returning to an a-sexual reproduction of the same in the name of (a genetic) immortality. In other words, having moved from a state of sameness and a-sexuality to a state of difference and sexual opposition, we are now engineering a type of immortality that will return us to our undifferentiated and a-sexual roots.[15]

It goes without saying that a comprehensive assessment of cloning's implications is well beyond the scope of this chapter and author. Nonetheless, suffice it to say that cloning will alter every aspect of human existence, radically renegotiating not only what it is to be, but also what it is *we are* in an era defined by genetic engineering. That said, I restrict the bulk of my remaining comments here to the implications of cloning for the issues of sex and gender, for I think it is these aspects of identity that are most forcefully engaged by an ad campaign that never intended to be, but nevertheless is a reflection on these issues.

Encouraged by both the timing of Meisel's campaign (it is contemporaneous with the first successfully cloned mammal and human embryo), the nature of its fundamental motif (sameness), and the retrospective nature of the product in aims to sell (Versace's Fall 2000 line is, like the phenomenon of cloning, reminiscent of an earlier moment: in this case, the 1970s), I return us to our analysis of *Four Days in L.A.* with the following proposition: let us read the campaign once again, only this time, let us interpret the series as an attempt to visualize a particular slice of life in the proximate, and on Baudrillard's account, familiar era of the clone.[16]

If cloning promises to free us from the fact of mortal finitude while at the same time introducing us to the "hell of the same" (see again, Valetta and Grenville), it may also terminate a culture in no small part determined by the once insurmountable fact of reproduction's (hetero)sexual nature. The final step in a process that began in earnest with the invention of the pill, cloning radically differentiates sexual and reproductive functions, and as such, its cultural consequences are extreme. Indeed, it can easily be said that if cloning frees us from the burden (release?) of death, then it also frees us from the burden of compulsory heterosexuality, and along with it the ubiquitous cult of feminine youth. Returning to Meisel's campaign with this in mind, the segregation of men and women therein acquires new significance. For, when one considers the campaign in light of the topic plainly suggested by the indistinguishability of its main models, one might conclude that if Meisel's men and women maintain their distance from one another in a campaign about twins and twinning, then it is at least in part because cloning has rendered entirely gratuitous the physical relation of women to men.

That said, some of the campaign's more suggestive photographs should come as no surprise, for what they offer us as visible *and paradigmatic* is a sexual relation that has always been an index of sexuality's fundamental indifference to the biological task of reproduction. The ad featuring Valetta and Grenville in the bedroom in scanty Versace couture is a case in point. With nary a man in sight—save the intrusive one implied by the stern and dismissive gaze of each outwardly facing model—Meisel's photograph, like the series more broadly, suggests a world both frightening and free, for if the uncanny sameness of his models alerts us to the tedium of the same, their proximity to one another in settings such as this at same time celebrates the irrelevance of biologically bolstered convictions about the "appropriate" nature of human sexuality. No longer the sole means of reproduction (a fact true since in vitro technology was introduced), the heterosexual act carries less associative weight than it has in the recent (but again, not distant) past, and from my point of view, the implied lesbianism of Meisel's "characters" is but one acknowledgment of this cultural shift.[17]

Also irrelevant in the era of the clone is a woman's biological clock, a fact Meisel's ads seems to suggest given their much-noted reliance on two models older than most. Although Valetta and Grenville are in truth nowhere near the age of infertility, they are nevertheless well beyond the age of today's typical fashion model, and in this way, we might say that Versace's ads are at the forefront of a shift that will entail (among other far more important things) an end to the heterosexist cult of feminine youth.[18] After all, in the era of the clone everyone is equally fertile, as every body part is, at least in theory, equally valuable to the process of reproduction.

As such, Meisel's futuristic (but also regressive) fantasy includes not only the suggestion of sexual unions that cannot procreate, but also a genuine indifference to the culture's preference for the female body that is visibly fertile.

If cloning will thus retool our notion of parenting (who parents with whom under what circumstances), it may also destabilize an entire ideology and culture based on the idea of essential sexual difference. In other words, if it is possible to say that the liberation of sexuality from reproduction will be one consequence of cloning, then surely, the radical liberation of sex from gender will be another. In saying this, I do not mean to suggest that sex and gender haven't always been separable—indeed, the difference between them is as old as hairstyles and makeup. All the same, the advent of cloning would be a conclusive step toward their differentiation—one that would continue to lay bear the theatrical nature of gender, rendering it visible as the ideological performance it's always been.

With this in mind, consider another image from Meisel's campaign. Referencing a traditional kind of portraiture in which wife is seated before standing husband, one image from the campaign shows Valetta and Grenville posed in the dinning room in exactly that way, and as such, we might say that the ad plays on our knowledge of patriarchal iconography in order to construct a meaning that is at odds with the very referent on which it depends. Once again, we see that traditional codes (this time, Western codes of sex-based authority) remain intact, even at the same time that the arbitrary nature of their application, which is also to say the limitlessness of their manipulation, is made visible. In other words, in the world constructed by Meisel someone still assumes the guise of authority (or passivity, or . . .), but who that someone is will be to an even greater degree a matter of personality rather than sex. Indeed, in the world constructed by Meisel, clothing will tell us something specific about the owner's fantasy of him or herself, rather than something general and potentially misleading about his or her sex as a whole.

Moreover, and more importantly, there *is* something that differentiates the performance of gender pre– and post-clone: With the advent of cloning, gender's performance will no longer be recuperable as a confirmation or subversion of *what is*, for in the era of the clone, *what is* is precisely what's changing. After all, if Baudrillard is to be believed, we are on the brink of a major evolutionary crossroad, one which may well render sexual organs and difference both gratuitous and obsolete. What's more, that consequence is arguably the least of it. For what is arguably at stake here is the fate of humanism, and more profoundly, the human species. Eradicating the very things that distinguish us from our primordial cousins (sex and death), the emergence of cloning marks nothing less than the end of man as defined by his essential characteristics. Seen in this light, what ought to be at issue in the current debate about cloning is not man's moral constitution, but rather our very existence, for just as bacteria gave way to protozoa, and protozoa gave way to us, so we, of our own volition, may well be giving way to the era of the clone.[19]

Ironies and Conclusions

If cloning is justifiably discussed in apocalyptic terms, here it needs to be said that the image of cloning painted by Versace and Meisel is more glamorous than morbid—a fact that might lead us to reflect on the role fashion may play in the epoch of the clone.[20] As noted, fashion has always been linked with performance, in the sense that costume has always enabled the individual to falsify or enhance his or her "natural" appearance, if in truth, such a thing does exist. In the era of the clone, I suspect fashion's performative dimension will become increasingly important, for as difference becomes a rarity, it will also become valued. So too, the role of the designer and all those associated with the visible dimension of identity. Indeed, for a fashion designer and/or photographer, what better fate than a world in which the theatrics of difference are paramount? A final means of differentiation in a world dominated by the same, fashion may well be our only way of constructing difference in the years to come, and as such, it seems likely that clothing will be a crucial and highly valued sign of individuality once the individual has been rendered genetically obsolete.[21]

With that in mind, we can better understand the tenor of Versace's perplexing campaign. Indicative of the industry's perverse fascination with a world in which fashion will be king, Meisel's meditation on the prospect of cloning openly concedes the appeal of this phenomenon for those "in the business"—a fact that helps us to explain the sheer number of fashion advertisements which have recently taken the double as their primary motif. Lacking the narrative dimension of Meisel's far more complicated campaign, many more advertisements reflect a kind of dumb fascination with the look and phenomenon of doubling, and in this way they are every bit the opposite of both the Versace campaign and Diesel's hyper-self conscious engagement with this same issue.

More sardonic and explicit than Versace in approach, Diesel's *Successful Living* campaign, the ironic theme of which is strategies for self-preservation, includes an ad which stresses the uncanny perversity of the clone, while at the same time openly probing the role fashion will play in a world devoid of real difference.[22] Featuring four, inanimate-looking versions of the same teenager dressed in different Diesel outfits, the copy reads as follows:

> I thought my youth was over, but then I discovered cloning. Now I can enjoy being young and attractive again and again. And if I discover a wrinkle, I'll just clone another me.
>
> —Louise Kemp-Welch (the 1st), born 1893

Although Versace and Diesel each address the tiresome cult of feminine youth, Diesel's ad is ironically focused on the psychology from which cloning stemmed, rather than on the potential consequences of its development. In this way, Diesel's ad is linked to several visual artists who have taken up this subject matter, most provocatively Jake and Dinos Chapman whose mannequin sculptures feature clusters of identical young bodies, unnaturally attached and deformed in ways that draw attention to both sameness and sex, whether through the proximity of identical bodies or the transformation of noses and mouths into distorted versions of male and female genitalia.

Exemplary of the Chapmans' work in this area, their sculpture *Zygotic acceleration, biogenetic, desublimated libidinal model* (1995) joins with Diesel in stressing the perversity of genetic manipulation, and lines up with Baudrillard and Meisel in its insistence that sex, and more specifically the act of sex is irrelevant (if not also physically impossible) in a world of cloning and clones. Of course, where the Chapman Brothers predictably depart from Meisel, is in their pointed indictment of fashion. Decorating the feet of each of these otherwise naked figures is a conspicuously identical pair of name brand sneakers—a detail I take to suggest not only our long-standing desire for sameness, but also the exploitation of that desire by those who sell the commodities that were (until recently) our best means of achieving that illusion. A pointed acknowledgment that the fashion industry is intimately linked to our desire for sameness, a work like *Zygotic acceleration . . .* leads us to consider the irony, and perhaps also the perversity of advertising campaigns that aim to thematize sameness' realization at the hands of genetic engineering. After all, there was fashion long before there was cloning, and what *is* fashion if not a crude form of cloning predicated on our desire to look alike?[23] Seen in this light, fashion emerges as the original manifestation of a desire science is now capable of gratifying, and in that sense a campaign like Meisel's can be seen as perverted and redundant in its conflation of fashion and the phenomenon of the clone.

If the Chapman Brothers can be credited with alerting us to the perversity of this conjunction, we might conclude by considering the possibility that Versace and Meisel are in on the humorless joke. Returning once again to the ad campaign that has been my primary subject in the preceding pages, I direct your attention one final time to the advertisements with which we began, for it is there, in the subtle form of logo worn as both brooch and belt, that we find an acknowledgment of the morbid connection between fashion and phenomenon of the clone. Indeed, if the Medusa's head is, in the first instance, the label that marks the clothes and advertisement as Versace (the Medusa head is their corporate logo), then it is in the second instance an emblem of fashion's self-conscious alignment with a culture that is aggressively courting the possibility of its own extinction.

That said, I end with a discussion of this modest detail because our relation to it is in some ways emblematic of the choice we now face with respect to emerging technology. On the one hand, embracing the culture of clone means avoiding the mortifying gaze of Medusa, who nevertheless resides within its borders. On the other hand, rejecting the culture of clone means resisting the lure of Meisel's identical models and facing the gaze of the Medusa head-on. If the latter seems the less appealing of these two options, in conclusion, consider this: in the precious moments between looking and dying there is knowledge, and as one awaits the inevitable consequence of having looked upon the mortifying sight of the Medusa, one will see in the form of her monstrous and androgynous face the unspeakable truth about the world and women one has shunned. Thus, if we tend to think of the Medusa as being emblematic of the terrible consequences that sight can bring, here, let us also remember that she can be equally emblematic of the consequence *of refusing to look,* even if only at an advertising campaign that may or may not have been a mortifying glimpse into our future.

Acknowledgments

A version of this chapter was presented in fall 2001 to the Women's Studies Faculty at the University of New Orleans, and again in March 2003 at the annual meeting of the Northeast Modern Language Association. Thanks is owed to those who invited me and those who attended. I would also like to acknowledge my colleagues and students both in the Fine Arts Department at the University of New Orleans and the Lamar Dodd School of Art at the University of Georgia. Their response to this campaign sharpened and enlivened my thinking, all the while validating my own sense that the campaign did indeed exert an uncanny fascination among those who look. Finally, thanks are owed to Jennifer Hirsh for her insight, friendship, and flawless Italian.

Notes

1. Meisel's advertisements for Calvin Klein are said to have inspired the look now known as "heroin chic." Moreover, and more specifically, Meisel's 1995 advertising campaign for Calvin Klein Jeans featuring spaced-out teens in shabby interiors was criticized for emulating the look and context of child pornography.

2. Banned in England, the advertisement featured a naked Sophie Dahl on a backdrop of purple velvet. Highly reminiscent of Bronzino's 16th century allegory *Venus, Cupid, Folly and Time*, the advertisement was contemporaneous with the Versace campaign under discussion here and shares with it this interest in the rhetoric of Mannerist painting.

3. An exception to this generality are the comments of Bruce Hainley (2000, 2001), who postulated that the campaign's appeal stemmed from its willingness to foreground adult females at a moment when the media is dominated by images of teenagers. Since Hainley's essay first appeared in the *Artforum's* November 2000 issue, many commentators have repeated his insight without expansion. Moreover, Hainley has himself expanded on

his original insights in the context of an essay written to accompany the subsequent exhibition at White Cube.

4. This is not the first time that White Cube has exhibited the work of a fashion photographer (White Cube had already exhibited the digitally altered photographs of Inez Van Lamsweerde) nor is it the first time modern culture has witnessed transgressions of the increasingly unstable boundary between advertising and art (Man Ray and Andy Warhol confused these boundaries long ago, to name only the most obvious examples).

5. As is well known, advertisements have a limited life span that moves them from an initial ubiquity to complete obsolescence in a matter of weeks. Transformed into art, Meisel's photographs thus transcend the conditions of their original circumstance, and do so in both practice and theory. At the level of practice, Meisel's exhibition keeps Versace's ads visible at the very moment they would have otherwise vanished, transcending in this way the average advertisement's life span through both the temporary solution of public exhibition, and the more permanent solution of the ads' amassed publication in an affordable and enduring catalogue. At the level of theory, the exhibition of Meisel's photographs in the rarified space of the gallery confers upon them the status of art—a fact that allows them to join that class of images traditionally associated with immortality and enduring value. For a discussion of the campaign's relation to art, see Campbell-Johnston (2001), Currah (2001), and Jones (2001). For a discussion of the relationship between Meisel's photographs and *contemporary* art and art history, see Lehrman (2001) and MacRitchie (2001).

6. I in no way wish to imply that I was not myself perplexed by Meisel's campaign. On the contrary, my initial experience of the campaign also resulted in an inarticulate fascination.

7. I am aware of the possibility that Meisel's description is purposefully vague, and take seriously the notion that he might wish to open up interpretive possibilities by restricting his commentary to a minimum. Also, this is as good a place as any to make the following disclaimer: although I use Meisel's remarks as a foil, I am ultimately unconcerned with his account of the series. My concern is not what Meisel wanted to do, or even what he thinks he's achieved. Instead, I am interested in the way the images function as indices of a particular moment, for which Meisel is only a (talented) medium.

8. This is in no way an exhaustive account of doubling's deployment in this campaign. Other ads also bear out this interest in more and less predictable ways.

9. Many reviewers nevertheless make reference to "Stepford wives" in their descriptions of the campaign.

10. Versace's contemporaneous campaign for their more casual line took androgyny as its explicit theme, often dressing and styling their male and female models in identical and sexually ambiguous ways.

11. Here, it's worth noting that Meisel's original conception included a still more effeminate male model. As Meisel observes in an interview with Vince Aletti (Aletti, 2001). "You never saw the original man. I did (the female model's) counterpart, but those pictures were all killed. They felt it was too strong and didn't think it was their type of person. I think they thought he was too effeminate..." Although I have nothing with which to verify this claim, I am intrigued by the possibility that the original men's model looked more like Meisel's androgynous female models, thereby leveling entirely the notion of sexual difference.

12. Baudrillard has written extensively on the phenomenon of cloning. See also Baudrillard (1993, 2001). For a general overview see Nussbaum and Sustein (1998).

13. Baudrillard's remarks here bear an interesting relation to Freud's theory of the death drive, as Freud also theorized our fundamental nostalgia for an earlier, undifferentiated state of being.

14. The fantasy of the double, of which the clone is only the most uncanny and recent manifestation, is as old as recorded history. However, Dolly is the first mammal to have been successfully cloned from adult cells—a feat accomplished at the Roslin Institute in Edinburgh, Scotland in March 1997. The first human embryo was cloned in November 2001. As Baudrillard (1993) noted: "Ours is the only period ever to have sought to exorcise this fantasy (along with others)—that is, to turn it into flesh and blood, to transform the operation of the double from a subtle interplay involving death and the other into a bland eternity of the same" (p. 114).

15. That the cloning became a reality in the shadow of the year 2000 is fact worthy of consideration, if only because cloning's regressiveness shares with the phenomenon of the millennium this temporal backwardness, as evidenced by the fact that we counted *down* the years, months and minutes to the millennium's end. On the peculiar temporality of the millennium, see Baudrillard (2000, pp. 33–57).

16. Needless to say, Meisel's campaign probes the issue of cloning through an investigation of wealthy White people, a fact that raises interesting questions about the role race and class will play in the era of the clone.

17. Of the essays I read, only Bruce's Hainley's catalogue essay made reference to the campaign's implied lesbianism.

18. Picking up on Bruce Hainley's determining remarks in *Artforum*, many authors noted the fact that Meisel gives us adults in an era when the media is dominated by teens. Although I agree that the ads present us with seemingly more mature figures, I think the issue cannot be reduced to nostalgia for the authority figures so lacking in contemporary culture.

19. I do not underestimate the amount of resistance (whether on the molecular or ideological level) the human species will generate in relation to this possibility. Here, I mark only the possibility that these objections will go unheeded.

20. Here, I do not mean to imply that Versace's ads are without their uncanny dimension—only that this aspect of Meisel's series takes a back seat to his appreciation of the vision he has constructed on Versace's behalf.

21. What an "individual" is, and whether or not one ever existed is an issue I leave open to debate. Here, suffice it to say that we will feel nostalgically about the individual's absence in any case.

22. At the time this chapter was published, the entire *Successful Living* campaign was available on Diesel's Web site www.diesel.com.

23. If fashion proceeds in the era of clone to do the opposite—that is, as fashion moves from exploiting the desire for sameness to an exploitation of our newfound desire for difference, that will be but a further irony in the highly perverse relationship between fashion and the science of cloning.

References

Aletti, V. (2001). Steven Meisel in conversation with Vince Aletti. *Steven Meisel* (exhibition catalogue). London: White Cube.

Baudrillard, J. (1993). *The transparency of evil: Essays on extreme phenomena* (J. Benedict, Trans.). London: Verso.

Baudrillard, J. (2000). *The vital illusion*. New York: Columbia University Press.

Baudrillard, J. (2001). *The impossible exchange* (C. Turner, Trans.). London: Verso.

Campbell-Johnston, R. (2001, July 25). On-the-wall-fashion. *The Times*, p. 15.

Currah, M. (2001, August 15–22). Steven Meisel. *Time Out*, p. 50.

Hainley, B. (2000, November). Oh, grow up. *Artforum*, p. 35.

Hainley, B. (2001). Sunny von Bülow-like. *Steven Meisel* (exhibition catalogue). London: White Cube.

Jones, J. (2001, July 30). Steven Meisel. *The Guardian*, p. 14.

Lehrman, K. (2001, June). Bronzino in the Valley of the Dolls. *Art and Auction*, pp. 96–105.

MacRitchie, L. (2001, July 24). Dedicated followers of fashion. *Financial Times*, p. 16.

Nussbaum, M., & Sustein, C. (Eds). (1998). *Clone and clones: Facts and fantasies about human cloning*. New York: W. W. Norton.

3

A (Bad) Habit of Thinking

Challenging and Changing the Pornographic Worldview*

Jane Caputi

The Pornographic Worldview[1]

A magazine advertisement for shoes (Fig. 2.1), curiously enough, doesn't show a shoe at all. Instead, it shows an apparently naked woman and man. She is cradling his foot in her hand and kissing it. There is nothing wrong with foot kissing, of course. But look closely at his hand on the back of her neck, holding her—maybe even forcing her—down. Is this simply an ad for footwear? Or is it also one for female subordination?

A music video, *P-Poppin* by Ludicris, is built around a strip club. It gets some pointed criticism from Marcus Flowers, a community educator at Atlanta's Men Stopping Violence: "The way that the women are paraded in front of fully clothed customers, their bodies for sale, reminds me of how half-naked slaves were exhibited to white buyers at auctions, as if they were animals" (Mendez Berry, 2005, p. 166).

It might not surprise anyone to learn that whole genres of pornography are devoted to what one Web site, www.sickestsites.com, approvingly describes as "women being totally degraded and turned into sperm ashtrays." "Sickest sites" applauds the pornography site "Meatholes" for showing one woman "reduced to tears with verbal abuse, forced ass-licking, toes forced into her mouth, and dirty sneakers pressed onto her tender pussy." These kinds of actions are understood by sociologists as "ceremonies of degradation," and such ritual demolitions of self-esteem

---

*This chapter was originally published in Marian Meyers (Ed.), *Women and Popular Culture: Representation and Meaning*, © 2008, Hampton Press, Inc.

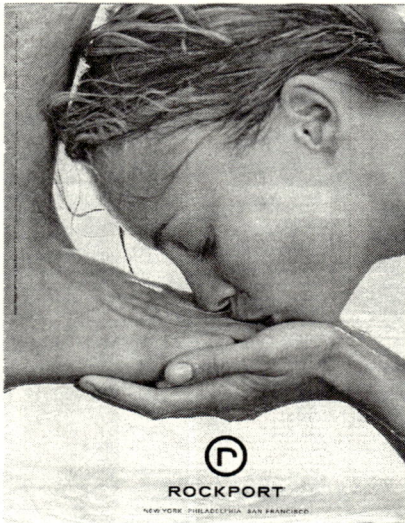

Fig. 2.1. Enforced submission

Fig. 2.2. Ritual degradation

are regularly done by abusers to victims in places like slave plantations, prisons, and torture chambers. References to these same types of ritual degradations show up not only in overt pornography, but also are coded into innumerable advertising images. Compare the Meatholes' enactment of dirty sneakers pressed into a woman's genitals with an image from a mainstream ad for sneakers, which shows a man's sneaker-shod foot pushed up against the mouth of a seemingly willing and aroused woman (Fig. 2.2).

As the title of this chapter indicates, it is not about X-rated pornography. Rather, the chapter is about a pornographic worldview, what Patricia Williams (1995, p. 123) called a "habit of thinking" based in the eroticization of domination and subordination as well as pervasive sexual objectification. Catharine MacKinnon and Andrea Dworkin (Dworkin, 1989, pp. 253–275) originally shifted the debate around pornography from questions of morality and chastity to those of power relations. They defined *pornography* as the "sexually explicit subordination of women" or those used in the place of women. Pornography, in this view, is not about the appreciation of women and the pleasures of sex but about the "denigration of women and a fear and hatred of the female body" (Kaplan, 1991, p. 322). Throughout this chapter, I explore the way these themes are ubiquitous in mainstream imagery. But first, I want to deal briefly with the charge that when feminists criticize pornography we play into the hands of right-wing forces.

Pornography's defenders argue that pornography radically challenges a moralistic and anti-sex worldview propagated by patriarchal religions. At first this seems to make some sense. Aren't those anti-feminist, family values types always railing against pornography? But let's think twice about this. The pornographic worldview is actually the secret twin of the puritanical one. Both worldviews rely on and uphold the *same* fundamentally sexist beliefs: that men are superior to women, and that women are in need of control and best suited for sexual and reproductive functions. Pornography as we know it is a direct result of patriarchal moralism's fear and hatred of women and of sex itself, which it also understands as something essentially taboo—"dirty," unintelligent, uncivilized, sinful, and shameful.

All of this counters millennia of human understanding that sexuality is a way of knowledge and pleasure and a force that—in its intimacy, creativity, potency, ecstasy, and dynamism—reflects and participates in the cosmic energy that powers the universe. In the ancient world, this understanding of sexuality as sacred and cosmic was represented by the figure of a Goddess, often naked, sometimes even with spread legs, a Goddess who is the origin of all life (Gadon, 1989).

But patriarchal religions, particularly in the Abrahamic traditions, depose that Goddess and then turn her into pornography (Caputi, 2004). In her place, they put an all-male, anti-sexual, or erotophobic God. This new religion tells us that women are in need of domination, and that male domination of women will be the basis of sex. This outrage is given divine endorsement in *Genesis* 3:16, when God curses Eve by telling her: "Your desire will be unto your husband and he will lord it over you." More recently, the popular Christian-oriented advice book, *The Surrendered Wife* (Doyle, 2000) presents this as a blessing. It promises that if women just "surrender" to their husbands in all ways—financially, sexually, psychologically, spiritually—they will have not only happier marriages, but also hotter sex. The same message is transmitted, albeit more graphically, in pornography where women are literally bound and gagged before being "fucked" (a word which, in our sexist culture, means both to have sex with and to do gross, violent injury to). In truth, the pornographic habit of thinking is not really deviant at all. Rather, it is part of a social network—which includes law, medicine, military, family, and religion—that long has worked together to subordinate women, primarily by defining, controlling, exploiting, and punishing female sexuality and by defining male sexuality in mechanistic and dominating ways.

A global feminist movement challenges that patriarchal network as it takes various forms in different traditions. By criticizing pornography I am by no means advocating censorship or some return to respectability and female "modesty"—a tried-and-true method of stifling women and controlling female sexuality. I support sexual freedom and sexual representations and simultaneously want the liberation of erotic imaginations from both pornographic and moralistic paradigms. Sometimes, however, it seems impossible for those of us enmeshed in it to imagine anything

Fig. 2.3. Active female sexuality
associated with sin

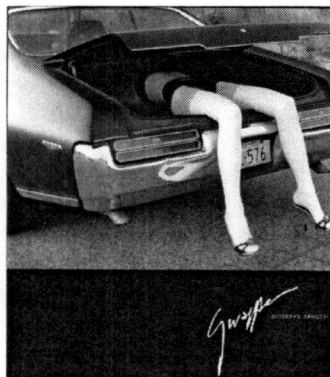

Fig. 2.4. Pornography of murder

other than what we've learned from conventional morality/ pornography. Everywhere we are told that without a certain measure of domination, submission, sin (Fig. 2.3), danger, possession, obsession, humiliation, objectification, and violence even unto death (Fig. 2.4), there wouldn't be any "sex" at all.

The paradigm of eroticized domination and objectification is not confined to interpersonal relationships but serves as a basis for all manner of exploitative and abusive practices. Scientific metaphors traditionally have turned on pornographic themes exalting masculine sexual aggression against what is conceptualized as feminine Nature and the planet we still colloquially understand as Mother Earth (Keller, 1985; Merchant, 1980). Many observers have found eroticized domination at the core of Nazism (Griffin, 1981; Sontag, 1980), torture (Brison, 2004; Caputi, 1987), the cult of nuclear weaponry (Caputi, 1993), militarism, imperial conquest (Smith, 2005), racism and slavery (Collins, 1998; Hernton, 1988). Pornographic thinking influences all of these larger social dominations, but it basically begins in our most everyday ideas about sex and gender.

Gender Pornography

Pornography depends on very conventional and moralistic notions of masculinity and femininity. Although there are complex differences along class, ethnic, and race lines (see, e.g., Collins, 2004), men and women conventionally are defined as opposite and inherently unequal. At the same time, men and women—and, the moralists thunder, only men and women—are ineluctably attracted to each other. This system links inequality itself to the erotic dynamic. The man is supposed to be taller, stronger, richer, older, and colder—in short, more powerful. The woman is supposed to be shorter, weaker, better looking, vulnerable, younger, warmer—in short, socially powerless. This scenario is played, for example, in one ad for lingerie. A woman clothed only in red undergarments looks up tremulously, lips parted, as a fully clothed man towers over her, holding something hidden, possibly threatening, behind his back.

A similarly sexist brand of heterosexuality also is pushed by a 1999 ad for L'Oreal "straight up" hair products. It shows a young, "clean-cut" White couple. The woman—with long, straight hair—gazes up, sweetly and trustingly, at her stern-faced boyfriend. He towers over her and is literally "in her face." The ad commands them to "play it straight." Certainly, that dictate refers as much to conformity to sexist heterosexuality—the male-dominant/female-subordinate kind—as it does to chemically straightened locks.

Those who uphold patriarchal family values claim that homosexual relationships threaten the very bedrock of civilization. Of course, because sexual inequality is the very bedrock of patriarchal civilization, they might have a point. Much of the antagonism to lesbian and gay marriage—unions among social equals—is based in fear of the idea of egalitarian, nonpatriarchal relationships spreading to heterosexual marriage.

Objectification

Objectifying others mean treating them as if they had no innate self, sovereignty, purpose, agency, or soul and using them for your own purposes, including for sexual gratification and for ego enhancement. Numerous images support this kind of dehumanization by making it seem as if women are literal objects—vehicles (Fig. 2.5), blow-up dolls (Fig. 2.6), furniture, collectibles, and so on. As objects, women

Fig. 2.5. Woman fused with car

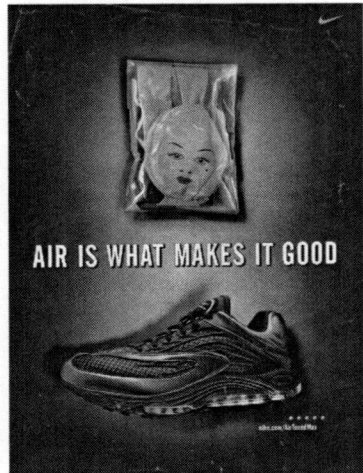

AIR IS WHAT MAKES IT GOOD

Fig. 2.6. Woman as sex doll

are denied autonomy and presented as perpetually accessible, something to toy with, something to possess, something to be consumed (Fig. 2.7; Adams, 2003).

Different ethnicities are marketed as specific types of objects in pornography. For example, Asian women are cast as submissive "Oriental Dolls," or dominant "Dragon Ladies," Black women as sexually loose "Jezebels" (Collins, 1998), and so on. In the oppressive class and race hierarchy, the most socially valuable women are young, light-skinned, slim, and usually blonde, representing the "gold standard."

As feminism has demanded sexual freedom for women, the pornographic culture responds by equating pornography with liberation. Everywhere, women and girls are encouraged to make themselves into sex objects, adopting the stripper or the pornography star as a role model. Black feminist theorist Patricia Hill Collins (2004) criticized the ways that Black popular culture characterizes men as thugs and women as "whores" and "bitches." Moreover, she suggested, the fixation on women's buttocks is reminiscent of the way 19th-century European men fetishized the buttocks and genitals of the South African woman they dubbed the Hottentot Venus, whom they stripped and displayed for profit.[2]

The age of the sex object keeps getting younger. Louise Kaplan (1991) argued that when women demand and express their intellectual, sexual and emotional freedom, society responds with both woman-hating pornography and the increased sexual objectification of girls (Fig. 2.8). In pornographic videos, women are marked with clothing and hair styles to suggest that they are children or teenagers (Jensen & Dines, 1998). So too, in advertising, grown women are posed as sexually available little girls (Fig. 2.9).

Fig. 2.7. Women as consumable objects

Fig. 2.8. Sexualization of girls

Fig. 2.9. Women presented as
sexualized girls

Sex and Violence

Objectification is a prerequisite not only for inequality but also for violence. Much overt pornography is explicitly devoted to rape and abuse, and everyday pornography also regularly shows women in situations that suggest that they are about to be raped, often facilitated by alcohol or drugs (Fig. 2.10).

Fig. 2.10. Scene suggesting gang
rape, facilitated by alcohol

Rape and other forms of sexual abuse are intended to silence victims. This is equally a concern of patriarchal religion. Saint Paul thunders: "Let a woman learn in silence with all submissiveness. I permit no woman to teach or to have authority over men; she is to keep silent" (1 Tim. 2: 11–12). Silencing women, not surprisingly, also is a central preoccupation of pornography. In 1976, for one of its jokes, *Hustler* magazine published a doctored photograph that depicts a woman's face whose mouth has been replaced by a hairy vulva. The copy beneath openly suggests rape as a way of silencing women's subversive speech:

> There are those who say that illogic is the native tongue of anything with tits. . . . It comes natural to many broads; just like rolling in shit is natural for dogs. . . . They speak not from the heart but from the gash. . . . The one surefire way to stop those feminine lips from driving you crazy is to put something between them—like your cock, for instance.

Pornography regularly features the binding and gagging of women, something reflected in scores of similar images in mainstream advertising that call for female silence. In one ad for gum, a teenage girl wearing a man's shirt and tie has a manhole cover shoved into her mouth; she is apparently being punished not only for having a "dirty mouth," as the copy below the ad reads, but for cross-dressing. Another 2004 ad for voting rights asks women not to silence themselves by neglecting to vote, but it simultaneously shows Christina Aguilera with her mouth sewn shut. Presumably, this image is meant to convey irony. But such a horrific image actually works to communicate the threat that is meant to induce women to silence themselves before someone else does it to them (Fig. 2.11). To understand more fully, it is necessary to recognize that this torturous image is not an isolated one. Similar ones are regularly reiterated in explicitly misogynist contexts. It is, for example, uncannily similar to one that advertised the 1998 hor-

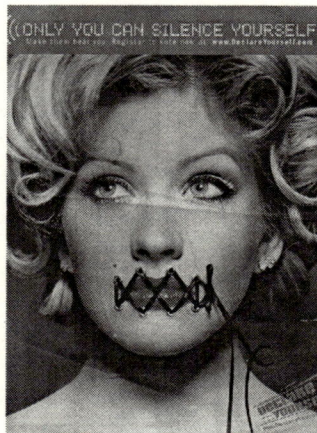

Fig. 2.11. Silencing of women

ror film *Strangeland*. This ad showed the face of a teenage girl whose mouth was similarly sewn up; a killer does this to his victims prior to raping and murdering them, in effect, permanently silencing them. The ubiquity of such imagery speaks loudly. It reflects not only the reality of *gynocidal*[3] violence against women, but also the intent of that violence and its representations—to terrorize women and girls and destroy our capacity to resist.

In the "snuff" genre of pornography, someone actually is raped, tortured, and killed. A faked film with the title *Snuff* was released in the United States in 1976, claiming to have been made in South America where, as its poster says, "life is cheap." This claim endorses the ways that economic oppression, racism, drug trafficking, and corporate greed make poor and/or racially stigmatized women especially vulnerable to prostitution, pornography, rape, and murder. These realities are horribly mirrored in the Mexican city of Ciudad Juárez and also in Guatemala, where hundreds if not thousands of women and girls have been tortured, raped, and murdered since the early 1990s.

In North American popular culture, White, male, serial sex killers, beginning with Jack the Ripper, have become cult heroes (Caputi, 1987) and "snuff" imagery has become the stuff of everyday entertainment, not only in horror movies (from *Psycho* on), television, and video games (e.g., *Grand Theft Auto*), but also in fashion advertising. Everywhere, we encounter images of women being shot, stabbed, strung up, and decapitated (Fig. 2.12). These images constitute a kind of virtual lynching, where mass audiences can enjoy the spectacle of sexualized murder of the stigmatized group. In one fashion photo from 2003, a seemingly dead woman wearing a green jacket is dumped by a river. The scene instantly reminded me of the "Green River Killer," Gary L. Ridgeway, who was convicted around that same time for raping and murdering 49 girls and women. According to prosecutors,

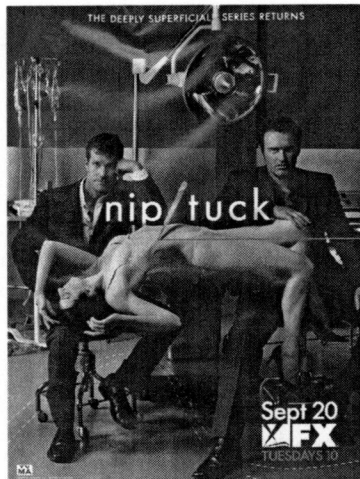

Fig. 2.12. Everyday snuff imagery

Ridgeway explained himself: "I'd much rather have white, but black was fine. It's just, just garbage. Just something [to have sex with and] kill her and dump her." Ridgeway, like other sex killers, uses the word "it" to refer to his victims. His point of view is reflected everywhere in popular culture where women are identified with objects—cars, motorcycles, dolls, tables, and household items. In one fashion series, the woman's presence is really an absence as she is represented only by a chopped up mannequin, her body parts used to make furniture. In the *Sky Mall* catalogue, available on any domestic flight, readers find a table whose "legs" seems to be a woman's in high-heeled shoes. The table is described as "playful and oh so much fun." Fun for whom? The serial killer Ed Gein actually used the body parts of his female victims to make furniture.

Pornographic Masculinity

James Gilligan (1996), who was the chief psychiatrist for the Massachusetts prison system, finds that men are more violent than women not because they are hormonally driven to aggression but because of the construction of patriarchal gender roles. These roles split the whole human psyche into two "opposite" and unequal sexes. These roles then ordain women to be sex objects and men to be violence objects. As such, men are mortified by any association with the feminine. The worst thing a man can be called is some variation of "girl," "wimp," or "pussy." Men are under enormous pressure to continually prove their "manhood" by showing dominance—militaristic, imperialistic, financial, intellectual, emotional, and physical. Gilligan also argues that poor and/or ethnically stigmatized men are kept from having access to social dominance, and so often resort to physical violence to prove manhood.

A seemingly innocuous ad for insurance stages a scene of high school humiliation around a trio of students. A young White man is mocked by a Black man and sneered at by a White woman for wearing a sweater identical to one the woman is wearing. This "wimp" temporarily loses not only his male privilege but also his White privilege. A similar threat to male voters' gender honor was mobilized by Republican supporters in the 2004 presidential election. As one bumper sticker warned: "Don't be a girlie man. Vote Republican."

One ad pitched to teenaged boys for Bitch skateboards handily pantomimes the basic process of becoming a man in patriarchal culture. Two figures—the universal signs for male and female—are represented; the male figure aims a gun at the female figure's head (Fig. 2.13). This, obviously, indicates hostility against girls and women. But another, hidden meaning may be that the teenage boy, in order to become a "real man," has to kill off his feminine-identified traits. Much popular imagery sends a message that the real man must be hard and so self-absorbed that he actually becomes incapable of relationship and connection except, of course, with machines, like his weapons, his car, or his computer.

Fig. 2.13. Bitch skateboards

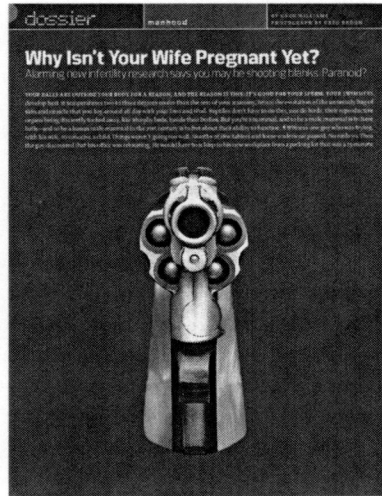

Fig. 2.14. *Details* magazine

The pornographic worldview—reflected in Freudian psychoanalysis, military marching chants, and innumerable images in popular culture—openly identifies men as violence objects, often equating the penis with a weapon. A frankly pornographic film called *Mr. MX* (after the nuclear warhead), focused upon a White man with a supposed 16-and-one-half inch penis. An everyday variant on this theme informs an illustration for an article on male infertility that appeared in a 2007 edition of *Details* magazine. It shows a large and fully loaded handgun aiming directly at the viewer. The headline reads: "Why Isn't Your Wife Pregnant Yet? Alarming new infertility research says you may be shooting blanks." (Fig. 2.14) In these visual metaphors, the penis is a weapon and the most potent ejaculation is a bullet or a bomb blast. Implicitly, then, a woman's vagina is a target or a war zone.

Pornographic Family Values

Nawal El Saadawi (1980) suggested that it is male insecurity in the face of "the innate resilience and strength of the woman" that first led men to oppress and subjugate women, to try to "conquer the indomitable vitality and strength that lay within women" (p. 100). This took the form of men trying to control, punish, and exploit female sexuality, which is why "good girls," in the family values framework, must be virginal, chaste, and under the control of father or husband. Of course, because heterosexual men do not want to restrict themselves to chastity, they also consign some women to the "bad girl" status.

The friendly sound of the phrase "family values" masks its underlying strategy of dominating, exploiting, and controlling women—sometimes through forced reproduction brought about by denial of birth control and abortion, sometimes by forced sterilization, especially of women whom racists see as undesirable (Smith, 2005). Some patriarchal systems work by mandating that women be veiled and covered; others promote a central image of women as nearly naked sexual objects. But both strategies, however different, are ways to control female sexuality and destroy female self-definition.

Traditionally, patriarchal cultures foster paternalism, granting the father basic ownership over his wife, or wives, and children. The father is supposed to protect them in exchange for their absolute loyalty, but he also has the right to physically abuse and sometimes to sell or even murder them (Millett, 1970). Feminism challenges this model worldwide, but much family values rhetoric indicates a desire to return to a time when women and children were understood as men's property or valuables and the father was the ultimate authority in the home.

Radical feminist theologian Mary Daly (1973) boldly pointed to the political implications of religious representation: "The symbol of the Father God . . . [makes] the oppression of women appear right and fitting. If 'God' in 'his' heaven is a father ruling 'his' people, then it is in the 'nature' of things and according to divine plan and the order of the universe that society be male dominated" (p. 13). The iconic 1950's television show *Father Knows Best* packaged that divine plan in the form of a situation comedy, and that phrase still is approvingly cited by family values spokesmen like Florida mega-church Pastor Bob Coy (2005). Coy regularly prescribes male rule as the direct expression of "God's" plan, closing one of his weekly televised sessions with this prayer to gender difference and men's preeminence: "As the wife does her thing and the guy does his thing as a husband, Lord, we'll find our homes are those havens of rest, a place where weary souls can come and discover that Father knows best." Ironically, a similar reference shows up in an overtly incest-friendly feature in *Playboy*. It is titled "Father Knows Best" and showcases a father who photographs his own daughter naked as an adult. As an added treat, *Playboy* includes a naked picture of the daughter as a 3-year old child that the father snapped when he took her with him to his pornography shoots and where she mimicked the older models.

Obviously, family-values spokesmen like Pastor Coy would not, as *Playboy* seems to be doing here, endorse incest. But father–daughter incest and other forms of sexist abuse are the inevitable underside of paternalist systems. What those who advocate male authority in the home don't tell us is that the patriarchal home is not very safe at all for many women and children. Domestic violence is the most common cause of injury to women and, like incest, it then gets turned into a specialized type of pornography. One pornography Web site, "Brutal Family," assures its visitors that there is only one family law—"Man says, woman obeys"—as

Fig. 2.15. Fashion imagery promoting
domestic violence

it shows naked women being beaten up by men. A three-part fashion spread in
Vibe also promotes a domestic violence sequence. In the first image, a man appears
to be yelling at a woman, who tries to cover her ears. In the second, he is grab-
bing her and appears to be slapping and shaking her (Fig. 2.15). In the third, he
is outside the door to the home, which is half-way open. Scarily, he seems to be
talking his way back in.

The Pornography of War and Conquest

The eroticized masculine domination over the feminine instituted in patriarchal
family relationships and everyday gender roles is regularly marshaled to support
war and colonization (Smith, 2005). Rena Swentzell (1993), a Native American
scholar, pointed to the atrocious belief in "power as an integral part of sexuality,"
and added that this "is what the Inquisition was all about. That is what the whole
conquest of the Southwest was about—power and control by males" (p. 167).

Historically, conquerors have conceptualized the land they sought as female
and often naked, as in one visual depiction of the "Discovery of America." This
classic 1600 rendition depicts a conqueror standing erect and holding a flag on a
pole. He is fully clothed and is associated with ships and gadgets. The land to be
conquered is represented by a naked and reclining woman, who is associated with
cannibals and animals.

The intimate connection between sex and conquest remains firmly established in American culture as revealed by events and images associated with the U.S.-led invasion of Iraq in 2003. Political cartoonist Ward Sutton shows the notoriously cocky Donald Rumsfeld, the first Secretary of Defense under President George W. Bush, masturbating to images of Baghdad being bombed. Whatever our political affiliation, everyone gets the joke.

In 2004, one pornography Web site, "Iraq Babes," devoted itself exclusively to images that purported to show American soldiers raping Iraqi women. Meanwhile, real harms were happening at Abu Ghraib prison in Iraq in 2003, where U.S. soldiers sexually abused and tortured Iraqi inmates, including by staging scenes of sexual humiliation (Danner, 2004) and photographing them. In May 2004, a number of these photos were released to the public.[4] The types of degrading abuses directed at the Iraqi prisoners are mirrored in the ordinary treatment of women in both pornography and mainstream imagery, where women routinely are put into shameful and vulnerable positions. In one of the photos from Abu Ghraib, naked men are made to pile on top of one another, with their buttocks in the air. Smiling and giving thumbs-up gestures are soldiers Charles Graner and Lynndie England, clearly enjoying this blatant demonstration of their power over the ritually abused Iraqis (Fig. 2.16). This torturous set-up is eerily mirrored in a photo in *Vibe* magazine, which appeared before the release of the Abu Ghraib photos (Fig. 2.17).

Two men are seated at a bar. To their left, a woman in a very short skirt and stiletto heels bends over the bar, exposing her "panties" and baring part of her buttocks. In the top-left corner we read: "BOTTOMS UP: Tyrese and Bobbito enjoy the show." Clearly, the two men are enjoying not only the woman's sexual display, but also the show of their power. They, after all, are seated, fully clothed, and facing the viewer; one grins and the other gives a "thumbs-up" gesture. In one

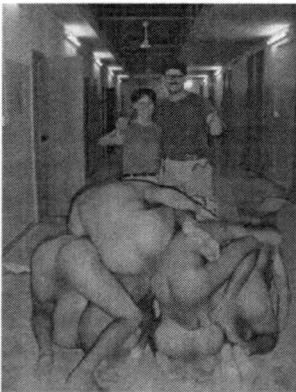

Fig. 2.16. Abu Ghraib

Fig. 2.17. Commercial ritual humiliation

Fig. 2.18. Abu Ghraib

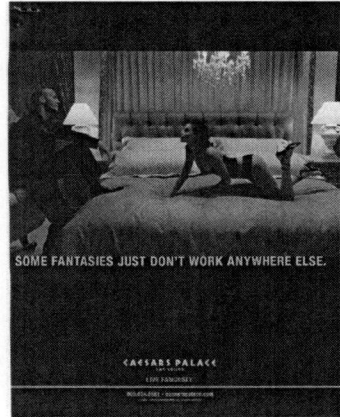

SOME FANTASIES JUST DON'T WORK ANYWHERE ELSE.

CAESARS PALACE

Fig. 2.19. Las Vegas

notorious photo from Abu Ghraib, the role of sexual dominator was taken by a woman, Lynndie England. In the pose of a dominatrix, England dragged a naked man on a leash (Fig. 2.18). The *New York Times* averred that Private England has come to symbolize the Abu Ghraib scandal. But we need to remember that the men in charge deliberately used a woman torturer because they knew that it would be far more humiliating for a man to be sexually tormented by a woman. Significantly, the ringleader at Abu Ghraib, Charles Graner, was England's lover, a former prison guard and allegedly abusive and adulterous husband, who sent off copies of this picture to friends saying, "Look what I made Lynndie do."

Everyday pornography regularly shows coded versions of the abusive dynamic so evident at Abu Ghraib—although usually with the man in the dominant role. One ad for Las Vegas has an uncanny resonance with the image of England dragging the man on the leash. In this image, there is no literal leash but one is suggested as a clothed man snaps his fingers and, in response, a lingerie-clad woman crawls across a bed on all fours to him. The accompanying copy, "Some Fantasies Just Don't Work Anywhere Else," suggests that Las Vegas is a special place, like a prison, where abusers can act out their desires (Fig. 2.19).

The Pornography of Bondage

In one publicity shot, Paris Hilton, naked save for high-heeled black boots, is elaborately bound in the cord from a microphone she is holding. Hilton at this time was involved with a man, Nick Carter, who allegedly was battering her, and some of her photos showed visible bruises. Carter claimed innocence and said that the injuries actually resulted from this photo shoot. Whatever the truth, this kind of image tacitly supports abuse, eroticizing female captivity, bondage and helplessness. Literally, this photo valorizes the point of view of a serial killer—someone like Dennis Rader, the self-named "BTK (Bind, Torture, Kill) Killer."

Bondage, literally, means a state of enslavement. Although pornography is supposedly about fantasy and sexual freedom, its imagery and practices are rooted in slavery. The eroticization of domination and the treatment of women as unpaid and forced domestic and sexual labor in the home began with the historical institution of slavery at the inception of patriarchal organization when elite men enslaved the women from conquered groups (Lerner, 1986). Later, men, too, were enslaved and even sometimes raped by masters and mistresses. But for women, "sexual exploitation marked the very definition of enslavement" (p. 89).

Patricia Hill Collins (1998) argued that contemporary pornography has strong ties to the treatment of Black women and men in U.S. slavery. Slavery eroticizes capture, bondage, punishment, whipping and rape; the master class justified itself by saying that slaves were like animals—and that it was acceptable to treat animals this way, which it also is not. These patterns continue in everyday imagery, such as one fashion ad, where a dark-skinned woman wears animal-print clothing and is posed with legs parted for accessibility. If you look closely, you can see that she is stapled to the fabric, looking like a doll, or a slave, for sale (Fig. 2.20).

Pornography, including everyday pornography, continually churns out fantasies sexualizing bondage, servitude, and submission, usually with women in the submissive position. In some contexts, both real and representational, privileged White women do play the master role—as in colonialism and racism (Fig. 2.21).

Fig. 2.20. Sexualized slavery

Fig. 2.21. White woman in sexualized "master" role

Fig. 2.22. Sexualized "slave" role

Concomitantly, the subordinated feminine role can be forced on men. One ad for sweatpants broadly suggests slavery and imprisonment (Fig. 2.22). Why is this heavily muscled, African-American man stripped from the waist up and then "emasculated," made to lower his head in submission? Ann duCille (1997) provided an answer, rooted in the historical institution of slavery: "Both male and female slaves were often exhibited and sold in the nude, their naked body fondled, and groped, and gazed upon by white men. . . . The dominant/submissive, master/slave power relation . . . was the perfect locus for playing out forbidden racial and sexual fantasies" (p. 308). Advertising then replays these sexual enslavement fantasies, albeit in coded forms.

The Pure and the Dirty

. . . keep pornography. . . dirty. The way it should be.

(Cromer, 2001, p. 28)

The religious historian Mircea Eliade (1969) wrote that sexuality's "primary and perhaps supreme valency is the cosmological function. . . . [E]xcept in the modern world, sexuality has everywhere and always been a hierophany [a manifestation of the sacred], and the sexual act an integral action (therefore also a means of knowledge)" (p. 14). In this view, sexual pleasure, rooted in our bodily nature, is something that can lead to wisdom and well as to spiritual understanding and connection with the divine. But all of this is reversed in many patriarchal religions that share a habit of associating sexuality, particularly female sexuality, with sin, "filth," and the forbidden. In this view, virginity and chastity are "clean," whereas sex is considered "dirty." This notion is the basis of the double standard, where women's sexuality is subjected to severe regulation and categorization, with women slotted as either "clean" virgins or "dirty" whores. The idea that sex can be something leading to wisdom is equally denied by pornography. Indeed, pornography *needs* sex to be "dirty," dumb, and forbidden, for without this taboo, sexuality and eroticism might be accepted and integrated into our culture in honest and open ways, and pornography as we know it would be obsolete.

A chilling ad from the 1970s is quite open about the abusive implications of making sex "dirty." The ad is for "Love's Baby Soft" fragrance. It depicts a heavily made-up child with an elaborate adult coiffeur (Fig. 2.23). A hand, one that looks far too big to be hers, reaches in front, holding a teddy bear, suggesting the presence of an adult abuser. The headline reads: "Love's Baby Soft. Because innocence is sexier than you think." This ad, while subtly endorsing child sexual abuse, also explains in part its thrill for those who practice it. When patriarchal religions make sexuality sinful and "forbidden," doing forbidden things actually can become more exciting, more compelling. And when sex is culturally understood not only as "power over" someone, but also as something that "dirties" or defiles, dirtying someone who is considered especially "powerless" and especially "innocent" or "pure" (e.g., a virgin or even a child) also can become especially compelling, especially for the most insecure and self-loathing men.[5]

Notions of purity and dirtiness also are manipulated to promote racism and genocide. One 1995 ad for soap shows an upright, young blonde woman in a white blouse, alongside the word *PURE*. It looks, on the one hand, like an ad for female chastity. On the other it might remind us of a neo-Nazi poster evoking racist notions of "purity" of

Fig. 2.23. Sexualized childhood "innocence"

blood. Those who claim to be the most civilized and "pure" regularly project all that they deny and fear in themselves on to people who are of other ethnic groups or races, whom they then castigate as "dirty" and "savage."

Alice Walker (1980) observed that although White women are represented as "objects" in pornography, Black women are represented as "shit." One cartoon in *Hustler* (1979) depicted a Black man wiping himself after defecating. Where he wipes, the underlying skin shows up as white. This utterly pornographic notion that dark skin is "shitty," whereas white skin is "clean" is reiterated in an ad for Diesel jeans from 1995. It shows a dark-skinned woman, prone on zebra-skin sheets and with jeans unzipped to signify that she is conquered, open to all. The small print says: "Right now, there are far too many dangerous animals running around, wasting space, wasting time, using the planet as a toilet! Take our advice. Don't be fooled by 'natural' beauty, stick em in practical, easy-to-clean metal cages." By associating this woman, and those like her, with waste, this ad basically presents a case justifying genocide, or what is euphemistically called "ethnic cleansing." Again, the makers of this ad might justify themselves by saying that their flagrant statements indicate they are being ironic. But, as with the supposedly anti-silencing image discussed earlier, this ad most effectively communicates fundamental racist and sexist symbolism. The ironic framing actually works to disarm some viewers, setting up a doublethink mechanism, and making the vicious messages even more potent.

Distorted notions of purity and dirtiness also are used to foment and justify homophobia. In March 2005, an extraordinary interfaith alliance of male religious leaders in Jerusalem formed to stop an international gay pride festival in Jerusalem. One Islamic leader stated the group's central concern: "We can't permit anybody to come and make the Holy City dirty." Once again, the scapegoating of another person or group as "dirty" is used as a way to exclude and demonize them, justifying oppression.

The idea that sex is "dirty" comes from an overall mind–body split in which the body and (female-identified) nature is seen as inferior and the (male-identified) mind and culture are seen as superior. This same split leads patriarchal cultures to disparage the Earth as mere matter, dirt, something for elite humans to exploit and use. In so doing humans forget that we are made of the Earth. The very word *human* is derived from the Latin *humus*, meaning earth or dirt. We are all equally dirty, equally human, and our body is inextricable from mind and spirit and is, moreover, "our most precious talisman," connecting us to the (Mother) Earth (Allen, 1990, p. 56). As we ponder the pornographic culture's body-hatred and concomitant notion of sexual "dirt," we can also consider the ways that violence against women and girls, as well as against peoples stigmatized as "savage," "shitty," "filthy," and "other," is part of an overall pattern of violence against the Earth and Nature.

Global Snuff

> What can be done, under patriarchy, to one female [or feminized] body can be
> done, under world patriarchy, to the entire body of earth. The pornographic
> images of women trussed up in chains and barbed wire, of female flesh bruised
> and bloodied and beaten raw, are really our species' maps of the mutilated earth.
> . . . The deadness of pornography is the deadness of the landscape created by
> patriarchy, in which nothing lives that is not hideously deformed, controlled,
> manipulated for the voyeur's eye, bound up for use. (Sjöö & Mor 1991, p. 411)

An illustration on the cover of a mid-1980s avant-garde rock compilation album,
"The Blasting Concept" shows a naked man strangling a woman with a rope while
raping her. Through a window, we see outside a corresponding blast—what seems
to be a nuclear mushroom cloud. How do we interpret such a horrific image?

One way is by recalling that in indigenous traditions throughout the world,
the Earth and Nature are recognized as a divine, feminine principle, although one
including both female and male, and often represented by a female body. This
perception is often expressed colloquially as "Mother Earth" or "Mother Nature."
In some traditions, this translates into respect. In the pornographic worldview, the
Earth and Nature are still recognized as a feminine principle, but now this means
that they can be objectified, raped, exploited, silenced, and sexually murdered.

Patriarchal religion, philosophy and science have long conceptualized Nature
as a pornographic object. Reflecting this tradition, one sculpture, "Nature Revealed
by Science" (Louis-Ernst Barrias) from just over a century ago represents Nature
as a sexually available woman, stripped and with her "mysteries" revealed. Popular
imagery continues to represent the Universe, the Earth and Nature as a passive and
vulnerable sex object, one available for penetration, forced to yield up her secrets,
and even implicitly murdered. An exceptionally violent ad for fax machines (Fig.
2.24) shows the face of a female figure symbolizing Nature being raped with objects
through eyes, ears, and mouth. This image is meant to convey that this particular
technology is so fast that it virtually breaks the laws of Nature.

One related ad for audio speakers shows a young woman, laid out as if dead,
her naked body covered with maps: She is the Earth, explored, mapped, conquered.
Correspondingly, images of the actual planet Earth are also shown as subject to White
male domination. An ad for a multinational corporation shows the Earth as a toy, with
four boy toddlers grouped around it. Three non-white boys sit on the floor, their eyes
unfocused. But the little White boy stands right behind the toy Earth and raises his
finger in a gesture of authority, signifying White male domination not only over men
of other ethnicities and races, but also over women and the Earth itself. (Fig. 2.25) More
explicitly violent images of the Earth also are common; in many ads, the planet is carved
up, objectified, targeted, and otherwise symbolically raped.

Fig. 2.24. Rape of Nature

Fig. 2.25. White male domination

All of this abusive imagery culminates in the figure of a futuristic "fembot"—an artificial, thin, and slick sex object (Fig. 2.26). "She" at first might seem to prophesy elite men's coming total control not only over the female sex, but also over Nature. But this is an illusion. A global feminist movement openly resists patriarchy. And Nature is not completely passive, malleable, and manageable. As militaries and corporations systematically damage or poison the ecosystem, the Earth responds by withdrawing such vital

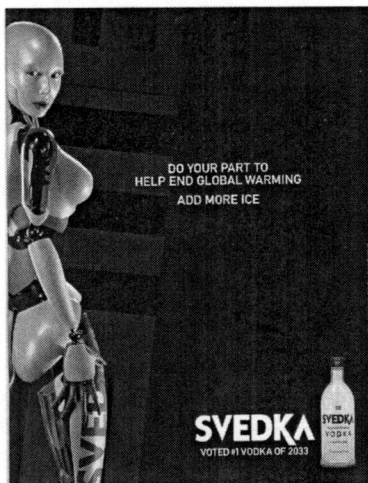

Fig. 2.26. Fembot

services as production of food and purification of water.[6] These egregious polluters do not so much control Nature as they hasten our own and other species' demise as the outcome of nuclear war, catastrophic climate change, the enduring toxicity of nuclear waste, and the contamination of the elements. The artificial sex object, the "fembot," does not really signify "mankind's" completed victory over Nature. What she does portend is desensitization, alienation, and sterility.

Reality Control

The novelist and essayist Toni Cade Bambara (1993) tells us that the experience of viewing racist and sexist popular culture fare for African-American women is a kind of "mugging" (pp. 132–133). bell hooks (1992) also argued, in even stronger terms, that such imagery can serve as a "murder weapon" (p. 7). Similarly, in his study of the pornography postcards of Algerian women manufactured by French colonizers, Malek Alloula (1986) argued that the postcard fully participates in the violence of colonization and is "no less efficient for being symbolic" (p. 5).

Pornography's defenders frequently admonish its critics by averring that pornography is simply a form of fantasy. Yet, hooks, Bambara, and Alloula take a very different view, declaring that the misogynist, objectifying, racist, and environmentally destructive imagery of everyday life not only endorses and normalizes violence but is itself a form of violence. Clearly, mass media representations, however heinous, are not the equivalent of an actual instance of abuse. Nonetheless, it is useful to draw out some of their correspondences.

Violence, including violence in intimate relationships, does not always take the form of physical blows. Abuse also takes an emotional/psychological form that is meant to destroy the self-esteem of the victim while enhancing that of the abuser. It appears as verbal assaults, belittlement, cultivation of anxiety and despair, mockery, blaming, accusation, humiliation, degradation, disrespect, and "reality control," which includes denying the harm of the abuse, creating an atmosphere of threat, and *blocking awareness of alternative ways of living and being.*

Psychological battery by a lover or a family member is direct and personalized and obviously will have much greater violent effect than commercial representations. Still, repeated negative, mass-mediated representation of a group is a public form of psychological violence and degradation. It, too, serves as a form of psychological destruction meant to squelch resistance and destroy self-esteem. It, too, feeds the sense of omnipotence of the dominators. And it, too, serves as a form of *reality control.* It tells us that this is the only world possible, that male domination is universal in time and space, and that the Earth is at the disposal of elite men. At the same time—and this is key—such violence *blocks awareness of alternative ways of living and being*; it stifles the development of a worldview other than the pornographic one.

Reclaiming the Erotic

In order to perpetuate itself, every oppression must corrupt or distort those various sources of power within the culture of the oppressed that can provide energy for change. (Lorde, 1984, p. 53)

On November 19, 1994, unknown vandals defaced bound volumes of women, gay, and gender studies journals at the University of New Mexico library. They took an issue of the journal *Lesbian Ethics*, crossed out that title, and replaced it with "God's Ethics." Underneath, they scrawled a swastika along with this pronouncement: "God made women for men."

This "God" is that familiar patriarchal father who "knows best" and who, allegedly, also made the Earth, animals and the elements "for men" to use and abuse as they like. But for much of human history, this was not the ruling view. Instead, there was respect for a "feminine principle" of nature—the intelligent, active, originating, and diverse life force in which both women and men participate. The feminine principle, often represented by a Sex Goddess, was understood and respected as the source of energy, desire, life and growth as well as decline and death, endings which became new beginnings in some form of rebirth.

In Goddess: Myths of the Female Divine, David Leeming and Jake Page (1994) trace an ancient history of Goddess reverence and an accompanying worldview which included respect for women and for sexuality. This was overturned with the advent of patriarchal civilizations, and covered up by rewritings of myth, and systematic denigrations, taking Goddesses and turning them into pornography (Caputi, 2004).

One Sex Goddess is Inanna of ancient Sumer (Fig. 2.27). Diane Wolkstein (Wolkstein and Kramer, 1983, p. 169) describes Inanna as: "the Goddess

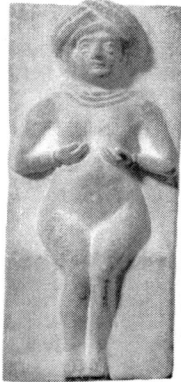

Fig. 2.27. Inanna of ancient Sumer

of Love. Formed from all of life, the Goddess of Love gives forth desire that generates the energy of the universe." Such a cosmology recognizes the body as sacred and perceives sexual desire not as "sin," but as a manifestation of cosmic dynamism. It knows the feminine principle as a unified and unifying force, as the source of life, and as something that must be respected. And that cosmology recognizes power as generative and creative energy, not as the ability to dominate everyone and everything.

Some of the most vital resistance to the pornographic way of thinking can be found in an ongoing feminist reclamation and recasting of these ancient traditions honoring the feminine principle and sexuality, what poet Audre Lorde (1984) calls "the erotic." Lorde claims that the erotic, a power source within our bodies as within the universe, is our conduit to cosmic forces of generation, ecstasy and relationship. The erotic is the energy source that enables us not only to desire sexually, but also to love, create, connect, resist oppression, and transform ourselves and our world. Patricia Hill Collins (2004) argues for the necessity of respecting the erotic and articulates a goal of "honest bodies that are characterized by sexual autonomy and soul, expressiveness, spirituality, sensuality, sexuality, and an expanded notion of the erotic as a life force" (p. 287). A diverse contemporary movement of artists, writers, activists, mystics, and environmentalists challenges the pornographic worldview by reclaiming an honest and erotic one (e.g., Anzaldúa, 1987; Caputi, 2006; Cisneros, 1996; Conner, 1993; Daly, 1984; De la Huerta, 1999; Ensler, 1998; Gadon, 1989; Griffin, 1981; Schneemann, 2002).

Pornography is a (bad) habit of thinking. It is a worldview, not the world. The pornographic passes itself off as the erotic, but it actually works by appropriating and then distorting the erotic energy that could otherwise be directed to enabling awareness, resistance, and transformation. Breaking the habit of pornographic thinking and activating the erotic, we can, in ways both large and small, empower ourselves to make another world—one that respects female sexual autonomy, finds objectification unattractive, and domination unethical and uninteresting, recognizes sexuality as a way of pleasure and knowledge, nurtures voice and listening, and instills respect for ourselves, each other, animals, the elements, and the Earth.

Notes

1. In 2006, I completed a film, *The Pornography of Everyday Life* that also incorporates much of this material. It is distributed by Berkeley Media, www.berkeley media.com. I would like to thank all those relatives, friends and students who brought some of these ads to my attention, including Mary Caputi, Dan Caputi, J.D. Checkit, Heather Stewart, Natalia Gago, Augusta Walden, and many others. I especially thank Ann Scales, Andria Chediak and Jeff Meyers for our many fruitful conversations on this topic.

2. Saarjite Baartman, a young Khosian woman who became known as the Hottentot Venus, was brought to Europe from Cape Town in 1810 by an English ship's surgeon who wanted to publicly exhibit the woman's enlarged buttocks.

Her body was displayed in England and France, including an exhibition of her naked body in a cage at Piccadilly, England.

3. *Gynocide*, originally used by both Andrea Dworkin and Mary Daly, and *femicide* were coined by feminists to define murders of women as a direct outcome of sexism (e.g., murders committed by men for reasons of sexual gratification, sense of ownership and punishment).

4. Both Iraqi women and men were abused, although only photos of the men were released to the public.

5. Perhaps something like this informed the motivations of two separate gunmen who staged gynocidal assaults on schoolgirls in late September and early October 2006. In the first case, a drifter, Duane Morrison, 53, took six girls hostage in a Colorado high school and sexually abused all of them before letting four go. When police stormed the classroom, he killed 16-year-old Emily Keyes along with himself. A few days later, Charles C. Roberts IV, 32, invaded an Amish school in Pennsylvania. He, too, sent away the boys and a few adult women, while keeping 10 girls with him. Roberts had brought an assortment of weapons, hardware, ties, wood, bolts and sexual lubricant, indicating that he intended to bind, torture, rape, and kill the little girls. As the police stormed the building, he tied them, lined them up, and then shot each in the back of the head before killing himself. Much public commentary on these crimes expressed the usual bewilderment. Few bothered to point out that girls had been deliberately selected; if all the victims were members of an ethnic or racial group other than that of their killer, these murders would have been instantly recognized as hate crimes. Rapes and gynocides are ritual enactments of male supremacy, in these cases, taking the form of "virgin sacrifice." For further discussion of the ritual aspects of such crimes and their relation to lynching, see "The Gods We Worship," in Caputi (2004).

6. The Millennium Ecosystem Assessment, a report compiled by 1,300 leading scientists from 95 countries, documents that pollution and exploitative practices are damaging the planet at such a rapid rate that the "ability of the planet's ecosystems to sustain future generations can no longer be taken for granted" (Conner, 2005). The planet, in response to this abuse, will no longer be so readily providing such "services" as purification of air and water, protection from natural disasters, and the provision of foods and medicines.

References

Adams, C. (2003). *The pornography of meat*. New York: Continuum.

Allen, P. G. (1990). The woman I love is a planet the planet I love is a tree. In I. Diamond & G. F. Orenstein (Ed.), *Reweaving the world: The emergence of ecofeminism* (pp. 52–57). San Francisco: Sierra Club Books.

Alloula, M. (1986). *The colonial harem* (M. Godzich & W. Godzich, Trans.). Minneapolis: University of Minnesota Press.

Anzaldúa, G. (1987). *Borderlands/ La Frontera*. San Francisco: Spinsters/Aunt Lute Press.

Bambara, T. C. (1993). Reading the signs, empowering the eye: *Daughters of the Dust* and the black independent cinema movement. In M. Diawara (Ed.), *Black American cinema* (pp. 118–144). New York: Routledge.

Brison, S. J. (2004, June 4). Torture, or "good old American pornography." *The Chronicle Review/ The Chronicle of Higher Education*, pp. B10–B11.

Caputi, J. (1987). *The age of sex crime*. Bowling Green, OH: Bowling Green State University Press.

Caputi, J. (1993). *Gossips, gorgons, and crones: The fates of the earth*. Santa Fe: Bear.

Caputi, J. (2004). *Goddesses and monsters: Women, myth, power and popular culture*. Madison: University of Wisconsin Popular Press.

Caputi, J. (2006). Cunctipotence: Elemental female potency. *Trivia: Voices of Feminism*. Available at http://www.triviavoices.net/.

Cisneros, S. (1996). Guadalupe the sex goddess. In A. Castillo (Ed.), *Goddess of the Americas La Diosa De Las Americas: Writings on the Virgin of Guadalupe* (pp. 52–55). New York: Riverhead Books.

Collins, P. H. (1998). *Black feminist thought: Knowledge, consciousness, and the politics of empowerment*. New York: Routledge.

Collins, P. H. (2004). *Black sexual politics: African Americans, gender, and the new racism*. New York: Routledge.

Conner, R. P. (1993). *Blossom of bone: Reclaiming the connections between homoeroticism and the sacred*. San Francisco: Harper.

Connor, S. (2005). The state of the world? It is on the brink of disaster. *The Independent UK*. Available at http://www.commondreams.org/headlines05/0330-04.htm.

Coy, B. (2005, Oct. 9). *The Active Word* [Weekly television broadcast]. Calvary Chapel, Fort Lauderdale, FL.

Cromer, M. (2001, Feb. 26). Porn's compassionate conservatism. *The Nation*, pp. 25–28.

Daly, M. (1973). *Beyond God the father: Toward an ethic of women's liberation*. Boston: Beacon Press.

Daly, M. (1984). *Pure lust: Elemental feminist philosophy*. Boston: Beacon Press.

Danner, M. (2004). *Torture and truth: America, Abu Ghraib, and the war on terror*. New York: New York Review of Books.

De la Huerta, C. (1999). *Coming out spiritually: The next step*. New York: Jeremy P. Tarcher/Putnam.

Doyle, L. (2000). *The surrendered wife: A practical guide to finding intimacy, passion, and peace with a man*. New York: Simon & Schuster.

duCille, A. (1997). The unbearable darkness of being: 'Fresh' thoughts on race, sex, and the Simpsons. In T. Morrison & C. B. Lacour (Eds.), *Birth of a nation'hood: Gaze, script and spectacle in the O.J. Simpson case* (pp. 293–338). New York: Pantheon.

Dworkin, A. (1989). *Letters from a war zone*. New York: E. P. Dutton.

El Saadawi, N. (1980). *The hidden face of Eve*. New York: Zed Books.

Eliade, M. (1969). *Images and symbols: Studies in religious symbolism* (P. Mairet Trans.). New York: Sheed & Ward.

Ensler, E. (1998). *The vagina monologues*. New York: Villard.

Gaard, G. 2004. Toward a queer ecofeminism. In R. Stein (Ed.), *New perspectives on environmental justice: Gender, sexuality, and activism* (pp. 21–44). New Brunswick, NJ: Rutgers University Press.

Gadon, E. (1989). *The once and future goddess: A symbol for our time*. New York: Harper & Row.

Gilligan, J. (1996). *Violence: Reflections on a national epidemic*. New York: Random House.

Griffin, S. (1981). *Pornography and silence: Culture's revenge against nature*. New York: Harper Colophon.

Hernton, C. C. (1988), *Sex and racism in America*. New York: Anchor Books.

hooks, b. (1992). *Black looks: Race and representation*. Boston: South End Press.

Hurston, Z. N. (1983). *Tell my horse*. Berkeley, CA: Turtle Island.

Jensen, R., & Dines, G. (1998). The content of mass-marketed pornography. In G. Dines, R. Jensen, & A. Russo (Eds.), *Pornography: The production and consumption of inequality* (pp. 65–100). New York: Routledge.

Kaplan, L. J. (1991). *Female perversions: The temptations of Emma Bovary*. New York: Doubleday.

Keller, E. F. (1985). *Reflections on gender and science*. New Haven, CT: Yale University Press.

Leeming, D., & Page, J. (1994). *Goddess: Myths of the female divine*. New York: Oxford.

Lerner, G. (1986). *The creation of patriarchy*. New York: Oxford.

Lorde, A. (1984). Uses of the erotic: The erotic as power. In *Sister Outsider* (pp. 53–59). Trumansburg, NY: The Crossing Press.

Mendez Berry, E. (2005, March). Love hurts: Rap's "black eye." *Vibe*, pp. 163–168.

Merchant, C. (1980). *The death of nature: Women, ecology and the scientific revolution*. San Francisco: Harper & Row.

Millett, K. (1970). *Sexual politics*. Garden City, NY: Doubleday.

Schneemann, C. (2002). *Imaging her erotics: Essays, interviews, projects*. Cambridge, MA: MIT Press.

Sickest Sites. Retrieved 2005 from: http://www.sickestsites.com/sadomasochism.htm.

Sjöö, M., & Mor, B. (1991). *The great cosmic mother: Rediscovering the religion of the earth*. San Francisco: HarperSanFrancisco.

Smith, A. (2005). *Conquest: Sexual violence and American Indian genocide*. Boston: South End Press.

Sontag, S. (1980). Fascinating Fascism. In *Under the Sign of Saturn* (pp. 73–108). New York: Farrar, Straus, & Giroux.

Swentzell, R. (1993). Commentaries on When Jesus came the Corn Mothers went away: Marriage, sex, and power in New Mexico, 1500–1846, by Ramón Gutiérrez, Compiled by Native American Studies at the University of New Mexico. *American Indian Culture and Research Journal, 17*(3), 141–177.

Walker, A. (1980). Coming apart. In L. Lederer (Ed.), *Take back the night: Women on pornography* (pp. 95–104). New York: Bantam Books.

Williams, P. J. (1995). *The rooster's egg: On the persistence of prejudice*. Cambridge, MA: Harvard University Press.

Wolkstein, D., & Kramer, S. N. (1983). *Inanna: Queen of heaven and earth*. New York: Harper & Row.

4

Lara Croft in Ads

Birgit Pretzsch

"Cyber-Goddess," "Icon of the 90s," "Virtual World Star": Lara Croft, protago-nist of the action/adventure computer game *Tomb Raider*, has captured the public imagination in the United States, Europe, and the global market in ways that no other virtual character has. Croft is a beautiful British amazon, fascinated by archeology and collector of antiquities. In pursuit of these she combats mythi-cal forces, outguns heavily armed opponents, and always emerges with the prize. She appears not only in the original computer games but also on Internet sites (of various fan and official Web sites); in magazines and newspapers; in product advertisements (i.e., for cars, women's magazines, *PlayStation*®, etc.); and even in a music video. She went on tour with the famous Irish band *U2*, she starred in two major Hollywood motion pictures and has body doubles to represent her at fairs and public relations events. In addition, the merchandising and licensing industries produce a vast array of products featuring Lara Croft. Arguably, no other computer game protagonist has lept out of the gamer subculture and acquired such a high degree of popular recognition—and market value—usually reserved for film stars or music celebrities.

In her genre she is revolutionary. Heroines who tackle problems without the aid of a hero are virtually nonexistent in the world of computer games (Louis, 1998). And with her impressive body squeezed into tight-fitting outfits, Lara is hard to overlook or ignore. But opinions diverge as to whether she is a liberating feminist icon or a reactionary object of male desire (see, e.g., Kennedy, 2002.). Is it to be celebrated that a strong, agile, and aggressive woman has gained such popularity, particularly among young men? Is she a suitable role model for girls, teaching them self-reliance, courage, and independence? Is Lara the perfect example of the ideal woman of the 20th (or even 21st) century in that she combines sexual attractiveness with assertiveness and a no-nonsense attitude? Or is it only a surface reflection of strength, popular precisely because it is contained within a virtual, controllable framework and furthermore made palpable by Lara's demonstrative sensuality and sexuality? Is her apparent assertiveness and independence undermined by her

71

sexuality? Does she automatically support the status quo instead of challenging it (as she would have to as a feminist icon) because she utilizes sex to sell? In short, are traditional gender boundaries reinforced or are they challenged? Since, among feminists there exist many disparate beliefs about what constitutes "woman" and which ideals individual women should strive for, the answers to these questions are bound to be as manifold as the directions of feminism.

As such, in this chapter, and informed by postmodern and feminist theoretical frameworks, I explore this question further—with a particular focus on the representations of Lara in advertising and marketing. In so doing, I also describe how identity, body politics, and reality emerge as three pivotal and interrelated topics in such an analysis.

First, using Claudia Springer's (1996) words, I understand feminism to mean "a philosophy that seeks to end patriarchy and institute in its place an egalitarian system. Feminism seeks to release all people, men and women, from narrowly defined ideas about gender" (p. 15). In order to achieve this aim, one must take a close, theoretically informed look at how these ideas of gender come into existence, are perpetuated, are protected from deconstruction and what ends they serve. One important area in which ideas about gender are reinforced and/or subverted is that of representation.

Representation frequently reinforces the notion of the male subject and the female object. But images do more than simply posit one gender as object and one as subject; they perpetuate meaning and power in gender relations. Discourses and images are vital in the construction and perpetuation of social and symbolic order (Bertens, 1995), an area that Michel Foucault (1972, 1978) theorized in great detail, especially when analyzing how power, discourses, and institutions interrelate. Thus, when defining discourse as "a social language created by particular cultural conditions at a particular time and place" (Tyson, 1999, p. 281) as a way to explain human experience in a culturally specific way, it becomes evident that discourse and ideology are closely linked. By mediating all areas of life, discourses control the production of knowledge: "they put a limit on what is sayable at any one time: they define what counts as 'legitimate' or 'illegitimate' statements" (Ward, 1997, p. 129).

But discourses do not simply reflect the ideological frameworks within which they come into being, they also influence ideology. Because there is no monolithic discourse to explain the complex dynamics of power within all cultures and subcultures, different discourses are constantly engaged in power struggles. This, in turn, opens up the possibility for opposition. As such, human beings are never merely victims of an oppressive ideological discourse, because alternative discourses usurp, or at the very least stimulate resistance to dominant ideological discourses.

Within this matrix of discourses, our identities and subjectivities are formed. And much like the process outlined here, our identities are never merely the product of society or our individual desires. Rather, they are constantly shaped and re-shaped in a mutually constitutive and dynamically unstable relationship within culture and discourse. Accordingly, this chapter also traces how Lara's identity has been created, and which social formations and ideologies are reflected in her social construction. I discuss how the discourses surrounding Lara interact with the shaping of our own identity, pointing out both elements of oppression and elements of opposition and resistance.

These ambiguities surrounding Lara's status as oppressive or liberatory become particularly apparent when analysing representations of Lara's body. Because the body is a vehicle for self-expression and self-creation, it reflects the power struggles outlined above. As Anne Balsamo (1995) pointed out:

> Transgressive body displays (of female bodies that are also strong bodies) are neutralized in the mass media through the representations that sexualize their athletic bodies—their sexual attractiveness is asserted over their physical capabilities. (p. 217)

Although Balsamo's statement refers to women body builders, it applies equally well to Lara Croft. Her strong, athletic, and weapon-wielding body continually competes with her sexually attractive and highly "feminized" one. The question then arises as to why an overtly sexualized body is in any way oppressive. Several feminist theorists have used Michel Foucault's notion of the disciplined body to explain how the female body is controlled via a normative gaze. In Western visual culture, women are bombarded with normative images of femininity, and several theorists posit that, although attempting to fulfill these norms, women's bodies are turned into docile, controlled bodies (Bartky, 1997), but, as others would argue, women are not just "cultural dupes and victims of cultural constructions of femininity" (Budgeon, 2003, p. 39) but also develop strategies of resistance and agency (for instance Bordo, 1989, 1993; Budgeon, 2003; Davis, 1995). These dynamic interactions of different discourses and ideologies are mapped onto Lara's body, and her liberating and empowering potential—a strong, independent, successful woman—is constantly undermined by her intimidating physical appearance. Here, I show that while challenging some traditional social codes of femininity, Lara immediately reinforces others. Lara's body is also constructed within the context of virtual reality using the most modern multimedia technologies. These new technologies have brought about many changes within society and in their wake many Western dualities have been blurred—such as human–machine, nature–culture, and real–artificial. And although technological progress is predominantly celebrated, it has also induced much anxiety and fear because it brings with it instability and a loss of certainty. This ambiguity is also mapped onto Lara. Through her multifarious representations, we can discern both the fears of society—along with its remedy of traditional certainties (such as what a woman's body should look like)—and the hopes of many feminist theorists that the questioning of reality by new technologies will open up the chance to question other certainties (such as the concept of gender).

Tomb Raider and Lara Croft

The three-dimensional (3D) action/adventure computer game *Tomb Raider* first appeared in November 1996 and was subsequently followed by *Tomb Raider* II, III, IV–The Last Revelation, V–The Chronic and VI–Angel of Darkness, in roughly 1-year intervals. All *Tomb Raider* games are produced by Core Design and published by Eidos Interactive, both of which are British companies. The target audience of the Tomb Raider games is males between ages 15 and 26 years, in the United States and Europe (Bradley, 1997a).

Lara Croft started out simply as the curvaceous protagonist of the game, but has become a formidable character in her own right, with a distinct background story, curriculum vitae, and lifestyle. She is an aristocrat, highly educated, extremely fit physically, and has chosen herself the life she wants to live. Lara is modern and not tied to any old-fashioned traditions. As an orphan living off her inheritance in the old family mansion, without family ties or obligations, she is free to do whatever she chooses (which in her case is the search for adventure). She therefore epitomizes the Western ideal of the independent, self-sufficient individual striving for success and happiness.

The key adjectives generally associated with Lara are *powerful, sexy, agile, charming, virtual, no-nonsense, independent, athletic, adventurous,* and *feminine*.[1] She does the job that needs to be done using her skills, determination, and an impressive array of weaponry. But while displaying these traditionally more male characteristics (reminiscent of Indiana Jones and James Bond), she still retains a very conventionally feminine side to her—she is charming, cultivated, sexy, and beautiful. A computer game magazine states: "Lara represents independence and strength of conviction in a really *female* way—although she's tough, there's nothing at all *butch* about her. She still retains her *feminine* qualities" (Bradley, 1997b, p. 25; italics added). This reflects traditional public opinion that in order to be *female*, one also has to be *feminine*, defined in contrast to *butch*, which in society at large is usually used in a derogatory manner. In order to make an aggressive, powerful woman acceptable—and convince the public that she is still "a woman"—Lara's corporeal characteristics and personality traits need to be overemphasised. The alternative is that her presence might be perceived as too threatening and would therefore lose its market value.

Merchandise

Because of Lara's enormous popularity and her huge number of fans,[2] there is an impressive array of merchandise available. The products, which all feature images of Lara, range from the conventional T-shirt, to mouse pads, calendars, watches and clocks, statues, decks of cards, stickers, posters, wallets, bathing robes, and so on. Not surprisingly, most of the images used are from the "sexy Lara" category rather than from the "Lara in action" category.

From this, it would appear that the merchandising industry feels her fans are more interested in Lara's erotic side and therefore uses highly sexualised pictures of her to sell their products. And notably, whereas there is merchandise aimed solely at men[3] and merchandise aimed at both male and female fans,[4] there do not appear to be any products specifically geared toward those women who wish to identify with a strong, courageous, and independent woman. For example, even though Eidos (publisher of Tomb Raider, 1999) claims to have chosen a woman as protagonist in order to attract girls and women as potential players of the game, the merchandise offered seems to contradict this assertion. On a personal and subjective level, I must admit that whenever I have contact with Lara merchandise I never have a sense of being addressed by the product, the advertisement, or character as such. The feeling is more one of catching a glimpse of a stereotypical world constructed for the pleasure of male viewers. If there is any chance to connect to Lara and get a sense of her empowering qualities and potential, it is always with a sense of reading her "against the grain."

Advertisements

The Game

When reviewing advertisements for *Tomb Raider* in different countries, such as France, Germany, the United States and Great Britain, it becomes clear that no single advertising or marketing strategy focuses solely on the game and its characteristics. As one reviewer said:

> The poster and media publicity reveal exactly what the EIDOS ad men see in Lara. They know that their target audience will latch onto a girl in short shorts and a crop-top more rapidly than any images of atmospheric 3D or logical problem solving. (Bradley, 1997a, p. 15)

In fact, much like the merchandising, advertisements for *Tomb Raider* are aimed primarily at a male audience, even though Eidos claims to have created a computer game that appeals to women as well. A striking example of this was the so-called "washroom campaign" for Tomb Raider, which involved poster ads of Lara placed in men's washrooms in bars and pubs all over Great Britain, in late 1997 (Bradley, 1997a). Male consumers were also the target of the German campaign that accompanied the release of *Tomb Raider II*, in which huge posters showed Lara batting her eyelashes and telling the viewer, "You can move me into 2,000 different positions. Try that with your girlfriend!" (Eidos, 1999, p. 110; author's translation). Not only does this slogan sexualize Lara and evacuate any of her strengths and abilities, it also positions the consumer as a heterosexual male or lesbian, completely ignoring any potential heterosexual female buyers.

Another example of the address to a heterosexual male consumer is an animated *Tomb Raider III* ad on the Internet (see www.eidos.co.uk, accessed September, 1999) which demonstrates the strategy of selling sex and adventure together. The animation involves six different panels. The first shows Lara with two guns and next to her the question "What more do you want?" The following four panels answer this question by showing Lara in action and emphasizing the quality of the game play. The last panel then adds the apparently necessary amount of sex, showing Lara's breasts squeezed into a tiny shirt, suggestively asking "More . . . ?"

In a series of three American TV[5] advertisements for *Tomb Raider II*, the emphasis is more on the game itself. All three start by showing locations usually associated with men (a basketball court, a man's toilet, and a stripper bar), all deserted. After showing several action scenes of the game, the copy "Where the boys are" is superimposed onto the empty locations. The spots imply that men have stopped doing what they normally do and are instead playing *Tomb Raider*. They are not where they used to be (sports fields, stripper bars, and men's washrooms), but instead are now joining Lara in her adventures. By linking the game to such stereotypically male pastimes and by directly overtly using the word *boys*, playing the game is constructed as a male occupation.

In another American advertisement,[6] the focus is more on the protagonist than the game itself. In it, the viewer sees the world through Lara's eyes. She enters a big laboratory, is introduced to her new adventure, and receives new tight-fitting outfits and some new "toys" such as a rocket launcher. The whole ad is reminiscent of James Bond: the way she is addressed as "Croft," the new gadgets she is shown, and the professor in a white coat with an English accent showing her around. Like Bond, she is linked to adventure, action, exotic places, impressive weapons, and sex. Unlike Bond, however, who always needed women to add sex to the cocktail to highlight his success, Lara herself represents eroticism and sexuality. This is especially evident via her clothing, which includes tight-fitting hot pants and crop-tops, and the phallic implications of the rocket launcher, which is referred to as "a girl's best friend."

Not surprisingly then, many companies quickly realized the potential of Lara's commercial clout and have subsequently capitalized on her symbolic value. Not only is Lara pleasant to look at, she is also independent and strong-minded. Her virtuality emphasises the company's up-to-date technology and its forward-looking philosophy. These factors, advertisers hope, mean that consumers are likely to trust her judgment concerning the products she is seen to endorse.

Seat

The French car company Seat produced a series of TV ads[7] featuring Lara. In the first commercial, Lara is being continually chased, first by a tyrannosaurus rex, then by two men on motorcycles, and finally by a helicopter. In each situation, she chooses a car from the Seat line-up and thereby manages to escape. In the last scene she sees a group of good-looking surfers trying to hitch a ride. Quickly exchanging the small car she has been driving for a large family sedan, she gives them a lift. The main emphasis of this commercial is on adventure, action, and risk. Lara is a tough woman, able to handle adverse situations. Only the last scene makes reference to Lara's appearance and attractiveness—when we see the surfers' broad grins and admiring gazes as they see who has stopped for them—and offers (male) viewers the chance to identify with the surfers.

The second commercial is similar in that Lara is on the run again, driving a car through the snowy Alps, followed by the bad guys on snowmobiles, shooting at her. Although the car manages the adverse weather conditions perfectly, the pursuers have more problems. In the end, Lara arrives at a little cottage, with three men sitting in the back of the car, wearing nothing but their boxer shorts, freezing. Leaning against the wall of the cottage are three surfboards, so presumably they are the three surfers she picked up in the previous commercial. The scene ends with Lara offering them the obligatory polite cup of tea. Here again, she is in complete control over the situation.

The third commercial makes a stronger reference to the game itself: We see Lara hurrying home to her mansion, because a player has put in the *Tomb Raider* CD-ROM and the game is loading. In order to get home fast enough, Lara again uses a Seat. In the last moment, she jumps into the game, ready for action. But Lara's sexualized body is not completely left out: In the first scene she walks onto the beach, carrying snorkelling gear, while wearing a bikini. Then she realizes the time and rushes off.

In a more recent commercial, the focus is solely on Lara's erotic side. Again we see her coming out of the sea, walking toward the beach, wearing a bikini, and seductively swaying her hips. Then we see a middle-aged man with glasses, sunhat, and a beer belly gaping at her. This is followed by cutting back and forth between the man—getting increasingly red and hot—and Lara's body (from neck to thighs), coming toward the camera. The camera position then shifts, so that it is behind Lara, slightly to the right and bearing up. We watch Lara walk toward the man, raising her harpoon. Owing to the position of the camera, we have Lara's bottom in full view, at times filling out half the screen. She makes the man get into the Seat right behind him, pushes the air-condition button, and locks the door. She triumphantly leans against the car and the man timidly knocks on the window. We are then informed that all Seats are now available with air-conditioning to "cool men down." In the last scene, the man is writing "I ♥ Lara" on the steamed-up rear window. The entire commercial is accompanied by a seductive musical score.

I find this commercial particularly interesting because Lara is once again overtly sexualized, and the viewer is encouraged to identify with the gaping man even though he is unattractive and undesirable. The camera follows his gaze and we see Lara from his perspective except when he himself is in the picture. When he is shown, he is depicted as a wimp, helplessly staring at her, and subsequently helplessly held captive in a locked car. Lara is in complete control of the situation. She does not hesitate once, nor does she get angry. She simply reacts in a matter-of-fact style with a touch of humour. She seems to be more amused than angry at his reaction and seems to be saying to herself, "Well, that's just the way men are." It is the representation of male sexuality in this commercial that I find most problematic. The popular myth of the ever-willing male is again perpetuated, along with the belief that all men invariably—naturally—react to a woman like Lara. Women have to be witty in order to handle men and it is their job to find ways of dealing with "natural" male instincts. No responsibility is given to men to handle these natural instincts appropriately. This popular construction of male sexuality is limited and reductive and reinforces tendencies to explain male (and female) behavior in terms of biological essentialism.

PlayStation

Another company using Lara is PlayStation (this is not surprising, because *Tomb Raider* is one of the top-selling PlayStation games). The following ad[8] is for several games (including *Tomb Raider*) that are on sale. A father wakes up his son, and excitedly tells him about the sale. The son is quite surprised, because he does not even have a PlayStation. The father rushes off, fights his way through the crowd of people and then spots Lara, sitting at a desk with *Tomb Raider* CD-ROMs stacked on it, looking rather bored. The father jumps the crowd barrier that keeps the fans at bay, rushes to her side, and takes a photograph of himself holding Lara, who appears rather irritated and annoyed. In the last scene we see the son holding this picture, asking his dreamily distant father if his mother knows about this, to which he gets the short and absent-minded answer "Who?"

As in the previous ad, Lara is portrayed as the good-looking, extremely sexy woman who drives men mad, leads them to disregard rules and proper social protocol or behavior and makes them act purely on animal instinct. But while, on the one hand, inviting the viewer to laugh at male foolishness, the commercial also encourages viewers to excuse such behavior because it is understood that men cannot be held responsible when it comes to women and/or sexuality.

Brigitte[9]

Lara shows a very different side of herself in a TV spot[10] for the German women's magazine *Brigitte*. The ad starts conventionally with Lara shooting at someone and then pursuing them. But then she spots a wedding dress in a shop window, stops to admire it, and forgets her original pursuit. As the *Lara Croft Magazine* states, this shows that "before all else, Lara is a woman" (Eidos, p. 117). She demonstrates that even though she is a tough woman, she can be feminine—and even romantic as well. We are thus again reassured that all women, no matter what our impression might be, are essentially feminine underneath. Even an independent fighter like Lara has the same dreams and desires deep inside (i.e., getting married) as every other woman.

On the whole, it can be said that the focus of these advertising and marketing campaigns is never entirely on Lara's action-oriented, independent side. Although she is shown to be in control and behaves more sensibly than her male counterparts, we are always reminded of her feminine side, usually represented via erotic imagery or—as in the last example—via romanticism.

The Question of the Body

> The endless depictions of the human body have in effect replaced actual human bodies in the public imagination. (Springer, 1996, p. 40)

> One implication of the new conceptions of power ... is the radical "deconstruction" of the body, the last residue or hiding place of "Man," and its "reconstruction" in terms of its historical, genealogical and discursive formations. (Hall, 2000, p. 24)

Changes in our culture, particularly the rise of consumer culture, have drastically changed our lives. In the Western world, the Protestant work ethic has largely been replaced by hedonism and consumption (Featherstone, 1983). Individuality is the key word and "everything" is within reach: "An ideology of personal consumption presents individuals as free to do their own thing, to construct their own little world in the private sphere" (Featherstone, 1983, p. 21). In these conditions, where the construction of identity is a central endeavor, the body has become inscribed with a whole set of new meanings: It is the vehicle for self-expression and self-creation (Davis, 1997).

Today's feminine ideal demands two very contradictory characteristics in a woman: She has to be warm and nurturing, charming and caring and at the same time tough, cool, successful, and in control, offering the best of "masculine" and "feminine" virtues (Bordo, 1989).

Lara is one of these women, seemingly offering everything a man may wish for today: She has the necessary "macho" characteristics, but she is in no way "masculine" as is used in a derogatory way of women. She may be self-determined, independent, in control, and strong (even carrying weapons) but she retains those characteristics that are associated with "femininity" in (Western) cultures: in the way she walks and moves, in the way her body is overemphasised and hyper-sexualized, and in the way she is often represented in traditionally feminine poses with a "feminine look" on her face (vulnerable, pouting or flirtatious). She might, therefore, seem an ideal of positive empowerment to many women. The popular associations with the term *feminist* have sadly become very negative, for both men and women. A feminist is very often seen as an unattractive, man-hating, and aggressive woman. Therefore, many women wish to disassociate themselves from this term, but still perceive themselves as equal to men and as independent. For many of these women, Lara seems to be the perfect role model: She does not threaten their perceived "female identity" (she is still a "real woman," neither afraid to be beautiful or sexy), but she is still independent and strong. Nevertheless, as Bordo (1989) pointed out:

[p]opular representations . . . may speak forcefully through the rhetoric and symbolism of empowerment, personal freedom, "having it all." Yet female bodies, pursuing these ideals, may find themselves distracted, depressed, and physically ill as female bodies in the nineteenth century, pursuing a feminine ideal of dependency, domesticity, and delicacy. (p. 28)

Paradoxically, the attempt to shape one's body according to conventional ideals actually offers many women a sense of control and mastery that they often lack in a male-dominated world. But, as Bordo argued, this sense of control—at least over one's own body—is illusory and turns one's body into one of Foucault's "docile" bodies, forcing women to spend their energies "improving," transforming, and subjugating their bodies to external regulation. Foucault has unmasked the body as "the primary site for the operation of modern forms of power—power that was not top-down and repressive, but rather, subtle, elusive and productive" (Davis, 1997, p. 3). As Foucault (1979) described it:

[What was then being formed was] a policy of coercions that act upon the body, a calculated manipulation of its elements, its gestures, its behaviour. . . . Thus, discipline produces subjected and practised bodies, "docile" bodies. (p. 138)

For feminists the link between these docile bodies, the processes of discipline and normalisation and social control—especially of the female body—has been particularly interesting and has been repeatedly analysed (e.g., Bartky, 1997; Bordo, 1989; Butler, 1993; Davis, 1997).

Bordo argued that this "discipline and normalisation of the female body . . . has to be acknowledged as an amazingly durable and flexible strategy of social control" (p. 14). Similarly, Bartky (1997), stated that modern disciplinary practices render a body feminine and seek to "regulate its very forces and operations, the economy and efficiency of its movements" (p. 129). These practices are not overtly imposed on women, there are no formal authorities or institutions who discipline transgressive bodies, so why, asked Bartky, do women conform to these practices—if we discard the notions that they are performed voluntarily or that they are natural?

Bartky posited that the very subjectivity of the subject is constituted by the structure of power. For her, woman is under constant surveillance. But this surveillance does not only originate from a central tower as in Foucault's Panopticon. Instead, the "conscious and permanent visibility" (Foucault, 1979, p. 201) induces in the inmate the need to perpetually survey his (or her) own self, internalizing the disciplinary gaze. Women have internalized the standards of femininity and therefore kept themselves under constant surveillance:

> In contemporary patriarchal culture, a panoptical male connoisseur resides within the consciousness of most women: They stand perpetually before his gaze and under his judgement. Woman lives her body as seen by another, by an anonymous, patriarchal Other. (Bartky, 1997, p. 140)

And Lara epitomizes these standards of feminity—beloved and admired by "every man": She manages the dual demands placed on women today, to be macho and feminine at the same time. She thereby helps to perpetuate a feminine ideal that women are desperately and unsuccessfully trying to achieve. In particular, her body represents an ideal that is hardly realizable: She is incredibly thin, has improbably large breasts, and is physically fit. She perpetuates a potentially limiting and inhibiting image of a woman's body.

Lara also takes commodification and idealization to an extreme. She is readily available, she is linked to consumer goods, and she is often reduced to a commodity. It could also be argued that an underlying current in the different forms of representation involves the notion that a woman's life, her body and mind can be bought and sold at will and used whenever the owner feels like it.

The hypersexualization of Lara furthermore makes apparent what Foucault (1978) described as the ever-growing discourse on sex.

> The discourse on sexuality creates the notion that sex is an absolute, abstract category. Sex and sexuality have become the titles used to cover all bodies and their pleasures. . . . All bodily pleasures are now understood in the terms of the degree to which they deviate from, conform to, improve or avoid sex. Sex is the dominant term, the standard against which "the body and pleasure" are measured. (Ward, 1997, p. 131)

In this sense, the discourse on sexuality objectifies and categorizes our experiences, which fundamentally affects our experience of both personal and social identity. The representations of Lara with their overt connotations of sexuality further enforce this idea. Following Foucault, it is possible to argue that the video game—and the other products Lara is used to promote—can only give pleasure when related to sexuality and the body.

The idea that female sexuality is dangerous is age-old and deeply embedded in Western, patriarchal society: "sexuality is dangerous, and sexual women pose a threat either because they are killers themselves or because they incite violence in men" (Springer, 1996, p. 157). Being both extremely sexual and quite a killer at the same time, Lara is the epitome of "woman." But her particular form of existence allows men to act out their desire to control and contain women and their sexuality. Women's bodies have always been perceived as "far more permeable, fluid and subject to 'leakage' " (Lupton, 1995, p. 101) than men's bodies.[11] This instability inspires both repulsion and desire—the female body offers emotional security but also threatens engulfment (Lupton, 1995). By playing the game or by consuming images of Lara, men have the chance to explore their fascination with female sexuality without a real threat, while at the same time controlling the process—either very directly in the game or indirectly through their choice to look or not to look. Female sexuality and women's bodies are thereby objectified and turned into a commodity, losing their perceived danger.

Even though Lara may challenge the common notion of femininity as weak, compliant, and dependent, the inherent threat is reduced by overemphasizing the biological difference between men and women, constantly reassuring the viewer of these differences which are necessary to justify male superiority. This overemphasis on biological difference in the representations of Lara raises another issue that postmodernism and feminism frequently deal with: the fact that Western thought is based on the concept of binaries and that these not only designate difference but also assign a value to the opposing elements. Both postmodernism and feminism have therefore raised a strong criticism of binary thinking, demanding instead the consideration of difference without hierarchy (Owens, 1985).

> The female body becomes a metaphor for the corporeal pole of this dualism, representing nature, emotionality, irrationality and sensuality. Images of the dangerous, appetitive female body, ruled precariously by her emotions, stand in contrast to the masterful, masculine will, the locus of social power, rationality and self-control. The female body is always the "other": mysterious, unruly, threatening to erupt and challenge the patriarchal order. (Davis, 1997, p. 5)

Anne Balsamo (1995) went even further, arguing that only "the construction of a boundary between nature and culture . . . guarantees a proper order of things" (p. 215). Blurring the proper boundaries through her masculine behavior, Lara's overtly feminine body is used to even things out. Because she is completely fictional, her body could have had any shape, but as Balsamo noted: "the gendered boundary between males and females is one border that remains heavily guarded despite new technologised ways to rewrite the physical body in the flesh" (p. 216). The dissolving of boundaries in other areas such as nature–culture and human–nonhuman, needs to be countered by a reaffirmation of perceived stabilities, such as biological difference.

The creation of characters such as Lara could help bring us closer to what Donna Haraway (1991) described as a post-gender world Using new technologies—Haraway used the cyborg as an example—we could rid ourselves of the self-imposed limitations inherent in our constructs of gender and our binary thinking. "Real" and "artificial" are challenged along with "natural" and "cultural." Haraway (1991) envisioned a world that "might be about lived social and bodily realities in which people are not afraid of their joint kinship with animals and machines, not afraid of permanent partial identities and contradictory standpoints" (p. 154).

The Question of Identity

> People can change their identities more frequently, experiment with them, select more options from a cultural supermarket with far less commitment than ever before. (Harris, 1996, p. 207)

> [T]he masculine desire [is] to fix the woman in a stable and stabilizing identity. (Owens, 1985, p. 75)

The concept of identity has undergone a shift in recent years after having been subjected to a thorough academic dissection and critique. The deconstruction of the term *identity* has taken place within several disciplinary areas, and as diverse as these new theoretical debates are, they are all, in one way or another, critical of "the notion of an integral, originary and unified identity" (Hall, 2000, p. 15). The idea of the self-sustaining subject, the "essential" or presocial self that has been at the centre of post-Cartesian Western metaphysics, has therefore been severely and irrevocably challenged.

Stuart Hall (2000) has summarized the main characteristics of the new conception of identity:

> [T]his concept of identity does *not* signal that stable core of the self, unfolding from beginning to end through all the vicissitudes of history without change; the bit of the self which remains always-already "the same," identical to itself across time. . . . It accepts that identities are never unified and, in late modern times, increasingly fragmented and fractured; never singular but multiply constructed across different, often intersecting and antagonistic, discourses, practices and positions. (p. 17)

The question of how identities are then constructed leads us to three central mechanisms: discourse, performativity, and exclusion. For Foucault "the subject is produced as 'an effect' through and within discourse" (Hall, 2000, p. 23). Therefore, identities are produced in specific historical settings, within specific discursive practices, by specific enunciative strategies, and within specific institutions. This means that language and wider cultural codes offer certain subject positions to us and identities are temporary attachments to, and "performative" enactments in and through, these positions (Hall, 2000; Redman, 2000).

The mechanism of performativity referred to here is related to Judith Butler's concept of performativity, which means that it is stripped of its associations with volition, choice and intentionality. In Butler's (1993) words, performativity needs to be re-read "not as the act by which a subject brings into being what she/he names but rather as that reiterative power of discourse to produce the phenomena it regulates and constrains" (p. 2). For example, certain cultural rituals are not simply performed *because* they are part of that culture, but rather the performance of these rituals *constitutes* the culture. Similarly, identities are not something materialistic to be unearthed within ourselves, nor are they something we can create voluntarily. Rather they are created in a complex and playful interaction with regulating discourses.

The endless performativity of the self and the rejection of any notion of processes of "closure" in the construction of identities contains both celebratory and threatening elements. A sense of liberation goes hand in hand with a sense of loss of orientation and reliability. This ambiguity is often reflected in a search for stability and structure in a world that is full of multiple meanings, fragmented experiences and a wide range of possible identities.

Lara epitomizes this ambiguity. On one hand, as an artificial character her identity only exists when it is performed. Because each person who interacts with Lara in some way—as gamer, as consumer or just as fan—creates his or her own fragment of Lara's identity, there cannot be any "unitary" and "directive" self somewhere within her. Lara can never be fully defined. There are only more and more layers of created fragments.

Her multimediality, her virtuality, and the technophoria associated with her are further elements of her tendency to celebrate multiplicity, fragmentation and rejection of closure. But even though this empty "form" of Lara—or maybe rather her theoretical construction—can be seen as celebratory, the content with which this form, or construction, is filled certainly epitomises the ongoing struggle to find reliability and stability. Lara has lived through a terrible tragedy (an airplane crash in which she is the sole survivor), and subsequently has found out what is really important in her life, namely adventure and independence rather than an aristo-cratic lifestyle. This sense of an essential self, which one needs to uncover and then be true to in order to lead a fulfilled and happy life, runs contradictory to newer concepts of identity introduced earlier, but it offers a (seemingly) straightforward and easy to understand road to happiness. But not only does she champion this find your true inner-self ideology, her identity is conservative in many other ways as well. Her behavior is predictable, her identity is continually presented—by the game manufacturers as well as the media and advertising industries—as firm and unchanging: There is no development in her character over time and it is reduced to some recurring characteristics such as her sexiness, toughness, and independence. Other parts playing a role in the formation of identity (such as sexual orientation, political and moral beliefs, spiritual attitudes, to name just a few) are neither mentioned nor considered to be of importance.

The possibilities offered by the fact that everybody can have access to Lara, that she has no "real" identity and that she can truly "be anything" are vast, but they largely go unused. The meanings associated with Lara could become multiple, contradictory and they could have the force to challenge boundaries. Fans could, for example, be offered the chance to officially present their versions of Lara, such as drawings and paintings or short stories,[12] but instead, the opposite is taking place as Eidos Interactive keeps a close lid on representations (in every sense) of Lara, and things that do not fit into the company's construct of its heroine are immediately sanctioned.[13]

As suggested earlier, the major changes that the new technologies and the second media age bring with them do not only bring about enthusiasm and fascination but also fear and disorder. This instability can be perceived as threatening because, for instance, biographies and identities are not stable and predictable (neither jobs nor marriages are necessarily "for life" anymore), politics have become so complex through globalization that they seem overwhelming, and the possible manipulation of the media gives rise to distrust as to what is true within this world. A common desire within this complexity is for easy, straightforward answers[14] and stable elements. When boundaries are challenged—as when feminists challenge gender boundaries—a counter movement aims to cement boundaries more firmly. This is what I perceive to be the case with Lara as well. Her potentially threatening instabilities (being computer-generated and therefore not real, challenging traditional gender roles, her possible death threat) need to be counterbalanced by her more stable characteristics, such as her rather simple and straightforward character (has found her true inner calling, is adventurous and action-oriented), her obvious sexuality (here she does not challenge traditional imagery of women but rather supports them) and her body, which is—through its oversexualization—also perceived as stable, even though it is just a construct of pixels.

The Question of Reality

If there is a common denominator to all these postmodernisms, it is that of a crisis in representation: a deeply felt loss of faith in our ability to represent the real in the widest sense. (Bertens, 1995, p. 11)

In the second media age "reality" becomes multiple. (Poster, 1995, p. 85)

The French philosopher Jean Baudrillard (1999, 2001) is particularly associated with theories of reality and simulation. He argued that there is no direct relationship between an image and reality and that simulation therefore cannot be the opposite of truth. Rather, the two concepts operate on different planes. This dissolution of the dichotomy real–simulation or authentic–inauthentic is closely related to the proliferation of different media and mediations that have permeated our society. Our daily experiences have become mediated by images, so that authentic experience becomes impossible (Landsberg, 1995).

But Baudrillard went even further in that, according to him, there is no real, essential, unmediated stance outside of simulation. He argued that, contrary to popular belief, images precede the real and produce it instead of reality producing the images. Even our construction of identity is deeply influenced by this: Because it is constructed by experience, how does the impossibility of authentic experience affect our sense of self?

Baudrillard argued that society's reaction to the simulation we experience is panic. Desperation and a longing for reality mean that we make fetishes of the supposedly authentic. In an attempt to assure ourselves of our reality and that of experiences, products, images and so on, we manufacture what Baudrillard called the hyperreal, meaning more real than real.

This underscores my earlier point that Lara needs to be particularly feminine (more real than real) precisely because she challenges at the same time—albeit through her artificiality—our concept of reality. Computer games are becoming more and more realistic, virtual reality for the masses is just around the corner, digital characters are becoming indistinguishable from real persons. All of these changes further enhance our increasing doubts about reality and authenticity. We are at the same time frightened and fascinated by their possibilities and these alternating currents are also visible in representations that involve new technologies.

Nigel Clark (1995), drawing on Marshall McLuhan, Walter Benjamin, and Baudrillard, argued that, whenever confronted with new experiences and drastic changes, people tend to "look backwards," toward the past in an attempt to master new challenges. Major changes and transformations lead to an insecurity—in order to deal with this insecurity and the discomfort that what we perceived up to now as reality has changed, we take refuge in the imagined certainties of previous times.

The digital media in particular oscillate between onward roll and backward glance, because they contribute strongly to the destabilization of our traditional sense of reality. This—frightening and new—destabilization is often countered by the deployment of these new media "as instruments for the containment, subjugation and recording of a universe of refractory messages" (Clark, 1995, p. 115). The representations of Lara can be seen as a prime example of this. New technologies—virtual reality but also genetic engineering and plastic surgery—threaten to make sexual difference obsolete, thereby undermining a pillar of patriarchy. In a desperate attempt to hold on to old conventions and securities, signs of masculinity and femininity have to be overemphasized.

This idea of playing and experimenting with identities has held an understandable fascination for feminists. Cyber-technology offers the possibility of getting outside of gender. As mentioned previously, Donna Haraway in particular envisions a world full of virtual space where identity is fluid and fleeting and social concepts and prescriptions of gender are a thing of the past—along with other limiting social codes.

Conclusion

In summary, Lara offers fascinating—but also potentially threatening—new territory (new technology, virtual reality) on the one hand, while on the other hand she also offers reassurance and stability. She seems to oscillate between reinforcing social codes—such as "correct" feminine attire or the need for women to exhibit "feminine" character traits—and challenging them—for example with her physical prowess, aggressiveness, and independence.

So, it would seem that the possibilities for a feminist subversion and challenge to patriarchy are present but go as yet mainly unused. The cyber-world is still male-dominated and clings desperately to old gender concepts, as can be seen in the construction of Lara. But, cracks in the patriarchal ideology are becoming visible, changes are taking place—albeit slowly. Lara sends out contradictory messages that have multiple meanings. I believe there is a chance here to find liberating readings of Lara, if we explore the cracks further and find ways of subversion. Women could use the playfulness that Lara offers in order to explore and to experiment with identity but also with the concepts body and of reality. I would argue that Lara, the way she is publicly presented, *is* a reactionary object of male desire. She establishes and cements more limiting borders than she challenges and her body and way of life might be attractive to men but not necessarily liberating and fulfilling for women. But I also perceive her potential as a feminist icon if other parts of her identity are explored more fully and if she was used to make political/feminist statements. But it is my firm belief that she should not be hailed the perfect heroine just because she is unique in her line of business and wields a weapon. Feminists can ask for more when looking for an icon.

Notes

1. See for instance Eidos (1999), Bradley (1997a, 1997b).
2. More than 28 million copies of the *Tomb Raider* games had been sold worldwide in 2002. (http://www.eidos.de/games/embed.html?gmid=153)

3. Bathrobes and T-shirts are only available in sizes XL and XXL for instance; mousepads carry erotic images and suggestive remarks ("Can you handle it?," "Only in your dreams, boy"), which seem directed at a male audience, as is the calender with Lara in typical pin-up girl poses.

4. Such as figurines, statues, watches, mugs, deck of cards, posters, stickers, wallets, and the like. but again most of them sporting erotic images rather than action-oriented ones.

5. These ads are completely animated.

6. This one is "real film" except for scenes from the game that are shown.

7. All of them completely animated.

8. This one is a real film, with an animated Lara faked in.

9. This magazine is aimed at modern, confident women (and men), regularly tackling issues of gender equality in a popular manner. It is one of the best-selling magazines in Germany.

10. Completely animated.

11. Interestingly enough, Lara's body is represented as very "contained": She does not sweat, she does not urinate or have bowel movements, she does not menstruate, she does not give birth, and she does not have sex. The only body liquid we ever see in contact with her is blood—when she is killed in the game.

12. See for instance www.network.ctimes.net/volc/

13. When the former Lara Croft body double Nell McAndrew got undressed for *Playboy* magazine in 1999, the text on the cover read "Lara Croft" while the image showed McAndrew in Lara's clothes. Eidos immediately intervened and the publishers of *Playboy* had to recall all the magazines and black out all evidence that linked Nell McAndrew to Lara.

14. Particularly well demonstrated by the U.S. current foreign policy concerning "terror," which is based on a very simplistic "good—bad" pattern ("axis of evil," "rogue nations"), offers simple reasons for warfare ("weapons of mass destruction," "bringing freedom") and refuses to consider any kind of more complex patterns of political interaction or behavior.

References

Balsamo, A. (1995). Forms of technological embodiment: Reading the body in contemporary culture. In M. Featherstone & R. Burrows (Eds.), *Cyberspace, cyberbodies, cyberpunk: Cultures of technological embodiment* (pp. 215–237). London: Sage.

Bartky, S. L. (1988). Foucault, femininity, and the modernization of patriarchal power. In I. Diamond & L. Quinby (Eds.), *Feminism and Foucault: Reflections on resistance*. Boston: Northeastern University Press.

Bartky, S. L. (1997). Foucault, femininity, and the modernization of patriarchal power. In K. Conboy, N. Medina, & S. Stanbury (Eds.), *Writing on the body: Female embodiment and feminist theory* (pp. 129–154). New York: Columbia University Press.

Baudrillard, J. (1999). *The revenge of the crystal*. London: Pluto Press.

Baudrillard, J. (2001). *Selected writings*. Cambridge: Polity Press.

Bertens, H. (1995). *The idea of the postmodern*. London: Routledge.

Bordo, S. R. (1989). The body and the reproduction of femininity: A feminist appropriation of Foucault. In A. M. Jaggar & S. R. Bordo (Eds.), Gender/body/knowledge (pp. 13–33). New Brunswick, NJ: Rutgers University Press.

Bordo, S. (1993). Unbearable weight: Feminism, western culture, and the body. Berkeley: University of California Press.

Bradley, D. (1997a). Introducing Tomb Raider. PC Format Gold, 4, 14–15.

Bradley, D. (1997b). Scoring with the heroine. PCFormat Gold, 4, 23–25.

Budgeon, S. (2003). Identity as an embodied event. Body & Society, 9(1), 35–55.

Butler, J. (1993). Bodies that matter: On the discursive limits of "sex." London: Routledge.

Clark, N. (1995). Rear-view mirrorshades: The recursive generation of the cyberbody. In M. Featherstone & R. Burrows (Eds.), Cyberspace, cyberbodies, cyberpunk: Cultures of technological embodiment (pp. 113–133). London: Sage.

Davis, K. (1995). Reshaping the female body: The dilemma of cosmetic surgery. London: Routledge.

Davis, K. (1997). Embody-ing theory: Beyond modernist and postmodernist readings of the body. In K. Davis (Ed.), Embodied practices: Feminist perspectives on the body (pp. 1–26). London: Sage.

Eidos Interactive Deutschland GmbH. (Ed.). (1999). Lara Croft Magazin. Hamburg: Future Press.

Featherstone, M. (1983). The body in consumer culture. Theory, Culture and Society, 1(2), 18–33.

Foucault, M. (1972). The archeology of knowledge. New York: Pantheon Books.

Foucault, M. (1978). The history of sexuality (Vol. 1). Harmondsworth: Penguin.

Foucault, M. (1979). Discipline and punish: The birth of the prison. New York: Vintage.

Hall, S. (2000). Who needs "Identity?" In P. du Gay, J. Evans, & P. Redman (Eds.), Identity: A reader (pp. 15–31). London: Sage.

Haraway, D. (1991). A cyborg manifesto: Science, technology, and socialist-feminism in the late twentieth century. In D. Haraway, Simians, cyborgs, and women: The reinvention of nature (pp. 149–181). New York: Routledge,

Harris, D. (1996). A society of signs? London: Routledge.

Kennedy, H. W. (2002). Lara Croft: Feminist icon or cyberbimbo? On the limits of textual analysis. Game Studies, 2(2). www.gamestudies.org/0202/kennedy/

Landsberg, A. (1995). Prosthetic memory: Total Recall and Bladerunner. In M. Featherstone & R. Burrows (Eds.), Cyberspace, cyberbodies, cyberpunk: Cultures of technological embodiment (pp. 175–189). London: Sage.

Louis, C. (1998). Lara und die tausend Helden [Lara and a thousand heroes]. EM, 1, 106–109.

Lupton, D. (1995). The imperative of health. London: Sage.

Owens, C. (1985). The discourse of others: Feminists and postmodernism. In H. Foster (Ed.), Postmodern culture (pp. 57–82). London: Pluto Press. (First published as The Anti-Aesthetic by Bay Press, 1983)

Poster, M. (1995): Postmodern virtualities. In M. Featherstone & R. Burrows (Eds.), Cyberspace, cyberbodies, cyberpunk: Cultures of technological embodiment (pp. 79–95). London: Sage.

Redman, P. (2000). The subject of language, ideology and discourse: Introduction. In P. du Gay, J. Evans, & P. Redman (Eds.), Identity: A reader (pp. 9–14). London: Sage.

Springer, C. (1996). *Electronic eros: Bodies and desire in the postindustrial age*. London: Athlone.

Tyson, L. (1999). *Critical theory today: A user-friendly guide*. New York & London: Garland.

Ward, G. (1997). *Teach yourself postmodernism*. London: Hodder & Stoughton.

5

Naturalizing Gender

Watered-Down Women and Grounded Men in Japanese TV Commercials

Todd Joseph Miles Holden

A 1999 Japanese television advertisement for Rokko no Oishii Mizu (Rokko's Delicious Water) depicted an actress in a white, floor-length gown drinking a glass of bottled water. Superimposed above a close-up of her face was a rippling line of liquid. As a full-length shot faded in, the actress was centered, holding the product, framed on either side by colored swatches, one orange, the other green, each looking like inverted brackets: > <. The final frame provided a portrait that, to the foreign eye, might seem an abstract expressionist painting wed with photographic realism. To a Japanese eye, however, or at least one familiar with Chinese lettering, this is clearly a signification aimed at linking women with water. And this is not simply because the actress is holding a bottle of the liquid in her hand. To understand this, consider the kanji for water, which looks like this:

水

The first stroke is the central post (mimicked in the ad by the woman's figure); then the ensuing strokes become framing angles: left, then right (i.e., the swatches of orange, then green, in the ad) on either side. This stroke order is reproduced here:

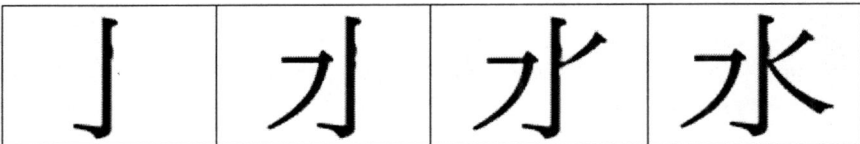

亅	刁	水	水

More often, such associations are less obvious. Nonetheless, in Japanese advertising they are ubiquitous. Images of women and water run to the hundreds in any given seasonal ad cycle. A group of teenage girls is excused from school and run to the beach to frolic in the tide; a middle-aged woman stands in her suit along the banks of a rushing river; a young woman takes a nude plunge in the ocean; a swarm of bikini-clad women smother a young *sarariman*[1] poolside. The list is endless as this chapter demonstrates, and, as often as not, the confluence of women and water has little to do with the product for sale. In the examples just recounted the products involved were, respectively, a flavored drink, rice wine, polo shirts, and instant noodles.

In the advertisement for noodles, not only is one *sarariman* smothered in smooches; another older, dour worker is physically assaulted by a female gang—this group less curvaceous, more muscular, leotard-garbed, bearing the countenance of professional wrestlers. What they do at the pool is far different than the previous scene: head-locking, pinning, pummeling the older man. After this thrashing, they hoist him over their heads and toss him in the pool. This ad provides a hint to the gender researcher, prompting the query: "What is men's relationship to water?" Not a very good one, it turns out. In ad after ad, men are shown under duress when water is in the mix. They are depicted fleeing from crashing waves, attacked unexpectedly by alligators, forced to compete against rivals in boats or in pools, and publicly ridiculed by women for becoming rain-soaked. Men are susceptible to female seduction in baths, ponds, hot springs, or on beaches—powerless when confronted by the mistress of water. The men in Japanese ads are rarely shown in peaceful co-existence with water—let alone harmony with it—as women so often are. Rather, the former are invariably displayed on land, upon which their lives are generally represented as stable, within their control, and less subject to duress.

Inductively, one could call this confluence of signs associating women and water (most obviously) and men and land (derivatively), a communication riddle. For, although the relationship between these elements is beyond dispute, the reasons for the couplings are not patent. As I suggest in this chapter, however, the explanation likely resides in deep-seated cultural notions about creation: the historic tendency to associate women in Japan with nature and men with the role of opposing and seeking to overcome natural forces. In a word, in their invocation of nature, Japanese television ads serve as repositories for cultural values concerning gender. In grounding men and women in particular natural realms, these ads also work as the kind of reproductive communiqués that Barthes (1957/1972) labeled *myth*.

In this chapter I explore such mythological communications. Applying qualitative content analysis to a pool of more than 5,000 television advertisements culled over the past decade, this chapter: documents gender-based differences in ads involving nature, details consistent patterns of behavior by men and women depending on specific natural contexts, decodes the meanings behind these behavioral/contextual associations, and explains ideationally what such a correspondence means.

Gender in Japanese Advertising

Of all analyses of gender and advertisements—certainly in the qualitative tradition—the most famous, by far, is Erving Goffman's (1968/1976) *Gender Advertisements*. This study concentrated on still photographs depicting men and women in various activities, poses, and interactions. Following coding and sorting, Goffman was able to demonstrate distinctive patterns of what he called *genderisms*—narrow, repetitive, internally consistent, staged depictions of the sexes. Conspicuous in this regard was women's relatively enfeebled status—in large part owing to their objectified, overly feminized, insularized existence. When depicted together, men often emerged as more centered and powerful. To show this, Goffman posited a set of categories that served to channel gendered discourse: *relative size, functional ranking, ritualized subordination, feminine touch* and *relations in the family*.[2]

Seeking to replicate this work in a different context (Japan), in a different medium (television), at a different time (the 1990s),[3] I utilized Goffman's approach on a large, systematically drawn sample. The sample, itself, now numbers in excess of 5,000 ads collected in six 1-month waves over the course of the past decade. Each wave aims at systematically constructing an "ideal week," of seven continuous, 20-hour broadcast days. These weeks, in turn, are pieced together from 1 month of recordings by which 4-hour broadcast blocks are taken from each of the four nationally affiliated commercial stations broadcast in Sendai, Japan, the most populous urban center in northern Honshu, Japan's largest land mass. Following recording, each block is assigned a number and then, utilizing a random number chart, placed in its appropriate position (i.e., in terms of day of the week and time), until the 7 days of that ideal week have been filled. From this 7-day pool, every ad is extracted and dubbed onto a "second-generation" tape. A team of three to five trained researchers then undertakes a qualitative content analysis of these ads. To do so, they employ a coding sheet with more than 80 codes, constructed from a combination of deductive assessment of the major thematic issues that have concerned advertising researchers over the years (such as age, race, class, hard and soft sell, advertising format, etc.), as well as an inductively informed inclusion of emergent categories over the course of successive research waves. Their coding decisions are made collectively, through a process of open discussion and consensus.[4]

Although it is fashionable among some scholars of language, literary, and cultural studies to assert that interpretations of any text are multiple and a nearly endless range of meanings are latent in any sign, the fact is that the associations described in work such as Goffman's or in the data that is described henceforth belies such claims. Without doubt, alternative interpretations may be offered, but one would be hard-pressed to assert that these meanings obviate the associations uncovered by the team of coders. More likely, it is the continued appearance of a limited range of signs (e.g., women empowered by water, men in competition or conflict with it) that lead in the opposite direction. Rather than assertions of "infinite openness," indeterminacy or irreconcilable subjectivity, this ad data pushes toward relative unanimity concerning meaning. Indeed, as this chapter demonstrates, what this data continually points toward is a set of cultural codes embedded within the ads—codes not conjured in the minds of those interpreting the symbols they have collected from advertising; rather, codes latent in the minds of those constructing ad text and communicating it through the medium of television. What this extensive pool of Japanese ads reveals is that gender representations unequivocally adhere to specific "rules"—both global and local—of encoding.

Above all, despite a different medium, a different context and a different era, Goffman's four genderisms (identified earlier) were (and remain) pervasive (see Holden 2000a). Deeper still, secondary discourse about social roles, sexuality, sexism, affection, emotion, intimacy, and personal character, although not identical with Goffman's findings, are highly circumscribed, consistent, and differ systematically (as between the genders). Importantly, when these local (i.e., Japanese) depictions deviate from the genderisms uncovered by Goffman, they nonetheless continue to differ (as between the two genders) in stereotypical, patterned ways. These findings, which have been detailed in Holden (2000a), include the partialing of female bodies more than those of males; an emphasis on women's sexual characteristics; a willingness to objectify women, often as statues, card-board cut-outs, pictures and the like; the depiction of women as sexually aggressive and men as sexually passive; and the presentation of women as freer of organizational ties, whereas men are consistently associated with organizations and hierarchies; and the communication of men as inexpressive, hard-working, and exclusively heterosexual, while women are more communicative and willing to make intimate physical contact with others, particularly children and other women.

One further genderism, as I suggested in the opening pages, is the relationship of gender to natural elements such as water and land. Specifically, I assert, content analysis should attend to the positive associations struck between women and water and men and land; so, too, as a corollary, the negative coupling of men and water. It is to these relationships—their manifestations and possible meanings—that I now turn.

Watered-Down Gender

Associations Based on a Comparative Case

It is best to think about water in Japanese TV advertising the way semiologists often do about signs: in terms of presence and absence. Doing so, one sees quite quickly that, as a general rule, when water is present, women invariably appear; absent water, men are apt to surface.[5] The most definitive evidence of this presence–absence, is/not confluence emerges when comparing ads prepared by the same company for the same product. Consider, for instance, a Kirin Lager (beer) ad that employed the form of a letter written (and narrated by) one spouse to another. In both husband and wife versions, the salutations were penned in the top left corner of the opening frames, indicating which partner was being addressed, and by whom. In the version featuring the husband's letter, the wife is shown resting on her veranda, clothed in a summer *yukata*.[6] She sips beer as a male voiceover explains how hard she works. "There is no retirement from one's position in the married couple," he intones. Cut to a two-shot, viewed from behind: A man stands immobile at a railing overlooking a body of water bathed in twilight. A woman leans into his shoulder, as if whispering in his ear, sharing an intimacy. Cut to a close up of the woman drinking on her veranda; smiling at the camera.

In the male version the establishing shot presents a middle-aged man sitting at his *kotastsu* (heated living room table) wearing a worn sweater. He pounds on his shoulders to relieve the tension. A woman moves behind him in the kitchen. We hear a female voiceover explaining how hard her husband works. Cut to a picture of him in his suit. It's daylight, inside a corporate environment. He rushes up to some important person off screen and delivers a deep, self-effacing bow. His eyes closed, he draws a long breath, showing signs of stress. Cut back to him sitting at home, quaffing his beer. He uses the identical glass used by the woman in the female version. The same anchoring phrase appears: "Strong, bitter—beer's tasty point." The commercial concludes with the husband raptly watching a baseball game and reacting with sudden excitement to a play.

Although water is far from central in these ads, one can see how its appearance in the "female version" assists in defining the female protagonist—one whose hard work is offset by respites in nature. By inversion, one can apprehend how the lack of water (or, more to the point, the omnipresence of a "grounded" world) frames the man's existence. Admittedly, the total number of such comparative portrayals is small. Nonetheless, this example is emblematic of the perceptual gulf that separates women and men in advertising. The former is invariably associated with the natural world—here reflected in the outdoors the wife relaxes in, the breeze that wafts through her hair, the gentle water she idles by with her partner; the latter associated with the artificial, built world—as reflected in the contrived corporate environment in which he daily toils. So, too, is a man's world bounded by and built from the constructed world of television—whose entertainment products he consumes vicariously within the insular living room of his home. One further note of difference to be divined from these ads: The male's entrees into the natural world are ushered in and secured via female accompaniment.

Gendered Sites of Power

One conclusion that can be drawn from the example just given is that contemporary Japanese television advertising wraps men and women in a discourse of power, one that revolves around—and is in large part defined by—the physical spaces they inhabit. In a word, women are depicted as efficacious—and therefore most powerful—in watery environments, whereas men are presented as most potent in landed contexts. And, in fact, this is what sustained coding and analysis reveals. Let's consider these confluences in greater detail.

Water as a Site of Female Action and Achievement. For women, water is often the site for activity that is absent from other physical spaces engaged by their daily lives. The act of consumption, of course (which is carried out in nearly every imaginable space portrayed in advertising), might be called a positive act—involving, as it does, ratiocination, assertiveness, and decision; however, other than consuming goods, a woman's daily grounded spaces bear little evidence of their emotional, intellectual, or physical strength. Water spaces, by contrast, elicit a full range of female action and achievement—from successful execution of tasks, to the display of special skills, to independent and original thinking. For instance, in an ad for a dating service, a woman walks pensively, at a moderate pace, along the beach with the setting sun in the background. Suddenly, her pace quickens; she utters to herself: "Compared to what you think, I like you (deeply)." As she breaks into a trot, then a gallop, the narrator exclaims: "The person you are searching for is here!"[7]

Release—emotional, as well as physical—also occurs at the water. In an ad for a language school, a high school girl is shown bolting from her English class, mounting her bike—which she pedals feverishly to the ocean—then, scaling a seawall, she spreads her arms wide and shouts into the ocean breeze: "I wish I were a bird!" In a commercial for shampoo from about the same period, a woman cavorts on the sand in a billowing skirt, turning circles, cackling with glee, lifting her hem and strolling casually through the waves. A late 1990s ad for Lacoste shirts focuses almost entirely on a woman removing her clothing in murky light, placing it on the craggy jetty, and taking a dip in the ocean waters. Another ad, for chewing gum, presents a young woman in a sleek, one-piece swimming suit, floating serenely on her back in the translucent water. A medium distanced, angled shot from high above, underscores how alone this woman is: luxuriating in complete solitude, her freedom from all social and physical attachment virtually total. A final ad worthy of note, from the mid-1990s, centers on a 30-ish woman in loose-fitting skirt and bright red top who launches, without any forewarning, into a full speed dash down a deserted beach. Following this run, she douses her head under a seaside spigot, then ravenously chugs a beer. In the final scene, with the sound of crashing waves and *The Gypsy King*'s "Volare" in the background, she lolls on a wooden bench: her legs crossed at the ankles, extended over the edge of the boardwalk, arms spread wide, her dress being rifled by the wind. Giggling to herself, as if in delirium, she suggests a state akin to drunkenness, self-satisfaction, or postcoital rapture. It is worth noting that in every one of these ads, women are depicted at the water alone; there is little evidence of others or built worlds. The settings are almost entirely natural and, aside from the props of bench or faucet, unspoiled by human hands.

Water as a Source of Female Power. Images coupling women and water are often highly stylized, emphasizing aesthetics, as well as feeling.[8] The young girl with her face in the sea breeze; the swimmer floating next to a bleach-white atoll; the runner gasping for breath while showering off beneath the gushing faucet, are all examples. Beyond imagery, however, these ads often contain indicators—inferable in the atoll ad—that a mystical connection exists between women and water. Events transpire or skills are displayed that defy reason. This is captured well in a 2004 ad for calorie-reduced (or "light") beer, featuring Lucy Liu.[9] In it she jogs across the surface of a lake and, although tripping, merely flips and skids across the surface (rather than sinking), astounding male on-lookers: fellow (landed) joggers and fishermen casting lines from nearby boats.

This is far from an isolated example. Water often serves as the milieu (the situs for expressing) or medium (the tool for demonstrating) ethereal female power. Consider the 1999 ad for Glaco car wax depicting a foreign, blonde-haired woman as superhero, with the "power" to resist the corrosive effects of water. Garbed in a red, tight-fitting, shiny leather one-piece bathing suit, she stands *akimbo* against a backdrop of torrential rain and flashing lightening. Within the context of the ad, women are analogized to wax. Their job: to protect the car (which, incidentally, has historically doubled in advertising as a symbol of male power) from the damaging rainwater. An angled close-up shows water gushing toward the hero's face; in response, she puckers her lips and blows the stream away. In a later scene she thrusts her fist at the fast approaching stream and redirects it away.

Although such ads are far from the norm, others do place women's supernatural, water power on display. For instance, in an ad for credit, three salaried women, bored with their mundane work-a-day lives, strip off their suits in a café, revealing colorful bikinis, then proceed to "swim" down the bricked sidewalk (presumably intent on reaching their desired destination: Bali). The mystical extends to the ability to wield and control water and it is through the social mirror of men that this magical power is recognized, magnified, even worshipped. For instance, in a 1998 ad for a yogurt drink a 20-ish male stands on his veranda admiring the woman next door, watering her plants. Transfixed, the man appreciates this (frankly, rather plain-looking) woman, carrying out a female's stereotypical "nurturing role." The power she wields over living things is delivered via the elixir, water. Importantly, although the woman is satisfied with her gardening, she seems blissfully oblivious of her considerable power.

The mention here of men prompts the important observation that female power often arises in connection with or as a result of male presence. Consider, once again, the instant noodle ad introduced at the outset—where one worker is physically assaulted at a pool, while the other is literally smothered by a gaggle of bikinied women who kiss, squeeze, and smother him amidst slithering limbs and glistening flesh. A reaction shot lingers on the man's delirium.

Encoded in this scenario is the idea that much of women's water-related power is seductive—an inexorable (sexual) force held over and enslaving men. A representative example of this was the mid-1990s drip coffee ad in which Nakayama Miho—at that time Japan's prototypical "girl next door"—enacted a ritualized seduction of her male partner at ocean's edge. With surf clipping her heels, she leaned forward, beckoning him, exposing her cleavage, and flashing a broad smile. After her tantalizing dance in the surf, the ad cut to a two-shot with the man "tamed," quietly sipping coffee with Ms. Nakayama. She received the camera's attention; her smile restrained, but satisfied.

This theme of woman as siren has been played out in numerous ads. Representative is a 2003 ad for a beer which begins with the tight shot of the naked back and neck of a woman. The audience sees her but hears a male's voice singing loudly in the background. As the camera pans back, the setting is revealed to be a hot spring. The frame continues to widen until, through the rising steam, one can discern a man regarding the woman from behind. He, too, is naked, soaking only meters away from her. His body is oriented completely toward her in the very large pool. She remains calm, studiously stroking her skin, apparently oblivious to the man's presence—despite the fact that they are sharing a bath. The commercial ends with his voice at lusty crescendo, as if he has lost all control under the spell of this regal female presence. Any number of examples can be marshaled from any ad cycle to demonstrate this theme of gendered enchantment and male-subjugation in water-based environments.

The power of women over men in liquid settings is not limited to the outdoors. It extends, as well, to worlds within built structures. For instance, in a shampoo ad from the early 1990s a young professional couple returns home after a day in their separate corporate worlds. As the man scrubs himself in the shower, the woman abruptly enters the shower room uninvited. Her partner reacts defensively—raising his leg and twisting away to hide his genitals.[10] Cut to a shot of the woman's towel dropping at her feet, followed by a two-shot in which her soothing fingers work their way through his scalp. This lathering serves to transform him into a willing, playful, becalmed mate. In a nearly similar ad from the same era—this time for bath fixtures—a foreign woman interrupts her Japanese partner's soak, again wrapped in a towel. The towel falls and she plops into the tub. He appears surprised by her boldness, especially when she leans over and plants a kiss on his reddening cheek. By ad's end, however, he is gleefully sharing his bath, offering a satisfied smile for the camera. Thus, in both ads women evince a power capable of transforming men from reticent to accepting.

Male Trouble: The Problem with Water. Although men may be the beneficiaries of water-inspired female sexual advances, it is also the case that they are never at full strength in or around water. These are the men of the scenes above: hurled into water, placed in hypnotic trances, forced to share their space, time, and possessions with female partners. More than these inconveniences, however, men invariably find themselves in situations they cannot control when water is in the equation. For instance, an ad for a medicinal cream from the early 1990s depicted a Japanese father being buried by his wife and children under mounds of sand at the shoreline. His total immobility serves to underscore the relative male disadvantage near water.

More than the loss of power is the discomfort engendered by water. Significantly, there is little of the peace, confidence, felicity, or happiness displayed by women under similar circumstances or, indeed, by men under dry conditions. This truth is exposed in the case of the man showering in relative peace, only to be disturbed by his live-in female partner. Or, as more often happens, it is demonstrated via elaborate burlesque—a sequenced set of actions demonstrating how distressed water makes men. For instance, when a young man wakes up with "bad morning hair," alarms suddenly blare, red "X"s flash overhead, and a geyser of water unexpectedly assaults him.

Emblematic of such sad fortune is the early 1990s ad for potato chips in which a boy and girl go for an outing at the beach. The theme is budding love, expressed symbolically through the chip. In the comic scenario, every time the boy musters the courage to hold the girl's hand, events intercede to defeat him. With each rebuke, the potato chip snaps crisply. In a final sequence, seated along the shoreline, he reaches out to touch his partner's hand just as she abruptly bolts for the water, unaware of his affectionate intentions. As the camera cuts to the image of his hand pathetically clutching at her handprint in the sand, he utters aloud "I like you." Now at the water's edge, against the roar of the waves, the young girl turns and asks in complete innocence: "What's wrong?," so oblivious is she to the great emotional tug she has exerted over the boy. Pitifully, he replies "Nothing," and the chip breaks into even smaller bits.

Another depiction, which similarly marks men as losers in water worlds, comes from a whiskey ad (of all things) from the end of the decade. In this ad, a man scampers from an unexpected rainfall, seeking refuge under a storefront awning. Waiting impassively for the shower to abate is a woman who casts a glance his way with an expression akin to: "Hey, pal, it's only water!" In the background a rock song blares: "Even if you get wet, don't worry!" Uncomfortable with the woman's disapproving scowl, the protagonist musters the courage to dash from the temporary refuge. In the subway, three young women—garbed in the outlandish *kogyaru*[11] fashion of the day—point and openly mock the drenched man: his hair matted, his suit wet, his soaked subway stub no longer usable in the turnstile. The song intones: "Even if they laugh at you, don't worry." As the ad concludes, the man stares up at a grey sky, with trepidation. The singer advises: "Even if you don't know, don't worry."

Male troubles with water do not only involve women. They can get into fixes all by themselves. There are ads in which men slip while ascending rocky peaks and dangle precariously over raging rivers; ads, as well, where they race along a beach, trying to beat the surf before it sweeps them off a craggy jetty. Ads have been known to place snapping alligators rising out of canals to assault male bystanders. More than one has depicted men aboard sloops on raging seas, enduring undulating swells.

From this, it is fair to say that Japanese advertising tends to view water as a man's natural adversary. There is an unswerving relationship of conflict and opposition in Japanese ads between these two. Unlike women who co-exist peacefully with water, men are presented as water's rival; water is an obstacle to be overcome, a site of test or challenge, an element to be rendered under human (or at least male) control. Water is where races occur, where strength is tested, where will and intelligence are called into play. In a country in which Zen once ruled, water is not an "is" for men to accept and work with harmoniously; rather, it is an obstacle, a task, a burden, a disturbance, something to be resisted and overcome. Emblematic of male repugnance for water is the ad for a vitamin drink in which two men dash down a shoreline, seeking to outdistance the on-coming surf. With waves crashing at their heels they scamper up a set of boulders, aiding one another to escape the peril; their ultimate liberation cause for celebrating the energy drink that enabled the feat.

Men's Grounded Discourse. Although the number of ads depicting men and water is notably less than those coupling women and water, almost none can be located in which men do what women do in water: luxuriate, escape, refresh, find inner peace. Rather, it is other natural environments—forests, mountains or deserts—where bonding occurs. Land serves as the situs for achievement, quest, performance and leisure. Men are active in all these natural settings—expressing their existence via efforts at dominion and control. Thus, we encounter them chopping trees in forests, riding horses across the plains, scaling craggy mountain faces, and piloting model planes across open fields. As a general rule, however, male activities transpire on *developed* land, for reasons I suggest later. For now, let's observe a basic antinomy engaging women and men: while the former conjures a *mystical discourse*—reflected in women who "swim" down concrete streets, or those who deflect torrents of rain with their forearms and breath—the latter elicits a *tangible discourse*—one in which power is measured via physical prowess, intellectual performance, the creation and practical use of products, and career- or class-based achievement. In a word, male sites of power are artificially constructed environments, stocked with concrete things—elements that have been molded by men and rendered subservient to male control.

Thus, men in ads are seen more often in offices and boardrooms, cutting pathways through urban concrete, driving cars or flying planes. They are depicted hitting balls on tennis courts or using tree limbs to extricate jeep tires from deep ruts in mountain roads; riding trains in foreign cities or running to catch baseballs through crowded sidewalk cafés; metamorphosed into giants who step over buildings as they carry giant products through the urban jungle, or peering down upon miniaturized women on rooftops.

The Absence of Water. As noted, few ads place men in lakes, streams, oceans, baths, or showers. When they do, men rarely actually contact the aquatic. A 2004 ad, for instance, situates a man on boulders above a rushing stream. It is from that vantage point that he manages to "fish" a fast-charging beer out of the whitewater. When actual contact with water occurs, men tend to extricate themselves before any further mishap can transpire. For instance, in a 2003 ad, a (foreign) man accidentally plunges into a lake on his skateboard. After scrambling to safety, he is shown manipulating his skateboard over a series of evenly spaced pylons at the close of the ad, thereby avoiding the lake's waters. Most typical of man's distanced relationship to water is the 2004 beer ad in which world footballer, Takahara Naohiro volleys a ball against a wall in the sun-bleached Mediterranean. During the course of this vigorous workout he directs his shot at a faucet; the forceful strike turns the handle and a stream of water is sent through a hose to cool him down. Epitomizing the essential separation between man and water, Takahara never directly touches the hose or the faucet that wets him down; and in a final scene he sits (fully dry) on a concrete stairwell, a shoulder-height wall interposed between man and the azure sea beyond.

Strategies and Representations

By now it should be clear: In advertisements in which water is present, women are represented as powerful, whereas men are depicted as relatively weak; by contrast, in ads staged on dry land, men are presented as potent. These findings take on significance when considering that land-based ads far exceed those involving water.[12] In this way, it could be argued that men are projected as more powerful than women via simple preponderance: "Their" domain receives more extensive airplay.

This recognition prompts the queries: Are other strategies at work that undercut or limit female power? Are advertising conventions structured so as to demarcate women? Are representational strategies employed which create, then confine, women to particular spheres of action? Part and parcel of this—do ads operate in ways that provide socially constructed, and carefully policed attributes regarding gender? The answers to such questions assume greater plausibility when we recognize that other semiological strategies—regarding water and land, women and men—are also employed. Here I wish to single out three that work to divest women of power and elevate men in stature.

Diminishing Women, Under(mining) Water

Advertising, in general, is heavily sexualized—and this is certainly true in Japan. Placing water at a creative director's disposal is like writing a prescription for divesting female actresses of their clothing.[13] And in the most extreme cases, mixing water and advertising lends impetus to the degradation of women; unquestionably it contributes to their increased sexualization. Bikinied, and more often of late, unclad women, are invariably profiled in Japanese ads. This can run the gamut from a solitary skinny-dipper, to groups of women frolicking in a shower shampooing one another; it can come in the form of a bare-breasted mermaid diving into and jetting through a river stream, to a naked fairy sitting within the pod of an unfurling blossom (before diving bare-backed into a calm pond). Entire ads can be devoted to nothing more than a pert 20-something year-old splashing a product called *hada misu* (skin water) on various naked body parts: knees, thighs, hips, shoulders, stomach. In between applications the model plays hide and seek with the camera, employing a sheet hanging on a clothesline, fluttering vigorously in the breeze. A 2003 ad for tomato juice featured 5 fully naked foreign models huddled together on a studio floor, their limbs arranged strategically to obscure nipples and vaginas.[14]

Sexuality and Water. There is, of course, a fine line between sexualization and sexuality, and it could be argued that much of what is going on relative to women in Japanese ads is an accentuation of their sexual prowess. What could be wrong with that? Isn't that a form of strength, of capacity, of efficacy? An argument can (and has often been) made that female sexuality—as a prelude or spur to fertility—has been installed at the heart of religions, consecrated in religious rites and artifacts. *Sheila-na-gig* is the word attached to female figures prominently displaying their genitalia as a means of signifying female sexual power. According to Fenkl (2003), these figures are vestiges of "older Goddess religions whose holy sites were usually taken over by later religions." Japan would seem to be one: a country with an early animist tradition that still observes fertility rituals in various communities, with rites and artifacts symbolizing female reproductive power.

That said, in the contemporary world, recognition of sexual function and capacity may seem a rather minimal basis for claiming prowess. Ultimately, it is neither a satisfying nor compelling way to construct human ontology. Certainly, men are not only sexual, but intellectual, productive, creative and physically active. In fact, many portrayals of women—even in their designated domain of water—possess little real power at all. Viewed as such, one might conclude that water has become woman's cage, rather than an enclave or refuge for expressing strength, autonomy and free-will; a place which—in its raw and natural state—serves as signifier for woman as primal beast. Whether water serves as sexual energizer or simply a milieu in which sexuality is experienced and expressed, it proves an overly simplified and rather limited domain for half of humanity's population.

If we cut beyond denotation to the significatory skin below, we see that, culturally, water is more than an excuse to show skin . . . much more. It is an opportunity to mythologize women. Because women are regularly depicted as mermaids, nymphs, or *kappa* (mythical river creatures), water relegates women to a status that is not real; more, they reside in a physical realm that does not exist. Ontologically, such portrayals threaten to erase women from the everyday equation.

Modifying Water, Enhancing Power

Men, as we have seen, have their own confinement to contend with: water, their source of oppression and opposition. In advertising this results in efforts to overcome such constriction. This is generally achieved via distance and control. We see the former, for instance, in a 1998 ad for canned coffee, with Tiger Woods[15] standing on a viewing platform opposite Niagara Falls. So, too, in the Takahara ad mentioned above, a wall provides protective separation between man and sea. As a mid-1990s ad for a lemon-flavored soda featuring the popular singing group *Da Pump* made clear—men may appear near water, but contrivances (such as a dock) will be furnished to avoid actual contact. In this way, it seems to be an advertising maxim that men engage water through the aegis of technology or the interposition of an instrumentality, such as a boat, a bridge, or a dock. Ads consistently show men regarding waterfalls from the interior of cars, spanning rivers via rope bridges, and traversing oceans in boats. When near the shoreline, seldom are they actually in the water—preferring, instead, to cling to grass or the sand.

What is more, when near water, there are factors which mitigate the potential power of liquid. One factor, suggested earlier, is "foreignness." Simply, the same rules do not appear to apply to non-Japanese men.[16] Another factor, surprisingly, may be activity and aggressiveness. In cases, for instance, in which men find themselves *near* water—although never actually in it—ads tend to emphasize what amounts to ritualized display—as if acts of physical exertion will work to ward off the enervating effects of water. Such is the case of the 1998 Nike ad featuring the Brazilian soccer team engaged in a spirited match on a beach.[17] Similarly, an energy drink ad featuring now-deceased K-1 boxer Andy Hug shows him kicking coconut trees at the shoreline until the fruit is dislodged. Importantly, however, never, in any of these ads are men depicted as being energetic *and then* taking a dip in or dousing themselves with water—as in so many of the ads involving females (e.g., the Kirin "Volare" ad, the Nakayama Miho ad, the teen-love potato chip ad), described previously, do.

In a word, Japanese ads do all they can to position men on solid land, as far from water, and in as powerful a posture, as possible. When contact with water is unavoidable, men do not succumb passively. They expend immense energy eluding it, or else working to control the conditions which will enable them to avoid actual contact with or immersion in it. Such strategies involve controlling instrumentalities built by human hands or else seeking to control women, the "mistresses of the wet." Their reluctance to actually engage with water stands in stark contrast to women, who so often embrace, co-exist with, or actually dwell in it.[18]

Controlling Women, Harnessing Water

This capacity to engineer solutions to the problem of water is generally embodied, as indicated earlier, in men wielding authority over machines or exerting dominion over inanimate objects: walls, boats, bridges, docks, umbrellas, and the like. There is one more strategy of control that appears possible: the subjugation of and intentional use of women to control water. Here I draw a distinction between the representational subversion of female efficacy, described in strategy one, above. Instead, I seek to highlight actual physical control over women.

This is raised in one ad in particular, broadcast in 1998. And, although the strategy has not been reprised in other ads since, one can see dimensions of this idea in the intensified willingness of men to engage water in the presence of women (an idea present in numerous ads). The ad I wish to highlight here was for a product called "Beer Water" (or reduced calorie beer). In it a muscular young man sunbathes atop a roof garden—a simulated natural space; in an urban venue dressed up with potted plants. The man sports blue jean cut offs and nothing else. His bare top exposes a fine set of abs and pecs. Overheated, he copiously imbibes beer. So, too, does he seek a shower. One dilemma: how to control a substance that, ontologically, men have no power over? In the ad his solution is simple: to wrap a garden hose around the arms, neck and torso of a life-size female cardboard cutout. It is she who controls the water, and he who controls her. The fact that she is a cut-out—that is, mute and defenseless to stop him from using her this way—is telling. As such, he can employ her as an instrumentality for delivering the water that he so needs to experience pleasure.

Assessed at the level of Barthes' myth, we could say that the second order connotation is that women—not men—possess a supernatural power, something akin to the snake charmer's flute. Anyone who can manipulate the instrument can produce a magical effect: controlling the dangerous snake (here the water) to do his bidding. According to this ad, it is a power that a male can only wield derivatively, via control of a female agent. In a word, the message flowing from an ad such as this one is: if one can control the being who controls water, then one can control water, itself.

Placing Naturalized Gender in Context

An earlier version of this chapter (Holden, 2000b) posed the question: "How unique are such portrayals?" Observing that women have been associated with water in a large number of cultures, stemming back to antiquity,[19] I presented extensive evidence of the same associations described on these pages in cultural contexts as diverse as the United States and Malaysia. Similar to Japanese ads, numerous examples could easily be located in both contexts in which women engaged in ritual cleansing, were portrayed as impervious to water, and even gained strength and seductive power from it. By contrast, men tended to be represented on land and, in cases where they were in contact with water, played antagonist and combatant. Space limitations have necessitated foregoing that demonstration; however, it can be asserted with confidence that such associations can be found in advertising around the world and, thus, are more than likely universal.[20]

While the naturalization of gender is ubiquitous, perceptions of the nature of gender and its specific manifestations vis-à-vis the natural world are not. Consider the so-called "third sex" in Japan. Rooted in the earliest animist epoch, in which gender-blended shamans reenacted creation rituals and worshipped production, the notion of mixed gender has taken concrete form in popular culture, most notably in traditional *kabuki* (theater in which all roles are played by men) and *Takarazuka* (an entertainment troupe in which all parts are played by women). In the music world and, derivatively, advertising, this has been popularized by cross-dressing entertainers such as past pop idol Izamu and singer Mikawa Kenichi. And when it comes to popular communications, water enters the mix in (mythically) telling ways. For instance, in the animated *Ranma ½*, we encounter a young man who, because of the misfortune of falling into a cursed lake in China, assumes the persona of a woman who died there, whenever he contacts water (whether bath, rain, pond, sprinkler, etc.). Of course, this moves us beyond the discussion of gender in advertising, but it does deliver us closer to appreciating the special view held toward gender in this particular cultural context, particularly as it pertains to water. Put simply, because water is the element capable of transforming man into woman—a claim not found in the U.S. or Brazil or France or any number of other countries around the world—naturalized gender can be said to be relatively unique in Japan.

Conclusion

The associations reported here are based on commercial representations collected over the last decade of the 20th century and into the early 21st. Because this reflects a fixed moment in time, one naturally wonders how much confidence we can have in assuming that such confluences will persist. I would venture, extremely confident. For, these are associations that have prevailed for hundreds—if not thousands—of years (as evidenced by Japan's earliest creation myths). And when talking about cultural myths that have endured this long, it is not likely that they will suddenly evaporate—not in 1 month, 1 year, a decade, or even a generation. The fact that a pervasive, powerful medium such as TV advertising continues to reproduce these associations means that it will take some very strong, persistent counter images—an unbroken gusher (pardon the pun)—to reverse this endemic cultural mindset.

Indeed, there is little sign of abatement. In winter 2003, one ad depicted two women immersed in a hot spring, while drinking hot chocolate. In the same ad cycle, another spot depicted two men sipping coffee at a campfire, under a full moon. The men were not in the hot spring; the women were not seated at the edge of the plain. By now readers of this chapter appreciate the pattern; it is possible to read the meaning via presence and absence—what is intentionally represented, what associations are selected; as opposed to what associations are intentionally ignored, what are rarely, if ever, conveyed. Consider the recent ad in which a woman steers a car through pouring rain with her male companion ensconced in the passenger seat. Another ad from this same period—also for cars—features a male driver tooling his jeep (laden with female passengers) over rugged terrain on the way to unearth dinosaur bones. The settings are more than qualitatively different; they bespeak ontological difference between each gender and their natural environment of choice.

A full menu of other examples can easily be located. From the four female singers frolicking with garden hoses, spraying one another with water (an ad for a yogurt-based dessert) to the offering in which a man scales the highest snowy peak to calmly sip coffee. For every woman diving naked into a stream after unfurling naked from a flower bud, there is a man pounding the pavement, briefcase in hand, heading to a closed-door meeting. In this way, advertising's present differs little from the cultural past; and this mode of representation seems certain to continue for years to come. Genderisms pertaining to women and water and men and land are deeply embedded in Japanese culture. They have existed for more than a millennium and will not easily be shaken.

Viewed through the prism of "media culture" (e.g., Kellner, 1995), this research reminds us of the verity that cultural ideas in any society are often encoded in certain sign-sets that are then transmitted through various media to message recipients in the information milieu, exerting possible deep social, political, cultural and moral impacts. As this chapter has shown, this is certainly true of gender in Japanese TV advertising. The continual reproduction of women and water and men and land is more than merely a stylized way of selling a product. It is more than a ritualized method, adopted unreflectively by ad crafters, merely because this has been the most-widely practiced mode of representation to date. Far from it, this associative set has clearly discernible roots in cultural mythology and links to stereotypical views of gender as it bears on autonomy, capacity, efficacy, entitlement and place in the social world. Such views almost certainly carry over and extend deep into the realm of social organization and activity, which is why this is a phenomenon whose persistence we ought to care much about.

Notes

1. The Japanese term for a white-collar worker; basically translatable as "salary man," a man who works within an organization for fixed hours, receiving, in exchange, a regular salary and benefits.

2. Although this was not a category name, it led to a set of conclusions about fathers and sons, mothers and daughters, and men in relation to their family units.

3. Although my work has not been the only study of Japanese advertising, the topic, itself, has been surprisingly underinvestigated. Tanaka (1990) explored the relationship between language and representations of women in one chapter, then later included another chapter on the subject in a book comparing British and Japanese print ads (Tanaka, 1994). Ford, Voli, Honeycutt, and Casey (1999) studied gender role portrayals, but also only in magazines. Virtually no work has centered on TV ads in the English language. Among Japanese researchers, too, this topic has been poorly attended to. One of the few extended treatments is by Ishikawa and Takishima (2000), whose collection studied both male and female images in print and TV advertising. Among the chapters were assessments of symbols, life stages, and sexuality. Shimamori (1998) wrote a book about women in print and TV ads, focusing on representations of "cuteness," career, autonomy, "Japanese beauty," and the like. Journal articles on the subject, although few, include: Nobejima (1998), Kumagai (1997), and Aoki (1986). Other texts, involving media representations of women more generally (i.e., not simply advertising) can also be located, for instance, Muramatsu and Gossmann (1998).

4. See Holden (1997) for a thorough account of the method of collection, treatment and analysis of this data.

5. Of course there are cases—which we shall review—in which this is not the pattern. Importantly, however, conditions can be specified which actually work to verify the stipulated pattern.

6. A traditional "robe" made of light cotton that either men or women can wear.

7. Water aside, this ad can obviously be assessed in numerous other ways. On the surface it seems to be directed at men, with the voiceover suggesting that there is a pool (pardon the pun) of available partners which normally one might not think is out there in the world. The women in this group, the ad suggests, are not only available, but ready and willing. To women, the ad communicates that there is a (socially) acceptable outlet for locating mates. It also implies (through the behavior of the protagonist) that it is permissible to be aggressive in the matters of one's personal life. The setting of the natural world—the ocean, a beach—may be a subtle suggestion that it is "natural" for women to think and act in such a raw, unrestrained, emotional way.

8. Some of this "feeling" element appears derivative of the sign "nature" and is not necessarily gender-specific. Men, for instance, are not excluded from expressing emotion as a result of physical sensation (kimochi or "feelings" in Japanese) due to contact with the natural world.

9. An American actress of Chinese descent who starred first in the long-running television series, Ally McBeal, then moved on to feature-length motion pictures such as Charlie's Angels: The Movie and Charlie's Angels: Full Throttle, Shanghai Noon, Chicago, and Kill Bill, Vol. 1.

10. For years, regular TV programming displayed women's breasts and male and female buttocks—generally on late night fare. There are still occasions—in "infotainment" programming featuring the Amazon or Africa, for instance—in which naked bodies are shown. In such cases, mosaic images are placed over genitalia. Advertising, however, remains a relatively censored province, although female bodies are routinely shown unclothed with arms, elbows, knees, and hands strategically situated to hide private parts.

11. Kogyaru (or "kogal") is a term that came into use in Japan in 1993. It refers to a young woman, generally of high school age, who wears particularly garish clothes, tints

her hair brown (and later blonde), and behaves in wild, attention-getting ways. Various incarnations of such a young woman were associated with the "loose socks" and *yamamba* (or mountain witch) fashion styles, as well as the *enjo kosai* (compensated dating) wave of social practice, which still persists today.

12. This claim is based on a nonstatistical reading of data culled over the past decade. It should be observed that numerous products "imply" water in the sense that liquid is a component of the product. Examples include beverages (which in 2002 was the fourth largest category of advertising expenditure, resulting in nearly 8% of all advertising) and make-up (the largest category of ad expenditure at 9.6%). In such ads, reference—both visual and verbal—is often made to water. While gender is relatively balanced in the former, the latter is obviously the province of women, where males rarely appear—and in all cases only in an ancillary capacity. Statistical sources: *Asahi Shimbun* (retrieved May 27, 2004, from http://adv.asahi.com/english/market/advertising.html) and Dentsu Online (http://www.dentsu.co.jp/ir_frm.html).

13. That said, a reading of the Cup Noodle ad, above, makes clear that not all representations of female power that arise in conjunction with water are soaked in the idiom of sexuality. The hyperaggressive wrestlers, for instance, are far from the classical pin-up. At the same time, many other instances of gratuitous hypersexualization—from full nudity to bare midriffs, hot pants, lingerie, and bikinis are routinely presented.

14. If this ad is to be coded as "water" it would be due to the image of red juice superimposed over the models at the close of the ad. Other than that, there is no connection between water and the product (or, for that matter, naked women and the product).

15. An American golfer of mixed (Thai and African American) ancestry, who began his golfing career at age 2 on a national TV show. At 21, his $40 million Nike endorsement contract placed him in the category of celebrity previously reserved for athletes like Michael Jordan and select movie stars. His prowess on the links became the stuff of legend: He won 29 tournaments in his first 110 professional starts, and became the first player ever to hold all four major professional golf titles at one time. Between 1999 and 2004 he held the world number one ranking; his 332 consecutive weeks the longest span of any golfer in history.

16. This might also apply to the cases of Lucy Liu and the blonde-haired rain-repelling super-heroine, described earlier, but the plethora of cases in which Japanese women do magical things with water should scotch the notion that it is solely "foreigners" who are the exclusive modifiers in the women/water/power equation.

17. Externally produced, but shown in Japan—lending some credence (as explored in the next section) that this women–water/men–land phenomenon may not be limited to Japan.

18. Thus it is that women in Japanese ads are frequently portrayed as mythical denizens of water worlds: mermaids, fairies, or *kappa*. The latter is most ironic, in the sense that historically stories have cast *kappa* as male.

19. This includes the Phoenicians, Egyptians, Greeks, Romans, Teutons, Irish, Kung Bushmen of Botswana, and Aborigines in northern Australia. See, on this point, Windling (2004) and the webpage *Women and the Sea: The mariner's museum* (retrieved May 28, 2004, from http://www.mariner.org/exhibits/women/myths/index.htm).

20. This begs the question "why do such associations 'universally' arise?" One might assert that, in an age of globalization, with media conveying images and ideas across national and cultural borders, shared meanings result. The greater integration of the global economy,

communication technologies, and an increasingly regularized advertising infrastructure has resulted in a "standardized" world (Holden, 1994). On the other hand, one could also argue that, in the case of a cultural myth like naturalized gender, the shared presence across geographic boundaries is more likely spurious: reflective of indigenous beliefs, based on hundreds (if not thousands) of years rooted in the local cultures. Such myths, though independently operative, are universal and relatively univocal.

References

Aoki, T. (1986). *Kokoku no naka no "Otoko" to "Onna": Seisa kara seisa e, soshite aratana jyenda-e.* [Women and men in advertising: From sexual difference to sexual brink—towards a new gender]. Tokyo: Senden Kaigi.

Barthes, R. (1972). *Mythologies*. London: Jonathan Cape Ltd. (Original work published 1957)

Fenkl, H. I. (2003). The Mermaid. In *The Endicott Studio Journal of Mythic Arts: An online journal for the exploration of myth, folklore, and fairy tales, and their use in contemporary arts*. (Summer). Retrieved May 28, 2004, from http://www.endicott-studio. com/jMA03Summer/theMermaid.html.

Ford, J. B., Voli, P. K., Honeycutt, Jr., E. D., & Casey, S. P. (1999). Gender role portrayals in Japanese advertising: A magazine content analysis. *Journal of Advertising*, *27*(1), 113–124.

Goffman, E. (1976). *Gender advertisements*. New York: Harper and Row Publishers. (Original work published 1968)

Holden, T. J. M. (1994). Standardizing information society?: A comparative study of commercial culture. *Interdisciplinary Information Sciences*, *1*(1), 93–102.

Holden, T. J. M. (1997). The color of meaning: The significance of black and white in television commercials. *Interdisciplinary Information Sciences*, *3*(2), 125–146.

Holden, T. J. M. (2000a). I'm Your Venus/You're a Rake: Gender and the grand narrative in Japanese television advertising. *Intersections: Gender, Asia and Globalization* (January). Retrieved March 26, 2005, from http://wwwsshe.murdoch.edu.au/intersections/issue3/holden_paper1.html.

Holden, T.J.M. (2000b, July). *Watered-down gender?: Portraying women in Japanese television advertisements*. Paper presented at the 22nd general assembly and annual conference of The International Association for Media and Communication Research, Singapore.

Ishikawa, H., & Takishima, E. (2000). *Kokoku kara Yomu "Otoko" to "Onna": Jyenda to sekushuarityi* [Reading "men" and "women" in advertising: Gender and sexuality]. Tokyo: Oyamakakushyuupan.

Kellner, D. (1995). *Media culture: Cultural studies, identity and politics between the modern and the postmodern*. London & New York: Routledge.

Kumagai, I. (1997). Shimbun kokoku wo jyenda-de yomu [Reading newspaper ads through gender]. *ShakaiBunka Gakkai*, *1*, 42–54.

Muramatsu, Y., & Gossmann, H. (1998). *Medeia ga tsukuru jyenda* [Media-made gender]. Tokyo: Shinyousha.

Nobejima, T. (1998). Nihon no telebi kokoku ni okeru jyenda-biyosha [Gender depictions in Japanese television advertising]. *Kokoku Kagaku*. Nihon Kokoku Gakkai, *36*, 1–14.

Shimamori, R. (1998). *Kokoku no Hirointachi* [Advertising's heroines]. Tokyo: Iwanami Shinsho.

Tanaka, K. (1990). Intelligent elegance: Women in Japanese advertising. In B. A. Eyal, B. Moeran, & J. Valentine (Eds.), *Unwrapping Japan: Society and culture in anthropological perspective* (pp. 78–96). Honolulu: University of Hawaii Press.

Tanaka, K. (1994). *Advertising language: A pragmatic approach to advertisements in Britain and Japan*. London & New York: Routledge.

6

Negotiating *Gaijin* Beauty

Japanese Women Read Western Models in Japanese Advertising

Fabienne Darling-Wolf

I had lived in a small southern Japanese village for only a few months when I was asked to pose on the cover of a small women's magazine. Flattered, I soon started fantasizing about a brilliant career in front of the Japanese cameras, until I realized that every female *gaijin*[1] who had ever set foot in the village had been asked to pose for the magazine in question.

I didn't quit my day job as a teacher. I did, however, develop a strong interest in Japanese popular culture and its complex relationship to the rest of the increasingly global cultural environment within which it has developed and in which it is now thriving. Considering the long history of Japanese cultural importation from the West starting with the 1868 *Meiji* restoration,[2] the presence of Western or westernized imagery in Japanese popular cultural texts is not particularly surprising. Nor—in light of Japan's spectacular post-World War II economic development—is the invasion of Japanese cultural products on Western markets.

Japanese advertising agencies, in particular, have, over the past few decades, managed to claim a major place on a global market until then largely dominated by the United States. In doing so, Japanese firms have had to learn to negotiate the constraints and demands of a growing international audience. One noteworthy consequence of this relatively recent entry into global geopolitics has been the presence of White Western and westernized Japanese models in Japanese ads, particularly those targeted at women.

Although this phenomenon is well documented and its significance occasionally investigated (Creighton, 1995; Ferguson, 1992; Gates, 1996; Lull, 1995), the voices of Japanese female consumers are conspicuously absent from most academic discussions on the subject. I attempt here to remedy this lacuna by exploring women's comments about advertising imagery gathered during 8 months of in-depth interviewing and participant observation conducted in the village where my brief modeling career took place. Located within the framework of feminist cultural studies, this work proposes to examine, in particular, how these women negotiated their gendered, cultural, and racial identity in their consumption of Western-influenced Japanese popular cultural texts. But before doing so, allow me to locate Japanese advertising in its larger sociopolitical context.

The Development and Significance of Advertising in Japan

In 1867, the first newspaper advertisement placed by a Japanese company in a Japanese-language newspaper appeared (Inoue, 1996). Although truly professional advertising agencies would not be founded until the 1880s and 1890s, following the birth of Japan's most prominent newspapers, advertising in Japan had clearly started developing before World War II. The post-war period, however, would be particularly instrumental in the development of this relatively new industry and the course and shape it would eventually take. As the occupation forces reorganized the Japanese media as part of their democratization policies, Japanese advertising agencies were often developed in tandem with American models (Inoue, 1996). In the 1950s, foreign-based advertising agencies began operating in Japan, and some of the bigger Japanese agencies, including Dentsu, Hakuhodo, and Asatsu, expanded outside Japan, in particular in southeast Asia. Today, Japan is the second largest market behind the United States in terms of total advertising expenditures (Inoue, 1996). According to Inoue, although foreign-based agencies have not managed to claim a significant share of the Japanese advertising market, their influence on Japanese firms combined with the historical context of post-war occupation can certainly be felt.

Even a cursory look at a few Japanese ads illustrates this influence. Japanese billboards and television commercials are teeming with the familiar faces of Western celebrities or—depending on the budget—those of unknown White models. In 1997, approximately 41% of ads in *Non-no* and 31% of ads in *an-an*—two of the most popular Japanese fashion magazines—featured White models (Darling-Wolf, 2000a). The percentages were even higher for other publications.[3] Although a continued casual observation of these magazines in more recent years reveals that these percentages have diminished, especially in magazines targeting a younger audience, White Westerners still enjoy a considerable presence on the Japanese media scene (Usher, 1999). Aside from visuals, English and occasionally French or Italian words are randomly employed on the printed page or the television screen with little attention to grammar or spelling. Even Japanese celebrities find themselves using foreign words, while Western stars are seen speaking a strange mix of "Japoglish." This specific set of circumstances has led scholars of the Japanese cultural environment to conclude that Japanese popular culture in general, and

Japanese advertising in particular, cannot be adequately understood outside the context of this country's complex relationship to the West (Creighton, 1995; Ivy, 1993, 1995; Maynard, 1999).

In his study of television advertising Michael Maynard (1999) asked: "What happens when one culture adopts the visual and verbal images of another culture?" (p. 30). Relatively few scholars of the Japanese cultural environment have actually ventured to answer this question. This is partly because of the fact that research specifically focusing on advertising in Japan is often comparative and generally employs quantitative methodologies not best suited for the subtle micro-analysis of imagery and language in popular cultural texts (Lin, 1993; Miracle, Taylor, & Chang, 1992; Mueller, 1987; Ramaprasad & Hasegawa, 1990). Studies of Japanese advertising have also tended to focus on organizational and structural aspects of this industry in order to better understand its economic success and particularities (McCreery, 2001; Moeran, 2001). Those who attempt to take a closer look at the possible significance of the presence of Western language(s) and imagery in Japanese ads quickly find that things are a lot more complicated than they may first appear to be. First of all, it is important to keep in mind that advertising always works within a specific cultural context (Maynard & Taylor, 1999), as well as within a highly intertextual media environment, particularly in the case of Japan (Darling-Wolf, 2000b), thereby creating a large pool of cultural meanings from which viewers or readers can draw upon in their process of interpretation. Thus, imagery and language may be significantly and actively negotiated by various groups and individuals (Ferguson, 1992; Gates, 1996). As James Lull (1995) said, "culture is context" (p. 66).

Keiko Tanaka (1990) noted, for instance, that English words used in Japanese advertising often take on new meanings in the Japanese sociocultural context. She gave the example of the word *feminisuto* (feminist) used to tout a gas company that claims to make "women's work"—by which they mean housework—easier. Pointing out that many feminists would find the uncritical equation of housework with "women's work" problematic, she concluded that, "Although there is considerable appeal to Western models and values, the net effect of this advertising does not appear to be the undermining of Japanese social attitudes. Rather, the prestige attached to certain concepts is subtly recuperated to reinforce many existing values" (p. 95). Millie Creighton (1995) further argued that rather than emphasizing similarities between Japan and the rest of the world, the use of Westerners in Japanese advertising aims at creating "visual quotations of what Japan and Japanese are not" (p. 136). She explained that "representations of the gaijin other create and highlight contrasting statements about the specialness of being Japanese" (p. 137). Foreigners and foreign places in Japanese advertising are indeed often "exoticized" with little attention given to the cultural integrity of the places or individuals the ads are supposed to represent (Maynard, 1999). In this sense, Westerners and the West are represented in Japanese ads as essentialized and "Other."

Scholars of Japan have also pointed to the fact that in the particularly postmodern Japanese popular cultural environment where the "no-meaning ad" is prominent (Creighton, 1995, p. 140), advertising texts are often perceived as playful fantasies in which viewers can freely engage. In fact, rather than being denigrated for their commercial nature and manipulative intent, ads in Japan are often discussed as works of art. For instance, in his book on Japanese culture, Ikegami (1991) deemed advertising "poetry with a sponsor" (p. 4). Similarly, in a speech at an advertising award ceremony, chair of the Tokyo Copywriters Club, Akiyama Shô, compared advertising to other modes of artistic expression:

> Advertising is not movies. Nor is it writing fiction. Advertising progresses by finding its own modes of expression. One has only fifteen seconds in which to speak. The message must be spoken in a single line. . . . Thus, as a form of expression it is different from movies and fiction. It might be described as "saying through labor in the middle of the night things which cannot be said in the open light of day." (cited in McCreery, 2001, p. 155)

Such a characterization has put particular emphasis on the playful and pleasurable nature of advertising and on the power of individual consumers to interpret advertising texts for their own gratification.

Contradicting this interpretation of advertising as harmless artistic fantasy is the work of scholars asserting that the media plays a significant role in the way individuals define their self-image and identity, particularly when factors such as gender or race are taken into account (Goffman, 1979; Williamson, 1978). As Michael Maynard and Charles Taylor (1999) noted, "The images one looks at contribute to the way one perceives what is acceptable, normative, or even 'perfect' " (p. 2). Thus, even within a highly intertextual and symbolic context, the presence of the Western Other—however domesticated it might be—may still be powerful especially when one remembers that ads are created with the specific purpose of selling in mind. As Maynard (1999) said, "The foreign-yet-Japanese text creates an intertextual (and often magical) effect which privileges the 'other' over the familiar. In this regard, selected foreign images assume value and exert power in their capacity to attract and persuade" (p. 310).

This may be particularly true when one pays specific attention to the role of westernized imagery in the construction of ideals of feminine attractiveness in Japan. Scholars agree that White Westerners—and in particular blonde, blue-eyed women—have long been the standard of beauty in this country (Kon, 1969) even if this standard is much more ambiguous than simple admiration (Creighton, 1995). This is the result of the post-war Western influence on Japanese agencies as well as the continuing domination of U.S. firms in the global advertising market, which typically construct ideals of feminine beauty as White and upper class (Bordo, 1993; Chapkis, 1986; MacDonald, 1995). For instance, because beauty advertising is one of the most global forms of advertising today (Leslie, 1995), ads for beauty products are particularly likely to use White Western models that have come to represent an international "standard" exportable around the world. But even in ads specifically designed by Japanese firms for the Japanese market, White Westerners seem particularly powerful. According to Nakamoto Chie, a manager at a Tokyo modeling agency, ads featuring White foreigners "have more impact than ones with regular Japanese" (cited in Usher, 1999, p. 3). Or as Ishii Hiroko, a creative coordinator with Japan's second largest ad agency concluded, "Japanese are still aspiring to the look of a foreign female" (cited in Usher, 1999, p. 3).

Beyond this anecdotal evidence, however, little research has actually focused on what Japanese women themselves think of the invasion of foreign faces and phrases in their popular cultural texts, or how they might negotiate and (re)interpret advertising imagery. Although numerous textual analyses have outlined the possible significance of Western models' presence in Japanese popular cultural texts (see e.g., Lin, 1993; Maynard, 1999; Maynard & Taylor, 1999; Rosenberger, 1996; Tanaka, 1990), few have paid attention to what consumers themselves have to say.

Such inquiry seems particularly necessary in light of the findings of numerous audience studies conducted by feminist scholars over the last 20 years or so, which have usefully challenged the notion that female readers are simply "cultural dupes" uncritically consuming media, and thereby swallowing oppressive ideological messages whole (see e.g., Bird, 1992; Brown, 1994; Brundson, 1981; Christian-Smith, 1990; Long, 1986; McRobbie, 1978; Press, 1991; Radway, 1984). By providing in-depth descriptions of fewer individuals' engagement with popular cultural texts, these analyses have helped problematize the concept of "the audience" as a broad unified mass, and significantly complicated the picture, especially within feminist media studies.

These studies, however, have, with a few notable exceptions,[4] mostly focused on texts produced and/or consumed in either the United States or Europe. Considering the current abundance of scholarly concern with processes of globalization (see e.g., Appadurai, 1999; Chuang, 2000; Crane, 2002; Cverkovich & Kellner, 1997; Sreberny-Mohammadi, 1996; Tomlinson, 1999), a greater focus on how audiences locally negotiate global processes of cultural influence is a still much-needed further step (Murphy, 2003). Furthermore, as I argued elsewhere (Darling-Wolf, 2003), the "classic" audience studies mentioned here have tended to remain caught in a limiting "domination vs. resistance" dichotomy. Although certainly a necessary recognition, their focus on women's ability to "resist" the "dominant" messages promoted in the media has made it difficult to further explore the complexity of the relationship between producers and audiences and the multifaceted nature of identity formation. Audience studies are yet to fully address, for instance, the interrelation of issues of race, class, gender, ethnicity, and/or sexual orientation, in audiences' negotiation of their favorite popular cultural texts. They have also tended to downplay the increasingly sophisticated ability of contemporary media production to commodify the very resistance they celebrate. In her article on this resistance–domination dichotomy, Sherry Ortner (1995) concluded that audience studies, which typically focus on individuals' relationship to one particular text in a relatively contained context (book or fan clubs, viewing groups), suffer from "cultural thinning." She argued for a return to "thick ethnography" as a means to more fully explore the multiple and often contradictory selves that our informants embody. By focusing on the entire media environment surrounding the group of women interviewed, and by engaging in extensive participant observation, this study attempted to produce the thicker descriptions Ortner advocated.

Speaking With Japanese Women

It is armed with several years of study of Japanese popular cultural texts and newly acquired knowledge of Japanese history, culture, and language that I moved back to the small town where I had previously lived. My goal this time was to integrate myself enough in the community to get a sense—through participant observation and in-depth interviewing—of how my female neighbors negotiated the Western and westernized representations of attractiveness bombarding them on a daily basis.

I had kept in contact with several women in the village who provided opportunities for socializing, which eventually developed into simply "hanging out" at their houses. After much initial awkwardness, and long after their families had agreed to participate in my research, these women slowly got used to having me there and stopped putting their daily tasks on hold to offer me tea and engage in conversation. About mid-way through my stay I was taking their daughters shopping, watching TV at their respective houses, and was even working in the kitchen of the community's Buddhist temple headed by one informant and employing several others. These women also recruited friends and more distant relatives to participate in interviews.

By the end of my stay, I had conducted 41 interviews lasting about 2 hours each, with 29 women ranging in age from 16 to 81 years. Six of these women lived in three-generational families with which I conducted extensive participant observation. Each of the women participated in six interviews—four with other family members and two with me alone. Other informants—the friends and family members of these six key informants—each participated in two interviews. The majority of these women still lived in a rural environment, but three of them had grown up in the village and moved to urban areas to attend high school or university. Three others were interviewed during a stay of approximately 2 months in Kyoto.[5] Most of these women belonged to the relatively lower echelons of the Japanese socioeconomic hierarchy, with the notable exception of members of the family heading the Buddhist temple who enjoyed a much higher social standing than most of my other informants.

Taking into account the highly intertextual nature of the Japanese media environment, I decided not to isolate a specific text—such as advertisements—to discuss with these informants. In other words, I was interested in finding out how the women I interviewed negotiated Western and westernized imagery as a whole, rather than how they read any specific representation. In order to do this, I let them lead me to texts they consumed and enjoyed—anything from television dramas, to books and magazines, to Japanese and Western films—and we then discussed their reactions.

This, of course, produced an amount of data far too great to consider in this short analysis. Consequently, I focus more specifically on these women's comments about advertising imagery mostly found in popular women's magazines and on television, while introducing a cautionary word about discussing the significance of such imagery in isolation from the larger context in which it appears. I also pay particular attention to the words of younger women who constitute the primary target audience for such advertisements.

Because I only interviewed a fairly small number of mostly rural women, I do not pretend in any way to assume that my informants' opinions are representative of those of other individuals in their cultural environment, or of Japanese women as a group. I agree with Kondo (1990) that "Collective identities like 'the Japanese' or 'Japanese concepts of self' no longer seem . . . to be fixed essences, but rather strategic assertions which inevitably suppress differences, tensions, and contradictions within" (p. 10). In fact, my informants very much resisted being pegged as "cultural representatives" and kept on insisting on their cultural specificity as southern, rural women. Nonetheless, as Bobo (1995) noted, although the people we interview may not be representative of an entire population, their experiences nevertheless provide insights into larger processes of identity formation and how these are negotiated at the local level under particular circumstances.

Furthermore, despite my efforts to view media representations "through my informants" eyes, this study was significantly affected by my position as a White Western scholar and necessarily reflects some of the biases associated with such a position. I may have found a place in this small community, but in a specific location as the village's *gajin*—literally meaning "outsider." This position and my racial identity are particularly significant here as we discussed racialized representations. My informants may, for instance, have expressed greater admiration for White features in my presence than they normally would have with their Japanese friends. On occasion, however, my racial identity itself became a research tool as I observed strangers' reactions to my conspicuous whiteness—as when old women stopped me on the street to touch my skin and comment to each other on how "white," "cute," and "beautiful" I was. Numerous ethnographers pointed out that even the most carefully crafted studies are always situated and partial representations of a particular situation at a particular point in time (see e.g., Abu-Lughod, 1991; Caplan, 1988; Ganguly, 1992; Mascia-Lees, Sharpe, & Cohen, 1989; Narayan, 1989). This study is no exception.

Negotiating *Gaijin* Ads in Mie's Room: Enjoying the Exotic White Foreigner

When I entered Mie's[6] room for the first time, she was sitting at the *kotatsu*[7] with her friend Madoka flipping through magazines, clearly having a good time. A quick glance around the room revealed a typical teenager's haven, with posters of Leonardo DiCaprio, Celine Dion, Claire Danes, and Sorimachi Takashi[8] on the walls, magazines and books stacked on the floor next to a purple inflatable alien, and a boom box playing J-pop.[9] The magazines on the *kotatsu* were *Roadshow* and *Screen*, both of which focus on Western cinema, and sport Western celebrities on their covers. Madoka asked the first question, "Have you seen *City of Angels?*" Luckily, I had just seen it on my flight to Osaka. The ice was definitely broken.

I would have many more occasions to share magazines, television programs, music, and movies with these two young women, and through the course of my interactions with them it became undeniably clear to me that media consumption can be a highly enjoyable activity. In fact, much of my informants' relationship toward popular cultural texts supported the thesis that advertising can be a pleasurable fantasy in which viewers freely engage. Their relationship to ads depicting Western or westernized models and/or using Western imagery and language, in particular, emphasized the exotic and escapist nature of these texts. Deeming Western models "images of fashion," 23-year-old Yukiko asserted that she found advertising imagery attractive even though she may never be able to afford or have the occasion to wear or use the kinds of products promoted in the ads. Mako, 25 years old, similarly explained, "We want to be like this stuff, but this is actually not our life. It's kind of apart from our real life. In that kind of thing we don't want to see real life, like you know, some short fat girl wearing these clothes, but that doesn't look good right . . . we are not Western people but, it's OK, because this is not our real life."

Thus, my informants' comments suggest that they enjoyed Western models and imagery for their exotic value. Japanese ads for Japanese products but employing Western celebrities[10] were deemed particularly enjoyable. For instance, an ad for a brand of green ice tea featuring Meg Ryan speaking a few words of Japanese—albeit with much difficulty—was the talk of the town for several weeks. The women I interviewed greatly enjoyed this transplanting of the exotic—Ryan stuck out like a sore thumb when interacting with Japanese actors—into their own everyday cultural context. The "domestication" of this extremely popular star who frequently travels to Tokyo, made the ad particularly pleasurable.

On the Evolution of Cultural Influence

Perhaps not surprisingly, the few young, relatively upper class women I interviewed who were living in an urban environment and had traveled to the United States or Europe were particularly undisturbed by the presence of White models on the Japanese popular cultural scene. Interpreting Japanese imitation of Western culture as a thing of the past, they argued that Western imagery was no longer the subject of unmediated Japanese admiration, and found other plausible explanations for its presence in Japanese ads. As 21-year-old Aya noted, "I think it's okay for me to see Western girls in magazines when they look good in these clothes. . . . If the designer is Western, the designer thinks of what fits Western style women so maybe the styles are better for Western women so the models are Western women." Her 25-year-old sister Miko added, "older society looked more to the Western culture. I think the Western model magazines are not doing as well. So I think it's been changing. It used to be, maybe five, ten years ago, Western model magazines used to be much more popular, people wanted to become like them, but now it's been changing."

These young urban women were also generally optimistic about Japan's ability to negotiate and integrate foreign influences without losing its cultural integrity. As Aya and Miko explained:

> I think Japan is going our own way now. Like TV games, they're Japanese. Maybe they originally came from the West, the technology and the standards maybe have been Western, but TV games, I see that as Japanese. We are creating all kinds of new culture. (Miko)

> We are going our own way. . . . Along the same lines . . . in Japan, the government first accepted Western styles, we first accepted all things for several years, but then we found that it's wrong or it's not good for us and we tried to change that. I think Japanese people are very flexible. They change things. (Aya)

These young women felt comfortable with the cultural exchanges happening in an increasingly global popular cultural scene and saw Japan as an active participant in the new culture emerging from cross-cultural interactions. For instance, Miko noted that "Fashion, skirts, pants . . . came from the West and developed in Japan. Now Sushi is Japanese food and goes to New York and now it's kind of new and we think it's different and that's okay, it's just another thing." Again, her younger sister agreed by pointing out that "We always want new things that we are excited about, so if two cultures meet then maybe another culture is born. We like new culture. It's interesting to be in a place where several cultures meet."

Lower class rural women were more likely to recognize their own admiration for Westerners. As 23-year-old Chieko said, "We admire Western people, it's true, I think.... Maybe these [White models] are not about being close or familiar ... they represent the kind of image that we want to be." However, even Miko, who assertively maintained that *in general* the Japanese admiration for the West was a thing of the past, asserted her *personal* fondness for White physical features when further questioned. As she explained, "I just think that White people are greatly beautiful. Just to see the White women, they are so beautiful. Not just the face, but the [body] style. We are short, our legs are short. But they have long legs and ... that's much better in the picture."

Race, Alienation, and Frustration

The contradictions embedded in Miko's statements are illustrative of the ambiguity all of my informants eventually expressed when discussing their feelings toward Western or westernized imagery. Although most of the women I interviewed asserted that they preferred to see Japanese models in Japanese ads, they also all, without exception, expressed their personal preference for White physical features. This unanimous show of support made me question whether or not my informants were hesitating to make negative comments about Westerners because of my presence in the room. Yet, although these women's desires to please me may have influenced their answers, a few incidents in the course of my fieldwork suggested that our close relationship was not the only explanation for their positive reactions. As mentioned, on several occasions, people I had never met came up to me to touch my face and comment on how white and beautiful I was.[11] Once, at the public bath, a woman remarked that Westerners "all have great bodies"—an observation clearly not empirically supported by the presence of my much-less-than-perfect naked body (I was, in fact, pregnant at the time). The popularity of cosmetic surgery to create rounder eyes and larger noses—advertised in most women's magazines—also points to a larger societal trend in the Japanese cultural environment.

Furthermore, the kind of physical features my informants deemed most important in order to be considered physically attractive in Japan were ones generally associated with a White racial identity, namely "high" noses, double eyelids, thinness, height, and fair skin.[12] They also recognized that the current standards of attractiveness were different from those in practice a few decades ago. As 47-year-old Takako explained, "In the old days, like in the Heiyan period, almond-shaped eyes were popular.... But now big eyes and differently shaped noses are more popular." Or, as 16-year-olds Mie and Madoka put it:

Mie: In the old times it was different, wasn't it? Fat women were considered beautiful.

Madoka: Like turtle shaped! There were many fat women then.

Mie: They liked eyes with single eyelids, elongated, small mouths, triangular faces.

The preference for White features was also evident in the kind of bodies my informants—particularly very young women—wished for themselves. When given a chance to engage in the kind of pleasurable fantasies arguably afforded by advertisements, the women I interviewed chose to dream about a very specific set of circumstances. For instance, when asked what she would do if all her wishes could be granted for one day, 16-year-old Harumi responded, "I would want bigger eyes, to be taller, have fair skin, a slender waist, make everything thinner to have good style." Mie and Madoka's fantasy was along the same lines:

Mie: I would be thinner, especially my legs and my arms.

Madoka: I would make myself thinner, with bigger breasts. . . .

Mie: I would change my eyes to double eyelids and have a high nose.

Madoka: I would change my nose to a high nose. I would make my hair very long and then I could have it cut as I like . . . I would change my hair every day.

Mie: I would change the color [of my hair] every hour. . . .

Madoka: I'd wear a dress like *gaijin* actresses do in the movies, one of those long full skirts, with a lace shawl.

Mie: I would go shopping in America.

This longing for bigger eyes and noses, and desire to go shopping in exotic foreign places suggest that these young women have effectively integrated Western and westernized imagery into their own cultural imaginary. This integration, however, was not always smooth and seamless. In fact, the ambiguity generated by White models' different racial and—in the case of lower class women—socio-economic identity, was particularly difficult to negotiate.[13]

Although the women I interviewed recognized the often pleasurable nature of advertising fantasies in which foreigners are domesticated and Japanese westernized, they also expressed frustration at the continuing presence of White models in the Japanese media. For instance, after admitting that they found White models in magazine ads particularly attractive, 23-year-olds Chieko and Yukiko concluded:

> Each country has to understand other countries and take things from them
> in order to grow. If they don't the world can't grow ... but maybe in Japan,
> we have taken too much from American culture. (Yukiko)

> Each country needs to grow, but does it mean that we need to take things only
> from white people's culture? [My interpreter translates "Western culture" and
> Chieko emphatically repeats "White people's culture"]. (Chieko)

Similarly, 44-year-old Abe-san deplored the presence of White models while at the
same time asserting their physical superiority:

> Everyone is White these days. In the past, it was different, but now everyone
> is White. Maybe it's because they have good bodies, you know compared to
> Japanese models, they have nice breasts, nice hips, longer legs, so they look
> nice with the underwear on, so maybe that's why they use White models.
> Japanese women might think that they can look nice in these kinds of things
> but they can't.

Ultimately, Japanese women's inability to ever live up to the standards of
attractiveness set forth by models of a different racial identity led many informants
to conclude that despite their pleasurable aspects, ads featuring White Westerners
were not appropriate models for them. They strongly expressed their preference
for Japanese models that they felt were easier to emulate. As 23-year-old Kumiko
noted, "[White models] look nice and they have good styles, so they're beautiful.
But I want the magazines to have Japanese models. Japanese models have a different style from these White models. I just can't imagine myself wearing these
kinds of clothes." Chieko expressed a similar frustration toward advertising for
clothing featuring White models: "Westerners and Japanese have completely different [body] styles, so if I try to wear these kinds of clothes, they generally don't
fit me, so I feel angry. I feel like I'm being deceived."

Thus, the women I interviewed experienced much frustration in their consumption of Westernized advertising imagery. Although they enjoyed engaging in
the exotic fantasies these texts construct, they also felt alienated by their emphasis
on standards of physical attractiveness they could never reach.

Analysis and Conclusion

Because of Japan's long history of Western influence and its unusual status as
a non-Western nation with a "first-world" economy, young Japanese women's
relationship to advertising texts is particularly complex. Ideals of attractiveness

promoted in much advertising in Japan are racially—and, often, culturally—different from those young women are likely to encounter in their own environment. Indeed, although images of White Westerners are present in the Japanese media, the actual Japanese population is far from as racially diverse, especially in rural Japan, as global advertising fantasies. Thus, the women I interviewed found themselves in the difficult position of reconciling their racial and cultural identity with representations of ideal femininity based on standards of attractiveness not only physically impossible for them to achieve, but also completely removed from their daily experiences. As critical media consumers struggling with the alienating nature of these texts, the young women I interviewed often harshly criticized the presence of White models in Japanese advertising for inevitably setting Japanese women up for disappointment. They did not, however, question the validity of White physical traits as inherently "better" models of attractiveness for women in general.

Furthermore, my informants' critical assessment of White models' role should not blind us to the fact that Japanese models often do not offer a much more realistic ideal than their Western counterparts. However, by establishing a clear contrast between Westerners and Japanese—Creighton's (1995) "visual quotations of what Japan and Japanese are not" (p. 136)—exotic representations of White models help construct Japanese ones as relatively closer and more familiar to the audience. Thus, although my informants assertively critiqued the standards established by white models as impossible to achieve, they did not extend their criticism to the ultra young, ultra thin, highly westernized—and often surgically achieved—Japanese ideal. This erasure of Japanese models' artificiality is one of the most interesting side effects of the continuing presence of Western models in a popular cultural environment in which producers work hard to make audiences feel close to Japanese celebrities (Painter, 1996).

Finally, we must also keep in mind that the context in which my informants negotiated their relationship to cultural texts is that of late global capitalism—a context in which the concepts of choice, participation, and resistance become particularly complex. As Hanno Hardt (1998) reminded us, "The authority of those who determine the agenda of media production is the authority of commodity production.... Therefore, the appeal to participation is an appeal to consumption of products or ideologies, and it exhausts itself in the relentless quest for commercial and political success" (p. 87). Arjun Appadurai (1999) similarly argued that in advertising, "images of agency are increasingly distortions of a world of merchandising so subtle that the consumer is consistently helped to believe that he or she is an actor, where in fact he or she is at best a chooser" (p. 229).

The recognition of the normalizing potential of capitalist ideology does not necessarily imply, however, that individuals are passive victims of false consciousness. On the contrary, as Theodor Adorno and Max Horkheimer (1969/1997) noted, "The triumph of advertising in the culture industry is that consumers feel compelled to buy and use its products *even though they see through them*" (p. 166, italics added).

The women I interviewed certainly "saw through" Western imagery, but they nevertheless continued to consume, enjoy, resist, and experience frustration from it. As they struggled to negotiate their relationship to an increasingly global popular cultural scene, they also negotiated their own cultural, gendered, racial, and class position in multidimensional and often contradictory ways. In this sense, their experiences illustrate, at the local level, the intricacies of processes of global cultural influence under late capitalist conditions.

Notes

1. Literally, "outside person." Common term used to refer to foreigners, in particular White Westerners.
2. The 1868 *Meiji* restoration marked the end of the Tokugawa era and the beginning of one of the most intense periods of Western influence in Japanese history aiming at turning Japan into a modern, more democratic state.
3. Percentages for other magazines included: *Vivi*, 47%, *éf*, 41%, and *Say*, 17%.
4. See for example Radhika Parameswaran's (1999) work on romance novels in India, or Antonio La Pastina's (2004) examination of telenovelas in rural Brazil.
5. The women I interviewed there were my roommates as well as one of their friends.
6. All names have been changed to protect informants' anonymity.
7. Small low table equipped with a heating lamp and generally covered with a quilt underneath that one can cuddle with on cold winter days.
8. Popular Japanese actor and singer (names of celebrities are given in the traditional Japanese order of family name first, followed by given name).
9. Name given in Japan to Japanese pop music.
10. Over the course of my fieldwork, DiCaprio appeared in ads for a car company, a cellular phone service, and a credit card. Arnold Schwarzenegger sold beer, Tiger Woods sold coffee, and Meg Ryan tea, to name a few.
11. This NEVER happens to me when in the United States or Europe.
12. Fair skin was revered in Japanese society long before Japan started interacting with the West, leading some of my informants to interpret preference for a fair complexion as a Japanese tradition. The current obsession with light skin—as illustrated by the popularity of whitening creams—is consequently a more complex phenomenon than simple Western admiration.
13. Although this chapter focuses on my informants' relationship to White models, new developments in the Japanese popular cultural environment prompted, in particular, by the recent explosion of hip-hop, suggest that current representations of the West in Japan are no longer mostly negotiated along a White–Asian divide. Young Japanese women today are presented with a wider array of racial identifications than was available at the time this fieldwork was conducted.

References

Abu-Lughod, L. (1991). Writing against culture. In R. G. Fox (Ed.), *Recapturing anthropology: Working in the present* (Vol. 5, pp. 137–162). Santa Fe, NM: School of American Research Press.

Adorno, T. W., & Horkheimer, M. (1997). *Dialectic of enlightenment.* New York: Verso. (Original work published 1969)

Appadurai, A. (1999). Disjuncture and difference in the global cultural economy. In S. During (Ed.), *The cultural studies reader* (pp. 220–230). London & New York: Routledge.

Bird, E. (1992). *For enquiring minds: A cultural study of supermarket tabloids.* Knoxville: The University of Tennessee Press.

Bobo, J. (1995). *Black women as cultural readers.* New York: Columbia University Press.

Bordo, S. (1993). *Unbearable weight: Feminism, Western culture and the body.* Berkeley: University of California Press.

Brown, M. E. (1994). *Soap opera and women's talk: The pleasure of resistance.* Thousand Oaks, CA: Sage.

Brundson, C. (1981). "Crossroads:" Notes on soap opera. *Screen, 22*(4), 32–37.

Caplan, P. (1988). Engendering knowledge: The politics of ethnography. *Anthropology Today, 4*(6), 14–17.

Chapkis, W. (1986). *Beauty secrets: Women and the politics of appearance.* Boston, MA: South End Press.

Christian-Smith, L. (1990). *Becoming a woman through romance.* London: Routledge & Kegan Paul.

Chuang, R. (2000). Dialectics of globalization and localization. In G.-M. Chen & W. J. Starosta (Eds.), *Communication and global society* (pp. 19–33). New York: Peter Lang.

Crane, D. (2002). Culture and globalization: Theoretical models and emerging trends. In D. Crane, N. Kawashima, & K. I. Kawasaki (Eds.), *Global culture: Media, arts, policy, and globalization* (pp. 1–25). New York: Routlege.

Creighton, M. R. (1995). Imaging the Other in Japanese advertising campaigns. In J. G. Carrier (Ed.), *Occidentalism: Images of the West* (pp. 135–160). New York: Oxford University Press.

Cverkovich, A., & Kellner, D. (1997). *Articulating the global and the local: Globalization and cultural studies.* Boulder, CO: Westview Press.

Darling-Wolf, F. (2000). Texts in context: Intertextuality, hybridity, and the negotiation of cultural identity in Japan. *Journal of Communication Inquiry, 24*(2), 134–155.

Darling-Wolf, F. (2003). Negotiation and position: On the need and difficulty of developing "thicker descriptions." In P. D. Murphey & M. M. Kraidy (Eds.), *Global media studies: Ethnographic perspectives* (pp. 109–124). New York: Routledge.

Ferguson, M. (1992). The mythology about globalization. *European Journal of Communication, 7,* 69–93.

Ganguly, K. (1992). Accounting for Others: Feminism and representation. In L. F. Rakow (Ed.), *Women making meaning: New feminist directions in communication* (pp. 60–79). New York: Routledge.

Gates, H. L. (1996). Planet rap: Notes on the globalization of culture. In M. Garber, R. L. Walkowitz, & P. B. Franklin (Eds.), *Field work: Sites in literary and cultural studies* (pp. 55–66). New York: Routledge.

Goffman, E. (1979). *Gender advertisements*. Cambridge, MA: Harvard University Press.

Hardt, H. (1998). *Interactions: Critical studies in communication, media, and journalism*. New York: Rowman & Littlefield.

Ikegami, Y. (1991). *The empire of signs: Semiotic essays on Japanese culture*. Amsterdam: John Benjamins.

Inoue, O. (1996). Advertising in Japan: Changing times for an economic giant. In K. Frith (Ed.), *Advertising in Asia: Communication, culture and consumption* (pp. 11–38). Ames: Iowa State University Press.

Ivy, M. (1993). Formations of mass culture. In A. Gordon (Ed.), *Postwar Japan as history* (pp. 239–258). Berkeley: University of California Press.

Ivy, M. (1995). *Discourse of the vanishing: Modernity, phantasm, Japan*. Chicago: The University of Chicago Press.

Kon, H. (1969). Mirror, mirror on the wall . . . Japanese beauties through the ages. *East, 5*(4), 18–27.

Kondo, D. (1990). *Crafting selves: Power, gender, and discourses of identity in a Japanese work-place*. Chicago: University of Chicago Press.

La Pastina, A. (2004). Telenovela reception in rural Brazil: Gendered readings and sexual mores. *Critical Studies in Media Communication, 21*(2), 162–181.

Leslie, D. A. (1995). The globalization of advertising agencies, concepts, and campaigns. *Economic Geography, 71*(4), 402–426.

Lin, C. (1993). Cultural differences in message strategies: A comparison between American and Japanese TV commercials. *Journal of Advertising Research, 29*, 40–47.

Long, E. (1986). Women, reading, and cultural authority: Some implications of the audience perspective in cultural studies. *American Quarterly, 38*(4), 591–612.

Lull, J. (1995). *Media, communication, culture*. New York: Columbia University Press.

MacDonald, M. (1995). *Representing women: Myths of femininity in the popular media*. New York: Edward Arnold.

Mascia-Lees, F. E., Sharpe, P., & Cohen, C. B. (1989). The postmodern turn in anthropology: Cautions from a feminist perspective. *Signs, 15*(11), 7–33.

Maynard, M. (1999). The power of foreign images: Intercultural signs in Japanese television advertising. In M. Prosser, & K. S. Sitaram (Eds.), *Civic discourse: Intercultural, international, and global media* (Vol. 2, pp. 301–311). Stamford, CT: Ablex.

Maynard, M., & Taylor, C. (1999). Girlish images across cultures: Analyzing Japanese versus U.S. *Seventeen* magazine ads. *Journal of Advertising, 28*(1), 39–48.

McCreery, J. (2001). Creating advertising in Japan: A sketch in search of a principle. In B. Moeran (Ed.), *Asian media productions* (pp. 151–167). Honolulu: University of Hawaii Press.

McRobbie, A. (1978). *Jackie: An ideology of adolescent femininity*. Birmingham: The Centre for Contemporary Cultural Studies.

Miracle, G. E., Taylor, C. R., & Chang, K. Y. (1992). Culture and advertising executions: A comparison of selected characteristics of Japanese and U.S. television commercials. *Journal of International Consumer Marketing, 4*(4), 89–113.

Moeran, B. (2001). Promoting culture: The work of a Japanese advertising agency. In B. Moeran (Ed.), *Asian media productions* (pp. 270–291). Honolulu: University of Hawaii Press.

Mueller, B. (1987). Reflections of culture: An analysis of Japanese and American advertising appeals. *Journal of Advertising Research, 27*, 51–59.

Murphy, P. (2003). Without ideology? Rethinking hegemony in the age of transnational media. In L. Artz & Y. R. Kamalipour (Eds.), *The globalization of corporate media hegemony* (pp. 55–75). Albany: State University of New York Press.

Narayan, U. (1989). The project of feminist epistemology: Perspectives from a nonwestern feminist. In A. Jaggar & S. Bordo (Eds.), *Gender/body/knowledge* (pp. 256–269). New Brunswick, NJ: Rutgers University Press.

Ortner, S. (1995). Resistance and the problem of ethnographic refusal. *Comparative Studies in Society and History, 37*(1), 173–193.

Painter, A. (1996). Japanese daytime television, popular culture, and ideology. In J. W. Treat (Ed.), *Contemporary Japan and popular culture* (pp. 197–234). Honolulu: University of Hawaii Press.

Parameswaran, R. (1999). Western romance fiction as English language media in postcolonial India. *Journal of Communication, 49*(2), 84–105.

Press, A. (1991). *Women watching television: Gender, class, and generation in the American television experience*. Philadelphia: University of Pennsylvania.

Radway, J. (1984). *Reading the romance: Women patriarchy and popular literature*. Chapel Hill: University of North Carolina Press.

Ramaprasad, J., & Hasegawa, K. (1990). Creative strategies in American and Japanese TV commercials: A comparison. *Journal of Advertising Research, 32*, 34–45.

Rosenberger, N. (1996). Fragile resistance, signs of status: Women between state and media in Japan. In A. E. Imamura (Ed.), *Re-imaging Japanese women* (pp. 12–45). Berkeley: University of California Press.

Sreberny-Mohammadi, A. (1996). Globalization, communication and transnational civil society: Introduction. In S. Braman & A. Sreberny-Mohammadi (Eds.), *Globalization, communication and transnational civil society*. Cresskill, NJ: Hampton Press.

Tanaka, K. (1990). Intelligent elegance: Women in Japanese advertising. In E. Ben-Ari, B. Moeran, & J. Valentine (Eds.), *Unwrapping Japan: Society and culture in anthropological perspective* (pp. 78–96). Manchester, England: Manchester University Press.

Tomlinson, J. (1999). *Globalization and culture*. Chicago, IL: The University of Chicago Press.

Usher, A. (1999). The old ad adage survives—sex still sells in Japan. *Japan Quarterly, 46*, 49–56.

Williamson, J. (1978). *Decoding advertisements*. New York: Marion Boyars.

7

Nimble Hands Weaving Culture
Representation and Sale of Turkish Carpets over the Internet

Damla Isik

> Meaning is a dialogue—always only partially understood, always an unequal exchange.
>
> —Hall (2000, p. 4)

Craig Owens (1994) made the following observation about the representation of "others" in American culture:

> [I]n our culture there is, of course, no lack of representations of women—or, for that matter, of other marginalized groups (blacks, homosexuals, children, criminals, the insane...). However, it is precisely in being represented by the dominant culture that these groups have been rendered absences within it. (p. 262)

Indeed, representations work to make absentees of those who are represented, and this process is not limited solely to marginal groups in the United States. Rather, as Edward Said (1979) argued, it affects other cultures as well. The more exotic the "other" is, and the harder it gets to categorize "other" cultures, the more need there is to ensure boundaries are created for the purpose of ideological mediation and control.

Moreover, within the commodity fetishism of today's global economy, representations of women's experiences at times are used to authenticate the process of production and consumption.[1] As Trinh T. Minh-ha (1989) noted, we live in a world where "genderless hands—in search of their fe/male identities—produce commodities in exchange for pay and where the law of the jungle happily prevails: Power belongs to s/he who succeeds, in the rat (extermination) race, to consume most before(/while) being consumed" (p. 108). In this "rat race," as Minh-ha's work shows, women's experiences can never be thoroughly defined and "yearning for universality, the generic 'woman,' like its counterpart, the generic 'man,' tends to efface difference within itself" (p. 97). Significantly, then, the representations themselves make absent the material reality of what/who they purport to represent.

In this chapter, I offer an analysis of both the visual representations and written texts that appear on specific Internet sites (2002; still active in 2004) designed primarily to market "oriental" carpets. In so doing, I discuss the lived experiences of Turkish village women compared with the idyllic and exoticized representations of carpet weavers that are prevalent on Internet Web sites. I begin by describing the lived experiences of Turkish village women weavers.[2] Then, I discuss how the stereotypical representations of village women as happy and content contributors to both family income and national heritage are used as a tool to sell a traditional image of Turkey to the Western consumer—be it the tourist or the carpet buyer. Finally, through a detailed analysis of the Web sites, I show how these depictions are also incomplete because the reality of women's economic and social lives is rendered absent.[3] The four Web sites were chosen randomly from more than 500,000 sites listed over the Internet that deal with the carpet industry. The four sites I analyze are representative of three specific types of Web sites: sites created by carpet dealers, sites created by travel agencies, and sites created by governmental organizations. Each of these types of Web sites analyzed here makes reference to Turkish carpets.

In his work, Marx identifies two types of value: use value and exchange value. According to Marx, the utility of a thing creates its use value; however, exchange value is more complicated. Exchange is characterized by a "total abstraction from use-value. . . . As use-values, commodities are, above all, of different qualities, but as exchange-values they are merely different quantities, and consequently do not contain an atom of use-value" (cited in Tucker, 1978, p. 305). Marx also refers to exchange value and states that "the value of commodities has a purely social reality, and that they acquire this reality only in so far as they are expressions or embodiments of one identical social substance, viz., human labour, it follows as a matter of course, that value can only manifest itself in the social relation of commodity to commodity" (cited in Tucker, 1978, p. 313). Hence, The value of a commodity can be expressed only relative to some other commodity (p. 314). Importantly, Marx notes that "human labour-power in motion, or human labour, creates value, but is not itself value. It becomes value only in its congealed state, when embodied in the form of some object" (p. 316). In the case of weavers, this object is the woven rug. However, this chapter also questions the consumption process and investigates the importance of images and representations of women weavers in the creation of value and masking of the labor process (see also footnote 3).

The Absent Reality: Economic and Social Realities for Women Carpet Weavers in Rural Turkey

Unfortunately, in the case of village women carpet weavers in Turkey, few anthropological studies have specifically addressed the local dimensions of carpet production, such as ownership, the production process, and the effect this production has on women and young girls (Hart 2005; Isik 2007). However, there are many economic and sociological studies that have described the social and economic reality of carpet weaving as a whole (Berik, 1987; Özbay, 1982; Youssef & Hetler, 1983). As Abadan-Unat (1986) stated, in Turkey there is a "huge gap between the economically independent urban woman and her dependent, unpaid, virtually illiterate rural sister" (p. 23).[4] In this work, which presents a detailed historical, economic, and social picture of the place of Turkish women within Turkish society, Abadan-Unat (1986) commented on the complexities involved:

> The second class status of women in the Middle East is also seen in Turkey. In recent years the position of the "woman" has improved more than that of the "young woman" who is still subject to strict social control. Clearly defined sex roles, division of labor and separate social networks may both help the woman endure the status difference and yet at the same time serve to reinforce and perpetuate this difference. (p. 186)

Perhaps the most useful theoretical stance in understanding women's economic position is seeing family relations as capitalist relations. Elisabeth Prügl (1999) complicated this perspective further by linking it to the broader concerns of nationalism and the nation-state. Prügl started out by noting that according to both Marxist and liberal economic theories, home-based work was destined to disappear as production moved to factories; however, as she stated, this was hardly the case. She gave the example of the 1965 International Labour Organization recommendation on the Employment of Women with Family Responsibilities, which was formulated "upon the explicit presumption that women were the primary caretakers of children. But, unlike prewar debates on industrial homework, motherhood and work were no longer constructed as contradictory. Women workers were no longer a social problem but emerged as 'supplemental income earners' " (p. 57). According to Prügl, crafts production redefined the home-work boundary and within the nationalistic rhetoric " 'preserving' crafts and 'developing' crafts became two aspects of the same coin: Backward crafts needed to become 'traditional' crafts in order to serve as symbols of national attachment" (p. 70). Hence, being a woman came to mean being a housewife tied to the home, and crafts production eliminated the inherent contradiction of income-earning activities and motherhood. Post-Fordist capitalist production redefined the home environment as a space where both family care and work could coexist and where "backward" crafts suddenly were symbols of tradition. This is exemplified in June Anderson's (1998) research as she discussed the revival of weaving in Turkey. She herself fell into the same romantic stance as she noted:

> Today's village carpets, like other folk-art genres, act as a connecting thread between the weaver and her cultural, regional, and personal identity. As a shared aesthetic, the designs denote her Turkish heritage. They connect past and present—a link in time. Regional variants connect the weaver to her family and community—a link to place. (p. 43)[5]

However romanticized, for the women of rural Turkey, agricultural work and weaving were the two avenues of production within the village setting, and as Gunseli Berik's (1987) work demonstrated, carpet weaving was a problematic endeavor. Berik suggested three major reasons why rural carpet weaving was a problematic activity for women in Turkey. First, rural weaving was an activity that was done alongside agricultural work and women regarded weaving activity as an important part of their lives as peasants and did not "consider themselves as 'workers'" (p. 3). Thus, as Berik noted, because general census questions in Turkey were designed to record single occupation, women weavers got classified as unpaid family workers instead of self-employed weavers or employees. Second, because weaving in villages took place largely at home, it was considered an activity that women took on to pass leisure time as opposed to legitimate work. This was important because not only did male kin and census takers see weaving as a leisure activity, so did the women weavers themselves. Consequently, although women earned money to support family income through weaving, they did not consider themselves workers or laborers. Last but not least, avoiding taxation was a major issue in the case of workshop weavers because of the social security contributions tied to labor. As Berik noted, "even where weaving is a full-time activity, there are perceived advantages to concealing women's employment . . . villagers are either ignorant of the tax code or fear that an income tax might be introduced, and hence the activity is not reported" (p. 3).

In summary, according to Berik, despite contributing to the household income, women did not consider themselves employed or even self-employed workers, nor did they exercise control over decisions concerning household expenditures and the ownership of their production. This corroborates the findings of the Hacettepe University Surveys of 1968 and 1973 conducted in one Turkish village which showed that only 23.3% of women participated in the sale of the carpets they produced, and only 28.8% had input into decisions over household spending. Hence, participation in paid work did not necessarily mean emancipation and greater autonomy for women, especially within peasant societies (Beneria & Sen, 1982). Berik (1987) concluded:

> The relative insensitivity of women's subordinate position to economic variables should come as no surprise. The discussion of social relations in carpet weaving and the nature of the activity explains why women's autonomy is insensitive to

the importance of their economic contribution. In rural Turkish society, carpet weaving is compatible with traditional female roles and is socially acceptable as women's work in terms of limited physical mobility outside the home. This study shows that weaving both in the home and at workshops in small rural communities [does] not challenge existing gender relations and the ideology embedded in the daily social practices, and therefore [does] not confer power on women. In general, the conditions under which weavers engage in paid work both depend on and reproduce their subordinate position as women. (p. 87)

Just as Berik's (1987) work showed how carpet weaving did not entail women's emancipation as workers, more recent studies demonstrate that it is also hard to see all women weavers as victims of capitalist production. Isik (2007) argues how carpet weavers in Konya have more control over the household budget and consumption due to their weaving income and at times use this income toward their daughters' education expenses. Hart (2007) shows how, despite hierarchies, carpet cooperatives may further complicate issues concerning the choosing and execution of designs and the sale of carpets. As much of the research discussed here demonstrates, making overarching generalizations about women's working conditions and place within the capitalist systems of production and reproduction may be problematic since conditions change depending on social, cultural, economic, and personal factors. In her work, Deniz Kandiyoti (1990) also stressed the fact that "the precise forms that household organization and dynamics will take cannot be automatically read off from processes of capital penetration," because this penetration builds on kinship relations and existing patterns of production. She thus noted that the effects of capital penetration are contradictory and complex. These complexities, which have economic and social dimensions that work to affect women's lives, are largely ignored in Web site representations which will be discussed in this chapter. As such, women's real experiences, women's voices and women's selves are absent from the neat, idyllic representations of the moment of weaving. Indeed, when the carpets become commodified the central issue is no longer the legitimacy of representing experiences, but the need to provide effective cultural and social glosses that exoticise in order to buttress what Karl Marx called the "exchange value" of products within the capitalist market (cited in Tucker, 1978).

Creation of a Stereotypical Heritage: The Timeless Carpet Weaver in Internet Sites

When I visited a typical travel site on the Internet that referred to Turkey's "timeless traditions" that lie at the "exotic cradle of civilization where Europe meets Asia," I was reminded of a story recounted by one of my mother's friends who had recently returned from a trip to Europe. Over dinner, she described how as a group of women they entered a restaurant for dinner in one of the major European cities, and had to battle with the waiter because he refused to believe they were all Turkish. She said laughing that the waiter insisted that Turks did not look like that, and more certainly, Turkish women definitely did not look like that! How could a Turkish woman wear European clothing and visit Europe? Impossible! Ludicrous! Unthinkable! And although I was able to laugh at this little anecdote back then, as more and more Americans tell me all they know about Turkey comes from *Midnight Express,* and that it must be difficult to live "there," the laughter subsides. As this chapter argues, stereotyping inevitably results in erasures or over-generalizations that limit our ability to see, understand, and question difference.

As Richard Dyer (1993) stated, we constantly forge new stereotypes to represent people and groups; however, the representations work in political and powerful ways to formulate a magical layer of meanings that are true, authentic, and original no matter who the onlooker is: "The stereotype is taken to express a general agreement about a social group, as if that agreement arose before, and independently of, the stereotype. Yet, for the most part it is from stereotypes that we get our ideas about social groups" (p. 14). It is this process of stereotyping that is at work on the commercial and governmental Web sites that market Turkish carpets and Turkish "traditional" culture. By using and repeating a specific set of visual images of village women and their experiences that is ahistorically constructed, such sites create templates to sell more products.

These stereotypical images represent Turkey as a place of "tradition." As the weaver of traditional carpets, the Turkish woman is the hard working, smiling and content village woman who is the maker of authentic tradition. A very good example of this is what used to be the *Turkish Rug Company*'s Web site (http://www. turkishrugcompany.com). At the time of this writing, this Web site, in only four pages, used 13 images that purport to chronicle a typical carpet weaver's work and life. In all the imagery, the setting was the village—sheep were grazing, women were preparing the loom, making the natural dye, or posing in front of a display of carpets and kilims, dressed up in the traditional costume of a village woman. Whether it was a travel Web site, a carpet dealer's Internet shop window, or a governmental site introducing Turkey to the world, all of these sites had one thing in common: a stereotypical and ahistorical representation of the "village woman."

Canoe Travel (http://acmi.canoe.ca/TravelWorld/turkey.html), which at the time of writing was a travel site supported by Canada's Internet network (Canoe), was designed to draw more tourists to Turkey. In so doing, it constructed a very specific image of Turkey and the Turkish people. Sharon Lloyd Spence's aptly named article *"Turkish Delight: Take a Flying Carpet Ride Through Istanbul and Cappadocia,"* featured on the site was an excellent example of how exoticization and orientalism prevented a more nuanced understanding of the workings of production and reproduction. Spence (2002) quoted a carpet shop owner: " 'It's not about money, my friend,' says Mustafa Belli, as his assistant unrolls one dazzling carpet after another onto the tile floor. 'It's about love' " (p. 1). As a writer for *Canoe Travel,* Spence made it a point to underline the humanitarian and communitarian aspects of carpet weaving and trading. Presumably, this was done because carpets and carpet weaving were a part of the tradition that was both timeless and part and parcel of the past; therefore, it was vitally important to gloss over the materialistic aspects of bargaining and pro-duction.[6] It was not about money as Mustafa stated, but about the dazzling carpets. Yet ironically, the power of money underlined much of the conversation between Mustafa and the prospective buyers of his "dazzling" carpets. Mustafa "insists we sit on his upholstered couch, as another assistant serves apple tea" (p. 2). As the trader and the consumer sipped their teas from "gold-rimmed glasses," Spence's husband made an offer of $500 for one of the carpets and Mustafa's answer, once again, deliberately overshadowed the power politics embedded in material culture; " 'You put a shotgun to my heart,' Mustafa counter-negotiated. 'This carpet best quality, from Hereke. A work of art! One year to make, maybe more' " (p. 2). This construction of the carpet as a "work of art" that is embedded in tradition and has a distinctive quality masks the labor process and the laborer who put 1 year of work into making it. Not only is the carpet itself removed from the process of weaving and the labor that goes into weaving it, but the weaver is also completely erased from the process of trade and commodification.

The journey Spence and her husband took into the Turkish delight gained a different perspective as she and her husband hiked to a village:

> [S]plendid carpets, thrown over walls, air in the sun. Ornately painted trailers pass by laden with vegetables, kids, veiled women, and dogs. A teenage girl shyly approaches our table.... Most young women in this village have a child on their hip and another by the hand, but it would appear this young beauty has other plans.... Wearing an apricot sweater and blue jeans, she looks like a runway model fresh off the plane from Milan. (p. 3)

This orientalist and romanticized picture displayed both carpets and women to the Western gaze. The holders of the gaze—Spence and her husband—dramatically enhanced the romantic picture of the village and its women while providing a par-ticular kind of commentary on what is being seen that emphasizes exoticism. The girl with the "apricot sweater" is equated with a Western model, just as the guide was equated with a Western actor, Sean Connery: "The next day we travel to Avanos, where a tour of the Sentez Avanos Hali carpet factory results in an introduction to Suat Hurmen, yet another Sean Connery double" (p. 3). This unique Sean Connery led them into the factory where, in a brief rupture in narrative, Spence was offered a glimpse into the complexity beyond the neat display of carpets:

> One room is piled high with silkworm cocoons, waiting to be unravelled into thread. Another contains huge vats of liquid plants and vegetables used for dyes. In the showroom, young women sit cross-legged at looms weaving silk and wool rugs by tying each knot by hand. I envy their skill, but not the long hours of eye and hand strain. (p. 3).

However, as befitting a travel narrative that is geared toward tourism, this brief but telling glimpse was pushed aside as more bargaining occurred over vari-ous carpets: " 'Look at the knots on the back of the carpet. Silk carpets of best quality are 10 knots per centimeter! Only from delicate woman's fingers' " (p. 4). Only from the delicate woman who almost always lacks a face and a name within the materialistic narratives of market oriented Internet sites.

The second Internet site I focus on is that of *Le Bazaar D'Orient* (http://www.lebazaardorient.com/ckinfo.htm). Specifically designed to market Turkish carpets, it presents the same visual and verbal imagery as the *Canoe Travel* site. Again a woman greets us. Sitting in what seems to be the backyard of her house, she is dressed in a traditional folkloric Turkish costume with her shalvar and her headdress. She looks lost in thought and engaged in the weaving process as the sun filters through one of the trees in her yard to shine on her loom. This is a very typical visual representation of the Turkish village woman whose presence is linked to the presence of the loom. Besides this visual template, *Le Bazaar D'Orient* provided the prospective carpet buyer with a mental template as well:

> Every carpet, with its patterns, resembles a collection of messages, beliefs and symbols. They are declaration of wish, on which all expectations are enshrined. Every pattern that is woven into a carpet is a picture of a feeling, a desire or a wish. So far as that every carpet represents a living history from the early ages to the present in which women have patiently and untiringly written their joys and sorrows in amazing codes and magic letters which are to be read line by line.

As its name suggests, *Le Bazaar D'Orient* is indeed the bazaar of the oriental image. Johannes Fabian's concept of the "denial of coevalness"[7] can be used to analyze the complexity of this web page. First, we have the frozen image of a woman carpet weaver to epitomize the woman-villager-other. And as if that is not enough to frame this oriental "other," we are presented with a mental description as well. The Turkish village woman is the traditional heroine who "patiently and untiringly" goes through the toils and troubles of life—toils and troubles that are not disclosed to the prospective buyer—in order to weave her "joys and sorrows" into her carpet. These joys and sorrows, ironically, are "codes and magic letters" to be deciphered by the seller and the buyer. Even her expressive agency is taken from her hands in a way that gives precedence to the decoding process of reading "line by line" what she toiled to preserve in her carpet. The Turkish village woman has no other agency, but to code for the pleasure of the decoder who may or may not comprehend her message. This alienation is further enhanced as the narrative continues to transfer the weaver's agency onto the carpet itself:

> carpet has long been a precious gift item, migrating on the routes of conquest and trade, carrying its patterns from one place to another, and this magic work of craft has finally traveled throughout the ages to our times with its colors, symbol-language and with all its beauty, becoming a subject of "flying carpet" tales.

Once again, the worker is totally alienated from her work both in a literal and symbolic way as the "flying carpet" takes over and miraculously gains an agency of its own. It is only the second paragraph in this web site, but already the woman-weaver is dismissed because the carpet is there, able to sell itself. The carpet is the one thing that supposedly not only "flies" through space and time, but also carries its immortal "beauty" and "magic" with it into the home of the prospective buyer.

To make the traditional and magical presence of the carpet complete, the web site made another sweeping generalization. To further ensure women were located squarely in the sphere of tradition, the Web site briefly mentioned the fact that women weave carpets for dowries. It suggested that "[a]t present carpet looms at villages have stubbornly resisted modern developments and resolutely carried on this traditional craft and historical custom." However, in an age of mechanical reproduction, most of the carpets that were sold in European and American markets either come from sweatshops in villages, or massive factories. This is completely erased from the rhetoric of the Web site.

It was not only the commercial sites that play with this imagery in order to market a traditional image—so did the nation-state. It is imperative to remind the reader that weaving is a complex social and economic process that is gendered. However, the government site, just like the commercial sites, did not mention this gendering or the problematics of weaving as a form of production. The Web site of the Turkish Cultural Foundation (http://www.turkishculture.org) demonstrated the complexities of the use of "tradition." The title read: "Our Traditional Cultural Heritage: Anatolian Turkish Hand-Woven Carpets and Kilims." In the title alone the points discussed in relation to the commercial Internet sites came once again to the foreground. Carpet weaving was a "traditional cultural heritage" that was timeless and always the same, and what made this tradition special and memorable was that the carpets were "hand-woven," meaning they required the toil and trouble of women and become symbolic wholes rather than fragmented creations of production, reproduction, marketing and consumption. Many tropes used by the commercial sites were replicated here in order to preserve the "authenticity" of Turkish cultural creation: "[c]arpet weaving, carried out on various types of looms without the benefit of modern appliances and demanding most meticulous handling at every stage of its production ... is one of the few Turkish handcrafts to have continued with the same scrupulous application to detail right up to the present day" (p. 2). This timeless creation was embedded in the identities of its producers (who were, ironically, completely absent from the general picture and masculinized): "[t]he Turkish craftsman possessed the ability to imbue his hand-woven fabrics with his own identity, his social position and communal traditions" (p. 2). Toward the end of the piece, The Turkish Ministry of Foreign Affairs admitted to the "creation" of an image through carpet weaving that has the ultimate goal of commercialization: "[c]arpet-weaving is of great cultural and economic importance and ... by using the 'Turkish Image,' [can] create a wide market abroad" (p. 4).

Indeed the "Turkish Image" is a careful and selective creation in order to both enhance capitalistic production and consumption and to create a Turkish culture that serves the nation-state's own legitimacy by underlining the importance of the peasant as the hard working, patriotic citizen of the Turkish nation and a keeper of the traditions of a Turkic identity.

In Turkish nationalism, both the peasant and the urban woman played an essential role in the formation of the Republic during and after the War of Independence. As Mert (2000) stated, during the formation of the Republic of Turkey, "the advocates of Westernist modernism who defined Western culture as an integral part of modernization started to clash with those who preferred to import only modern technology" (p. 50). The Republican regime was founded by a westernist modernist military and civil bureaucrats and Westernization was the official strategy. Islam was held to be responsible for the Ottoman decline and "backwardness" (Arat, 1998; Tapper, 1991; Zürcher, 2001).

Republican ideology also relied on populism "that idealized the ordinary man or peasant. At the same time, however, in the eyes of the ruling bureaucratic elite, ordinary people were the carriers of the culture of social 'backwardness' and had to be enlightened and transformed, even if it incurred their opposition" (Mert, 2000, p. 50). It was right-wing politics that transformed the "Ottoman subject" into "Turkish citizen." However, only the westernized urban bureaucrats fit the perfect image of the Turkish Republican citizen. The peasantry needed to be "civilized" and "taught" by the Republican elite. Hence, the image of the "downtrodden," "backward" weaver was a part of the Republican elite's civilizing mission (see also İncirlioğlu, 1998, Mert, 2000, Swedenburg, 1990, for more information).

One web page cited earlier (but no longer in existence) demonstrated the importance of this image in the context of globalization. *The Turkish Rug Company*'s Web page relied heavily on the rural, Turkic image in order to sell its carpets. On the first page, a woman could be seen weaving a carpet in what looks like a confined environment. She was no longer in her backyard; however, she was still dressed traditionally and was diligently working on the carpet. On the very same page was a young woman standing in front of what looked like a display of carpets, wearing "traditional" clothing from head to foot—she was no longer simply a young woman, but rather a symbol of "authenticity" who stood beside the carpets and yet, visually, was almost a part of them. The second page was used to visualize, for the reader, the various processes of carpet weaving. Starting with the picture of the grazing sheep, the pictures showed us another "traditionally" dressed woman who is spinning the wool while all her other "traditionally" dressed sisters posed near her for the picture. Next, we saw the making of the traditional dyes by another woman (or was it the same woman? We could not quite see her face, but it did not matter because weren't all women the same, after all? Weren't they the eternal symbols of "tradition"?)

Once again, the boundaries between capitalist production, marketing, "traditional" usage of carpets, village space and the space of the factory or the sweatshop were blurred:

> [w]hen the beautiful dowry rugs are completed the villagers hold a celebration and they are placed in the young girl's dowry chest ready for her wedding day. Each village girl is exceedingly proud of the dowry rugs that she has woven with endless effort and infinite patience to create a work of art that will last of centuries. (p. 4)

This image used the experiences of village women to conceal the workings and complexities of market production.

Putting It All Together: Making the Absent Present

Roland Barthes (1998) underlined the problematics of exoticism and its a-historical stance when talking about cultures:

> exoticism here shows well its fundamental justification, which is to deny any identification by History. By appending to Eastern realities a few positive signs which mean "native," one reliably immunizes them against any responsible content. A little "situating," as superficial as possible, supplies the necessary alibi and exempts one from accounting for the situation in depth. Faced with anything foreign, the Established Order knows only two types of behaviour, which are both mutilating: either to acknowledge it as a Punch and Judy show, or to defuse it as a pure reflection of the West. In any case, the main thing is to deprive it of its history. We see therefore that the "beautiful pictures" of The Lost Continent cannot be innocent. (p. 96).

The importance of Barthes' statement lies in its realization that in creating and situating exotic pictures, we unavoidably create an alibi that helps us erase the sides of the frame that we do not want to see. In the case of the carpet weavers, such an alibi inevitably erases the varied and complex networks of production and consumption. As the Internet sites discussed in this chapter show, behind these various representations of the village woman is the desire to market a "traditional" and "pristine" culture that is imagined by the sellers and the buyers of the carpets. Even the government Web site tries to package the "traditional" culture of Turkey as a way of drawing more tourists into the country.

As Barthes (1998) demonstrated, all cultural practices (such as wrestling, eating steak, and having a certain hairstyle) act as signs. All facts, events, and actions speak to both the participant and observer and become significations that can be coded in various forms and require decoding. The Internet sites discussed here may have been chosen randomly, but their signification is far from random.

When we consider the women who are the weavers of the carpets in Turkey, we need to keep in mind the diverse structural factors that ultimately affect women's activities, workload, and decision-making power. Despite the fact that I have not dealt in depth with the processes of weaving in Turkey, it is still easy to see from the overview I have presented that images work to hide complex and diverse realities. Representations indeed make absentees those who are represented. Agricultural patterns, placement of villages and the economic strength of the villages all shape women's experiences and their different processes of weaving. Women's experiences can only have a meaning within a discursive social, cultural, and political space that is at the same time historically situated.

The magic hand that weaves captures the attention of many photographers and tourists in Turkey; however, usually that hand lacks a face. Even if faces exist, they represent merely frames through which the beauty of the carpet is seen. Such representation presents itself in a majority of websites. In several photographs that can be found via the Internet children, women, and men hold carpets to the eye of the photographer; sometimes even their faces are hidden behind the carpets they hold while they become frames for what is economically profitable. One such case is a photograph in the *Oriental Rug Review* (Askoy, Bischof, & Hofmacher 2002) which shows two men holding up modern Cengiz yastiks (pillows) that cover their faces and transform them into carpet-faced legs lacking identities. Carpets become the real-life faces of a diverse culture frozen in time in different villages.

In this short piece I have tried to portray both what is absent and present in the image of the Turkish village woman. As the quote from Stuart Hall that opened this chapter aptly states, meaning is indeed only "partially understood" and is an "unequal exchange" as seen in the Internet dialogue between the carpet producers, government officials and the global consumer. Through the process of representation, both the face and the work of the carpet weaver become a trademark of "traditional" culture that bolsters global sales of carpets and the packaging of the Turkish nation as unique and timeless. Unfortunately, this foregrounds a romantic view of the village woman, which usually ends up hiding the everyday concerns and problems she may have.

Notes

1. In his *Capital*, Karl Marx pondered on the "mysterious" nature of a commodity:

> A commodity is therefore a mysterious thing, simply because in it the social character of men's labour appears to them as an objective character stamped upon the product of that labour; because the relation of the producers to the sum total of their own labour is presented to them as a social relation, existing not between themselves, but between the products of their labour. (cited in Tucker, 1978, p. 320)

It is this inherent problem of things representing realities, but at the same time lacking them, that leads Marx to develop the concept of "commodity fetishism." His use of "commodity fetishism" becomes an attempt to explain a refusal, or an inability of the human being to fully comprehend a symbolic system of value. For Marx, the important question is how and why the sign of value becomes marked on a specific commodity. Once a commodity is fetishized it is hard to grasp the process of labor that is embedded in its production, and value becomes marked by the equation of different commodities of equal value that has to be established by exchange.

2. As stated, I will only provide a brief discussion of village women's position in Turkey. For a more detailed analysis see: Abadan-Unat (1981), Delaney (1991), Göle (1996), and Kağıtçıbaşı (1982, 1996) (see footnote 5).

3. Although I apply Marxist analysis in this chapter, by foregrounding the importance of representation, I go beyond the Marxist focus on the labor process as the sole place where value is created. Marx's disregard for the processes of exchange and consumption is criticized by Appadurai (1986/2003). As Appadurai noted, "even though from a theoretical point of view human actors encode things with significance, from a methodological point of view it is the things-in-motion that illuminate their human and social context" (p. 5). Hence, for Appadurai processes of exchange, the creation of demand and the circulation of the product are as important as the labor process. By focusing on Internet sites, my chapter also foregrounds the importance of representation and circulation of imagery in creation of value in the production and consumption of Turkish carpets. For more detailed information on Appadurai's focus on exchange and demand see Appadurai (1986/2003).

4. Although one can be critical of Abadan-Unat's (1986) clear-cut generalizations and demarcations between the "rural" and the "urban," it is still important to note the lack of data available on women's working and economic conditions in rural Turkey. This lack can be felt in various edited volumes in economics of women and work like Çınar's (2001) and Rives' and Youssef's (1997) edited volumes that discuss women and work. Kasnakoğlu and Dayioglu (1997) openly acknowledged the lack of data in the rural context and, thus, choose to focus on urban Turkey. Since the writing of this chapter, there has been at least two ethnographic studies that concentrated on rural labor politics in Turkey's traditional carpet weaving industry. One is my own ethnographic fieldwork (Isik, 2007) that focuses on the production and sale of handwoven carpets and *kilims* (flatweaves) in Central and Western Anatolia. The other is Hart's (2005) research on a carpet cooperative in Western Anatolia. Both these works offer a more detailed, ethnographic analysis of carpet production and labor politics in Turkey. Here, my primary focus is on Web sites and sale of carpets, which, due to time constraints related to publication, could not include information from these two detailed ethnographic studies. For more information please see: Isik (2007) and Hart (2005).

5. An extensive analysis of economic theory is beyond the scope of this chapter, but other works further complicate the theoretical stance that sees family relations as capitalist relations. Respectively, Ökten's (2001) and White's (1994) research further complicates the focus on the capitalist relations within the family space by making visible the structures outside the family space that contribute to women's lack of control over her workload, time, and income. Ökten's (2001) research shows that home-based work is not only compatible with capitalist, post-Fordist relations of production, but also with the basic female role in an Islamic society. Her focus is on political Islam in Turkey. She notes how political Islam in Turkey espouses perspectives on women's role that reinforce rather than depart from the traditional status quo. She noted how:

according to miners surveyed in the small town of Soma, a man's primary role is to work in the mines and earn money; a woman's role, on the other hand, consists of homekeeping. In another survey in Bornova, on the periphery of the metropolitan area of Izmir, 94% of respondents were housewives. Fifty-eight percent of these housewives expressed no desire to work outside the home, and 24% could not work because their husbands would not permit it. (p. 282)

The working conditions in the informal sector allow other agents to organize and dominate women's working conditions easily. Agents "who may be firms or individuals, organize the production of the homeworking women on behalf of small enterprises which may be workshops, wholesalers, or retailers" (p. 275). Hence, women's work within the informal space not only reproduces traditional gender roles, but also enables further control over women. Agents and work conditions that are almost always completely outside of her control determine a woman's command over her time, work load, and income. "The working conditions in informal enterprises require the reproduction of traditional social organizations for survival, because the most effective cost reduction factor for small enterprises is the exploitation of labor through family, kinship, neighborhood ties and traditional female roles" (p. 284). White (1994) provides an excellent case study of the different ways in which such capitalist, post-Fordist relations of production affect women's working conditions and lives. She states that the aim of her research is to look at power relations in small-scale commodity production in urban Turkey: "Since much of this production is aimed at the world market, what is revealed is not only a syncretism of capitalism and local culture but also a basic mechanism by which international business takes advantage of the cultural construction of labor and of the production process to create a pool of cheap, expendable, primarily female labor" (p. 1).

6. It is important to note that defining a certain "traditional" aspect of the culture helps in marketing that culture's artistic products because, in the case of carpets, the buyer not only pays for a very well weaved carpet, but a carpet that is a product of traditional motifs and a traditional, pastoral, romantic way of life.

7. In his *Time and the Other: How Anthropology Makes its Subject*, Johannes Fabian (1983) coined this term to criticize the fact that most ethnographies foreground the eternity of "the other." "The other" is eternally "primitive." Despite the fact that fieldwork is a discursive process that takes place between the ethnographer and his or her subject, and despite the fact that this means sharing time and space (coevalness), ethnographic rhetoric denies the subjects contemporaneity and a historical presence by keeping them eternally primitive and eternally same. For more on this subject see Fabian (1983).

References

Abadan-Unat, N. (1986). *Women in the developing world: Evidence from Turkey*. Denver, CO: University of Denver Press.

Aksoy, B., Bischof, M., & Hofmacher, J. (2002). Carpet studies in central Anatolia: A practical approach. *Oriental Rug Review, 15*(6). Retrieved January 2002, from http://www.rugreview.com/6bischof.htm.

Anderson, J. (1998). *Return to tradition: The revitalization of Turkish village carpets.* San Francisco: California Academy of Sciences.

Arat, Z. (Ed.). (1998). *Deconstructing images of "The Turkish Woman."* New York: St. Martin's Press.

Appadurai, A. (Ed.). (2003). *The social life of things: Commodities in cultural perspective.* Cambridge: Cambridge University Press. (Original work published 1986)

Barthes, R. (1998). *Mythologies* (A. Lavers, Trans.). New York: Hill & Wang.

Beneria, L., & Sen, G. (1982). Class and gender inequities and women's role in economic development—theoretical and practical implications. *Feminist Studies, 8,* 157–176.

Berik, G. (1987). *Women carpet weavers in rural Turkey: Patterns of employment, earnings and status.* Geneva: International Labour Office.

Çınar, M. (Ed.). (2001). *The economics of women and work in the Middle East and North Africa.* Amsterdam: JAI Press.

Delaney, C. (1991). *The seed and the soil: Gender and cosmology in Turkish village society.* Berkeley: University of California Press.

Dyer, R. (1993). *The matter of images: Essays on representations.* London: Routledge Press.

Fabian, J. (1983). *Time and the other: How anthropology makes its subject.* New York: Columbia University Press.

Göle, N. (1996). *The forbidden modern: Civilization and veiling.* Ann Arbor: University of Michigan Press.

Hall S. (Ed.). (2000). *Representation: Cultural representations and signifying practices.* London: Sage.

Hart, K. (2005). *Aci Tatli Yiyoruz: Bitter or sweet we eat. The economics of love and marriage in Orselli village.* Unpublished disseration, Indiana University.

İncirlioğlu, E. O. (1998). Images of village women in Turkey: Models and anomalies. In Z. F. Arat (Ed.), *Deconstructing images of "The Turkish Woman"* (pp. 199–225). New York: St. Martin's Press.

Information about Carpets and Kilims. Le Bazaar D'Orient. (2008, September). http://www.lebazaardorient.com/ckinfo.htm.

Isik, D. (2007). *Woven assemblages: Globalization, gender, labor, and authenticity in Turkey's carpet industry.* Unpublished dissertation, University of Arizona.

Kağıtçıbaşı, C. (Ed.). (1982). *Sex roles, family, and community in Turkey.* Indiana: Indiana University Press.

Kağıtçıbaşı, C. (1996). *Family and human development across cultures: A view from the other side.* Mahwah, NJ: Erlbaum.

Kandiyoti, D. (1990). Women and household production: The impact of rural transformation in Turkey. In K. Glavanis & P. Glavanis (Eds.), *The rural Middle East: Peasant lives and modes of production* (pp. 183–194). Birzeit University.

Kasnakoğlu, Z., & Dayioglu, M. (1997). Female labor force participation and earnings differentials between genders in Turkey. In J. M. Rives & M. Yousefi (Eds.), *Economic dimensions of gender inequality: A global perspective* (pp. 95–117). Westport, CT: Praeger.

Mert, N. (2000). The political history of Centre Right Parties: Discourses on Islam, the nation and the people. In Y. Stefanos, S. Gunter, & K. Vorhoff (Eds.), *Civil society in the grip of nationalism: Studies on political culture in contemporary Turkey* (pp. 49–99). Istanbul: Orient-Institut.

Minh-ha, T. T. (1989). *Woman native other: Writing postcoloniality and feminism*. Bloomington: Indiana University Press.

Ökten, A. (2001). Post-Fordist work, political Islam and women in urban Turkey. In E. Mine Çınar (Ed.), *The economics of women and work in the Middle East and North Africa* (pp. 269–288). Amsterdam: JAI Press.

Our Traditional Cultural Heritage: Anatolian Turkish Hand-Woven Carpets and Kilims. Republic of Turkey Ministry of Foreign Affairs. (2008, September). http://www.mfa.gov.tr/grupe/cj/cja/carpet2.htm. Available at: http://www.archive.org/web/web.php.

Owens, C. (1994). *Beyond recognition: Representation, power, and culture*. In S. Bryson & B. Kruger (Eds.), Berkeley: University of California Press.

Özbay, F. (1982). Women's education in rural Turkey. In C. Kağıtçıbaşı (Ed.), *Sex roles, family, and community in Turkey*. Bloomington: Turkish Studies, Indiana University.

Prügl, E. (1999). *The global construction of gender: Home-based work in the political economy of the 20th century*. New York: Columbia University Press.

Rives, J. M., & Yousefi, M. (Eds.). (1997). *Economic dimensions of gender inequality: A global perspective*. Westport, CT: Praeger.

Said, E. W. (1979). *Orientalism*. New York: Vintage Books.

Spence, S. L. (2002, February). Turkish delight: Take a flying carpet ride through Istanbul and Cappadocia. *Canoe Travel*. http://acmi.canoe.ca/TravelWorld/turkey.html. Available at: http://www.archive.org/web/web.php.

Story of the Rug. The Turkish Rug Company. (2008, September). http://www.turkishrug-company.com/Story_of_the_Rug.htm. Available at: http://www.archive.org/web/web/php.

Swedenburg, T. (1990, January). The Palestinian peasant as national signifier. *Anthropological Quarterly, 63*(1), 18–30.

Tapper, R. (Ed.). (1991). *Islam in modern Turkey: Religion, politics and literature in a secular state*. London: I. B. Tauris.

Tucker, R. C. (Ed.). (1978). *The Marx-Engels Reader* (2nd ed.). New York: W. W. Norton.

White, J. B. (1994). *Money makes us relatives: Women's labor in urban Turkey*. Austin: University of Texas Press.

Youssef, N., & Hetler, C. B. (1983). Establishing the economic condition of women-headed households in the Third World: A new approach. In M. Buvinic, M. A. Lycette, & P. McGreevey (Eds.), *Women and poverty in the third world* (pp. 216–243). Baltimore, MD: Johns Hopkins University Press.

Zürcher, E. J. (2001). "Fundamentalism" as an exclusionary device in Kemalist Turkish nationalism. In WS. Van Schendel & E. J. Zürcher (Eds.), *Identity politics in central Asia and the Muslim world: Nationalism, ethnicity, and labour in the twentieth century* (pp. 209–222). New York: St. Martin's Press.

8

Was There Really a Crisis?

Female Images in the Recontextualization of Political Issues in Indonesian Television Advertisements

Wiwik Sushartami

A television advertisement for a Tropikana dietary product that ran in Indonesia in mid-1998 opens with the following caption: "Warning for those who stock sugar." It continues with a visual of the back of a woman wearing a red sleeveless dress. She is shown greedily enjoying her meal, and as she eats, her body expands until eventually, now shown from the front, she turns into a sack of sugar. A male voiceover warns, "This is the danger. Your blood sugar will rise, your body will become fat and you will easily fall ill. Now, there is Tropikana Slim corn sweetener. Low in calories, sugar free."

The advertisement was broadcast during a period that coincided with the crisis of the New Order government and its eventual downfall. This period marked a highly reflexive time in Indonesian society in which identity meanings and constructions were contested and reworked. Under the New Order rule (1966–1998), women had been recognized as "complete" only through matrimonial relationships, and the official discourse on gender roles and identity in Indonesia tended to be largely silent on single women, who fell outside this category. However, with the booming of the advertising business as part and parcel of the development of television industries in Indonesia since late 1980s, images of young, single women have become abundant. Television ads broadcast by Indonesian private television stations in 1998–1999 showed that images of single women occupied a larger part of the advertising market, although those of middle-class domestic housewives and mothers were still to be found. These television advertisements depicted single women engaged in the workplace, public life, and in relationships with men. More images of single women rather than married women were used to sell a wide variety of products ranging from household goods to institutional and telecommunication services. These ads demonstrated new constructions of femininity through images of urban, middle-class, single women.

As the meanings of ads are always "relational and contextual" (Goldman, 1992, p. 5), this chapter finds that Indonesian television advertisements that ran in the years 1998–1999 also accommodated events related to the upheavals of the time. This chapter also finds that in these ads more single women than married women were made visible. These single women were portrayed taking part in public activities. Although most of the depictions picked up loose associations with the general atmosphere of the time, this chapter focuses on three particular ads that showed a strong association to three specific events: first, the reification of the issue of the shortage of a staple food in an advertisement for a dietary product; second, the recontextualization of the case of mass rape during the May 1998 riots in Jakarta in the presentation of a television advertisement for a telecommunication service; and third, the significance of women and the press in the issue of East Timor's independence deployed in a television advertisement for cellular cards. The texts, pictures, and sounds in these three ads explicitly made correspondence to what was happening in Indonesia at the time concerned.

Following an analysis of these three television advertisements, this chapter finds a contradiction. On the one hand, these ads provide a space where a new identity construction can be generated by making single women visible. On the other hand, they arguably used images of single women to obscure and recontextualize political issues into playful nonpolitical narratives. In other words, the use of the images of single women in the reconstruction of these events—decked with necessary symbols of consumerism—has risked the progressive potential of engendering new female identity.

I begin with a discussion of contemporary gender studies in the Indonesian context.

Gender and the State: Contemporary Theories

Local societies in Indonesia, as in other Southeast Asian countries, have long been perceived as containing manifold gender relations between women and men. Atkinson and Errington (1990) suggested looking at different rules of cultural worlds in the Southeast Asian region as local constructions of gender relations in this region demand understanding in their own terms. Compared with the contemporary gender construction in the United States, which emphasizes the conceptions of body and sex as major attributes for gender constructions, gender constructions in the Southeast Asian region seldom place anatomy or physiology in a central position (Errington, 1990). The concept of a universal public–domestic dichotomy that is predominantly based on the social organization and position of men and women falls short of recognizing the various gender relations in this region (Rosaldo, 1974). Within the scope of local Indonesian societies we can find a variety of gender relations, as in the matrilineal Minangkabau of West Sumatera (Blackwood, 1995), the egalitarian gender relations in the Wana society of central Sulawesi (Atkinson, 1990), or matrifocality (or prominence of mothers) among the matrilineal Minangkabau, patrilineal Acehnese, and bilateral Javanese (Tanner, 1974). Gender relations in these local societies repudiate body, sex, and sexuality as the major attributes for gender constructions.

Because local communities are increasingly recognized as sites of heterogeneity and contestation, there has been a shift of orientation where the State is increasingly perceived as the force of cultural homogenization and gender oppression (Steedly, 1999). Nation-building constituted from an imagined community (Anderson, 1983) demands not only an imagination of a shared experience in identifying with an extended community, but also historical practices in which social difference is perpetually invented and performed. Yet, despite the nationalist ideology bearing on the idea of common unity, nations have reached to the sanctioned institutionalization of gender difference, a concept to which I return referring to the practice of the New Order State. In this way, nationalism augments the people's identities through social contestations that are always gendered (McClintock, 1997). This can be realized in the imagery of familial and domestic space and the symbolization of domestic genealogies (McClintock, 1997). As such, we can speak of a nation as mother- or fatherland.

The familial assemblage is important for nationalism because it offers a natural figure in which national hierarchy is sanctioned with a common unity of interests and a figuration of time in which the national history can be shaped into a single narrative. Utilizing the image of state as family, the New Order embraced "State Ibuism" (Suryakusuma, 1996), or literally state-motherism, as its official gender ideology, in which women were perceived as dependent wives who exist for their husbands, their families, and the state. Within this notion, the relationship between women and men followed the predominant gender ideology that put men as the primary source of power and women as the medium of that power. In this statist imaginary of gender relations, the category of single women simply never exists.

What follows is an outline of the state-endorsed gender practices of the New Order that restrained the category of single women to provide an historical context to situate this analysis.

Indonesian Single Women: Beyond Definition

The years 1965–1966 signified an important period in the political history of Indonesia as they marked the transition from the Old Order (1945–1966) to the New

Order. One central event marking this shift was the incident of the September 30, 1965 movement of the Indonesian Communist Party (*Gerakan 30 September PKI*, or G30SPKI).[1] As a result, in early 1966, General Suharto, then second president, instigated the mass killing of hundreds of thousands of people suspected of colluding with *Partai Komunis Indonesia* (PKI), the Indonesian Communist Party (Vatikiotis, 1998). The New Order then dismantled many communist-oriented organizations, including *Gerakan Wanita Indonesia* (hence Gerwani), the Indonesian Women's Movement. Gerwani was a grassroots women's organization that took an active part in a national effort to improve the quality of life for women (Wieringa, 1996). By 1965, Gerwani had openly declared their leaning toward the PKI. This move turned fatal as at the time all communist and left-wing political parties were banned. Gerwani, as a member of the Communist Family, was also suppressed. Members of Gerwani were said to have taken part in the kidnapping and killing of army generals and the brutal mutilation of their genitals. These women were sent to jail without trial and many were said to be tortured and sexually assaulted by the officers while in detention.[2]

The early months of 1966 thus signified an end of this large women's organization. By associating radical women's movements with communism and sexual perversity, the regime not only castigated leftist women's movements, but also demonized women who stepped outside their expected social and familial roles. This eradication of radical women's movements cannot be understated in terms of the regime's attempt to build the totalitarian State and assert national stability as a requirement for development.

When Suharto seized power in 1966, Indonesia was experiencing a negative growth rate, 600% inflation, a national debt of more than US$2 billion, and no foreign reserves to speak of (Vatikiotis, 1998). The new State's propaganda of National Development promised not only a new hope for the Indonesian people, but also detachment from its recent history, and from the memories of the bloody turmoil preceding its inauguration. Modernization, or the preferred term *pembangunan* (development), became the buzzword of the New Order State.[3] With the booming price of crude oil, the primary traditional commodity in Indonesia in the 1970s and 1980s, the country's growth rate rose from minus in 1967 to 7% to 8% per year (Vatikiotis, 1998). This ushered in not only infrastructure development, but also the development of the print media and advertising in Indonesia (Brenner, 1999). The increasing literacy rates among the people and growing financial strength of the middle class also influenced the rise of publications and the consumption of print media.

Beginning in 1970, the State established *Keluarga Berencana*, a family planning program. It then became a part of the development strategy of the government to control population growth. By regulating "sex through useful and public discourse" (Foucault, 1990, p. 25), the New Order State took a strong role in defining sexuality in Indonesia. In other words, the official discourse on femininity under the New Order government was focused primarily on the reproductive and productive functions of the female body and sexuality. This practice, however, had a greater impact on married women than single women, as only the former were acknowledged in the official discourse. As a consequence, single women, officially considered virginal and sexually unavailable, were made involuntarily absent from the category of "real" women. This official regulation that annulled single women's sexual availability is also sanctioned by the society at large. At the level of social life, premarital sexual relationships are considered immoral. Single women who have indulged in premarital sex, as proven by pregnancy, are still stigmatized.

The issue of ambiguous "gender difference" implicated in the active involvement of members of Gerwani in political activities during the Old Order, became the main reason for the New Order to regulate a normative rigid dichotomy between men and women from the 1970s. The New Order found it necessary to institutionalise an ideal of gender difference through two key institutions: *Pembinaan Kesejahteraan Keluarga* (PKK, Family Welfare Guidance) and *Dharma Wanita* (Sen, 1998). PKK is a "functional unit of local government whose main task is to implement the Applied Family Welfare Programme and its many projects at the neighbourhood and village levels" (p. 41). *Dharma Wanita* is an organization for female civil servants and male civil servants' wives. By 1974, its membership had become compulsory for these women. This regulation was then followed by the introduction of the *Panca Dharma Wanita*, or the five duties of women, in which women's roles are constructed through their participation as "reproductive agents" outside the fields of economic and political achievement.[4] In the state's propaganda of women's roles, again, the category of women was mainly translated into those engaged in matrimony.

Throughout the 1980s and 1990s women were portrayed in Indonesian media in a variety of ways. In the 1980s, the representations of women in print advertisements focused predominantly on the depictions of middle- and upper-class women in their domestic roles (Tomagola, 1998). In the 1990s, working women, represented primarily by professional rather than proletarian women, were iconized as symbols of Indonesia's modernity in the global economy and culture (Sen, 1998). Although Tomagola still finds the continuation of a rigid dichotomy between men–women and public–domestic in print advertisements, Sen offered a theory on the transformation of gender identities based on the division of classes. She argued that the emergence of "new middle-class identity" creates a challenge for the state-sponsored gender ideology as these gender conceptions are contested and reworked by members of this class. In other words, Sen brought up the issue of the ambiguous identity as a result of the burgeoning phenomenon of successful working women.

The New Order eventually fell in May 1998, after 32 years of power. Its downfall was preceded by chaos and unrest in the capital city of Jakarta and several other big cities. As a consequence of the economic crisis that hit some countries in southeast Asia the exchange rate of the Indonesian Rupiah in the second week of February 1998 dropped to the level of Rp10,000 against US$1.00, more than quadrupled from its exchange rate in July 1997. As the exchange rate of Rupiah sank, the prices of goods rose. People started to panic because not only was the price of staple goods skyrocketing, but they were also disappearing from the market. The failure of the government in handling the weakening national economy in the wake of the harsh economic crisis in the region heated the social tension.

Riots in Jakarta between May 13 and 15, 1998, not only brought political change to Indonesia, but also spurred a prolonged debate on rapes during these riots. The issue of mass rape was not exposed until June 1998 when a voluntary team for humanitarianism, *Tim Relawan untuk Kemanusiaan,* reported findings that many Chinese women were raped and tortured with some even killed during the riots. It was believed that a certain army commando instigated the rapes.[5] This soon became an international issue when it caught the attention of many foreign countries.[6] In July 1998, *Tim Gabungan Pencari Fakta* (TGPF), the joint fact-finding team, was formed to investigate the case.[7] Unofficial reports and stories circulating described most of the victims as young women or teenage girls.[8] Thousands of Indonesians of Chinese descendants, mostly women and children, fled the country to neighbouring Singapore.[9]

During this time, cases of violence against women in other parts of the country such as Aceh of North Sumatera, Papua, and East Timor were also exposed. The cases of mass rape in East Timor received more attention than in the other places as these were highlighted in the struggle of East Timorese Independence. East Timor was formerly a colony of Portugal. In December 1975, Indonesian troops attacked this region and annexed it as its youngest, popularly known as the 27th, province. Since then, there had been a growing separatist movement against which the Indonesian armed forces (TNI) implemented a heavy-handed counter-attack through a declaration of *Daerah Operasi Militer* (DOM), military operation zone. The implementation of DOM in East Timor eventually did not only repress the separatist movement, but, as a consequence, also made victims of innocent people. One of the highlighted human rights abuses conducted by the Indonesian military was rape and other forms of sexual abuse against East Timorese women. As the most common form of gender-specific torture perpetrated against women, rape "constitutes a violation of both sexual and reproductive rights" (see Aditjondro, 1997). Women in general were particularly vulnerable to gender-specific human rights violations, including rape and sexual harassment, while those who were involved in any political movement encountered the highest risk.

This social and political unrest happened in tandem with the development of media, especially the broad expansion of television and advertising industries. The events have provided the symbolic supply for the advertising industry to recreate meanings and to sell products. As ads creatively absorb any social happenings, namely those that are widely shared by the broad public, we can expect that the Indonesian ads in that time would also take up those related issues as background stories. As space does not allow a lengthy discussion of advertisements and their meanings, the following presents a brief discussion on television advertising, the commodity sign and contextual frames to serve as a frame for the analysis that follows.

Framing Advertisements

Together with the expanding range of consumer goods at the beginning of the 20th century, the producers of these goods found it necessary to create new markets. In order to establish these new markets, the public needed to be educated as consumers, that is, through advertising and media (Williams, 1993, p. 336). Advertising helps the production and reproduction of the exchange value of commodity goods. Once advertising has obliterated the original use value of goods, the commodities are then free to take on any social or cultural association. By using social and cultural symbolism advertising becomes the key medium to manipulate people and persuade them to consume.

The logic of ideological manipulation in mass produced commodity culture is in parallel to Marxist theory where ideology is perceived as a false consciousness that is utilized to conceal the reality of oppression that the working class bears and maintains the ideology of domination of the ruling power. Following capitalist logic of the mode of production, the masses, targeted at the lowest common denominator, are then manipulated to participate in the mass-produced commodity culture (Featherstone, 1991). On the other hand, reasoning from consumption logic, goods are also used to define social relationships within a certain social structure. Some commodity goods gain high status once they move from production to consumption at the point where their symbols are consumed and give satisfaction to the consumers. In consumer culture, the foreground for social categorization may no longer be based on the mode of production, but on consumption. At this point, commodity becomes stripped of its commodity status and attached to the exchange value. This is when the commodity needs an image to construct its "commodity sign" (Goldman, 1992).

Advertising, as a key medium in promoting consumerism, eliminates the logic, context, and history of signs, symbols, and images; it abandons the origin of class society (its economic, politic, and gender relations) and invites us to embrace those references as a new currency of commodity signs (Bertelsen, 1998). This in turn contributes to the construction of a new historical subject. Advertising and media, in this case, provide dissemination of the images of new subjects.

To understand an advertisement, we need to first recognise the "framework or context within which meanings are rearranged" (Goldman, 1992, p. 5). Goldman further argued:

The organisation of meanings in ads is governed by *frames*. To study ads is to study the framing of meaning. All meanings and activities exist in a social context—meaning is always relational and contextual. Remove an activity from its context and its meaning changes. Advertisements photographically isolate meaningful moments, remove them from their lived context and place them in the ad framework where their meaning is recontextualised and thus changed. Every image that appears in advertisement has been framed. It could not be otherwise. (p. 5)

In other words, to understand the connection between the meanings and the images employed in a particular advertisement, it is imperative to first know the larger context within which it is produced and consumed. Without such understanding, we could never understand, for example, the political nuances of why in the ad outlined earlier, the woman's body turns into a sack of sugar.

Single Women in Indonesian Television Advertisements

Tropikana Slim

In February 1998, police officers in Tangerang, west of Jakarta, found two companies stock-piling 222,471 sacks of sugar, the equivalent of 11,000 tons of sugar, in their warehouses (*Gatra*, 1998b). The reason these merchants were stocking commodities and delaying sales had to do with the unstable currency at the time. As mentioned earlier, the economic crisis had hit Indonesia severely and caused the current exchange rate of Rupiah to drop to its lowest level, in turn causing the prices of goods to rise. Even worse, goods were also disappearing from the market. Middle-class housewives reacted against the disappearance of staple foods in the market with panic, as they rushed to shops and supermarkets to buy up the entire stock of items such as milk, cooking oil, sugar, wheat flour, and so on (*Gatra* 1998a). Desperate people started to loot and rob shops and warehouses. Among those looters, housewives and mothers were also reported to be bringing home goods for free.

The television advertisement for Tropikana Slim, a dietary product targeted at and consumed by the middle class, absorbed and incorporated the issues of staple food, riots, and women's panic into the representation of a single woman eating greedily, and the sinister analogy of her expanding body with a sack of sugar. It ingeniously commodified the events into a new sign value securely detached from its contextual meanings, thus depoliticizing the meanings and contents. It relocated popular fear of a sugar shortage with a single middle-class woman's fear of becoming overweight. The caption "Warning: for those who stock sugar" bridged the association between the issue of the sugar shortage, a middle-class single woman, her expanding body, sugar sack, and dietary product. This caption was equally applicable to both the merchants who stock sugar and the single woman who eats too much.

The advertisement also criticized the single woman who eats too much for not falling into step with the State-sponsored concept of "mother," who invariably and readily gives up her needs to meet those of her family, or "state-ibuism" idealism. The State's partiality to this gender ideology was apparently based on the premise that nations are often realized through the imagery of a family. In this imagery, an ideal mother should always be willing to give up her food for other members of the family when needed. This ideal imagery could be found, for example, in a television advertisement for a popular brand of instant noodle—Indomie—that ran in the same period. This ad showed an image of a mother preparing and serving two bowls of instant noodles for her husband and son. Although both her husband and son were shown happily eating the noodles, she was shown contentedly serving them. The ad is then closed by her receiving kisses from her husband and son on both her right and left cheeks. Obviously, a woman who eats greedily on her own, unaware of her surroundings, would never be seen as a "real mother" and so needs to be punished—by being turned into a sack of sugar.

Indosat 001 International

The use of images of single women in a television advertisement to sexualize a political issue was apparent in an advertisement for Indosat 001 International telecommunication service which ran in October 1998. PT Indonesia Satellite Corp (Indosat) is the State-run operator for international telephone services and is one of the biggest advertising spenders in Indonesia, spending US$2.3 million on advertising in 1998. This particular television advertisement made reference to the mass rape during the May 1998 riots in Jakarta.

On November 4, 1998, the TGPF released a report on the investigation of mass rapes during the crisis ("Laporan Akhir," 1998). TGPF noted that many sexual crimes took place during the riots in Jakarta and its surrounding areas; Medan of North Sumatera and Surabaya, East Java. The investigations found that there were 52 victims of rape; 14 victims of rape with battering; 10 victims of sexual attacks; and 9 victims of sexual harassment. Needless to say there may have been more as these numbers reflect only official reports of the rape cases. Although not all of the victims were of Chinese descent, the team concluded that most of them were. As a consequence of the riots and their attendant rapes, there was a mass exodus of Chinese descendants to the neighbouring country of Singapore.

TGPF also found three groups of people identified as the agents of riots: the provocateurs, the active mass, and the passive mass. The active and passive masses were only identified as provoked onlookers or passersby. In the category of provocateurs, TGPF found small groups of 10 people or so who instigated the masses by acts of vandalism, burning, and looting. These groups worked in a very organized manner. They moved fast and were facilitated by vehicles and communication tools such as walkie-talkies and hand phones. In another report, it was found that the riots were directed through a special radio frequency, to which only the elite Special Command Troops (*Kopassus*) and the Armed Force Intelligence had access (Kelompok, Dipandi, & Frekuensi, 2006).

Indosat's television advertisement immediately deployed the issues of rape and mass exodus to promote its products and services. The advertisement was set in Sukarno-Hatta International Airport in Jakarta. It opened with some shots of the airport signboards displaying "*Kedatangan*" (arrival), "Singapore," and "Immigration." A female voice was heard announcing a flight arrival from Singapore. Then the advertisement showed a smiling young woman officer walking and carrying a telecommunications gadget in her hand. Some women and children were shown behind a big glass window happily waving their hands. Among them was a woman who was obviously Chinese. A male voiceover said: "Invite your families and relatives to come together back in Indonesia with Indosat 001."

This advertisement creatively adopted and incorporated the discourse of the riots and accommodated it to the urgency of telecommunications service. It invited the audience to remember the May 1998 riots, yet erased the horror associated with them. It promoted telecommunications tools not as a means to instigate riots or social movements, but instead to call and gather back the families who had fled the country. It showed a young woman officer holding a walkie-talkie instead of the images of strong, well-built men holding walkie-talkies to move the masses during the riots. Instead of displaying crying victims of the riots, this ad portrayed a smiling Chinese woman waving her hand, welcoming her family back after they had fled the country. It distorted the harsh reality of mass brutality during the riots by projecting the image of a smiling and friendly female airport officer at the scene of a family reunion. It also relocated the horror and tragedy of the events into a benign visualisation of a young female officer and some young women visitors, happily waving their hands behind the glass window. As such, while in the case of mass rape, the female is signified as the victim of rape, in this advertisement the female was symbolized by the hospitable, unscathed, single woman officer in a family reunion.

That said, there was no crisis; all these women were smiling. The images of young, single women in this ad neutralized the horror as they served to give meaning to the act of fleeing and returning as reconciliation.

Telkomsel's Halo Cellular Card

An advertisement for Halo Cellular Card from Telkomsel (*Telekomunikasi Selular*, or Cellular Telecommunication) which also ran in the second half of 1998 showed the image of a young female journalist and local children in Dili and highlighted the issue of the struggle for independence in East Timor.

Telkomsel, a division under PT Telekomunikasi Indonesia (Telkom), provides prepaid and post-paid cellular cards and is the main provider of domestic telecommunication services. In August 1999, Telkom launched its Satellite Telkom-1 that covers all of Indonesia, including remote areas that are unreachable with wired telecommunications.

Telkomsel boasts that its Halo card has better coverage than its competitors in all the Indonesian provinces. Accordingly, this advertisement pictured various activities performed in a range of geographic locations throughout the country. This also creates an image for the audience of Indonesia as one nation. The advertisement opens with tall buildings and highways in Jakarta, and then shows a professional businessman in a black suit speaking on a cell phone from outside his office building. Next, we see a family in an executive train to Semarang, central Java; a young businesswoman in Batam, Riau Province; a businessman in Balikpapan, east Borneo; and a man on his boat in Manado, Sulawesi (popular because of its Bunaken water marine life). The advertisement also shows a female journalist wearing a brown vest among local children in Dili, East Timor, and a site manager in a mining company in Timika, Papua. A female voiceover introduces the product as having innovative facilities such as easy payment service and broad coverage.

Of the three images of women in this ad, the depiction of the young woman journalist in Dili, East Timor, is particularly interesting as this television advertisement was first aired in the second half of 1998, when the issue of East Timor's independence was intensifying. This segment of the ad was probably inspired by popular knowledge about the struggle for independence of the people in East Timor. Yet, because the State had for so long dominated the dissemination of information throughout the country, it was likely that the stories circulating about the struggle had to a large extent been shaped within the State's discourse. The State's propaganda of national unity operated best in its act of repression against all forms of separatist movements. As such, although the ad was likely sympathetic toward the East Timorese struggle for independence, the ambience of its images was still resolved around the widely circulating narrative about an integrated nation and the anxiety of the separatist movement. Happy elementary school children in national school uniform were shown welcoming the journalist, waving small Indonesian flags. The journalist approached them, a camera just visible hanging around her neck, and then she turned around to receive a call on her cell phone. The image of happy children going to school in national uniform and carrying Indonesian flags symbolised the joyful moment of unification within the country. This image anticipated the unease about the secessionist attempts.

As the struggle for independence in East Timor was heightened by the findings of many cases of sexual abuse by Indonesian troops against local women, the use of images of women could be understood to heighten the association of this ad to the actual event. The feminization of the East Timorese occupation and independence was pertinent precisely because the images of women, both as victims and survivors, have been made predominant in the struggle. However, this advertisement shifted the feminization of the East Timor struggle for independence into the image of an independent young female journalist. The feminine identity was, thus, no longer associated with the victims of sexual abuses in East Timor, but with the affluent single woman working as a journalist.

The use of the image of a single woman journalist was also in accord with the social norm, as single women journalists often have more privileges than their married colleagues when it comes to outdoor assignments (Soemandoyo, 1999).

Apparently, it did not occur to the executive producers of this advertisement, and perhaps most Indonesians, that East Timor would ultimately gain its independence through a referendum on September 4, 1999. This development may have caused the withdrawal of this television advertisement from broadcast as I noted that after that date the ad no longer appeared on TV screens.

Conclusion: Rethinking the Feminine Single Women

In conclusion, this chapter has shown that images of single women, regardless of the official denial of this social category, appeared in television advertisements in Indonesia in the period of the late 1990s. The various images of young single women in these ads helped people to perceive gender in a new way as a fluid variable, which shifts and changes in different contexts and at different times, and not as a fixed attribute in a person (Butler, 1990). Yet, the production of a gendered person cannot be disentangled from the production and maintenance of political and cultural intersections within the society concerned. It was within the discourse of reform in Indonesia that the identity of single women was, paradoxically, celebrated and ridiculed.

As this chapter demonstrated, some advertisements have ignored the appalling sociopolitical turbulence of the times, reconstructing particular events instead as benevolent events. Images of single women were used to obscure the harsh reality and political significance of these issues and recontextualize them into playful non-political narratives. The television advertisements manipulated the severity of the sugar shortage event, the mass rape tragedy in the riots of 1998, and the struggle for independence in East Timor into pleasant images of ordinary middle-class single women, such as the rapacious eater, the hospitable airport officer, and the female journalist going about their lives in modern Indonesian society.

It is argued that the construction of these images of important social events in Indonesian society is in line with the political culture of the New Order government that silenced women's political participation and cultivated apolitical middle-class aspirations. This is not to say that the New Order dictated how women had to be portrayed in the media, however the State's policy and practice had "set the tone for what could or could not be said—and even what *should* be said" about women to the public (Brenner, 1999, p. 14). The use of the images of single women further loosened the significant political meanings of these issues. In other words, these television advertisements worked in a recuperative manner. They drew on current social and political events but used the images of single women to empty them of their politics and horror and reconstruct them as politically "neutral" signifiers. The meaning of reform as equated with freedom of expression has thus been replaced with freedom to consume.

In presenting these findings, this chapter demonstrated that popular notions of femininity in Indonesian television advertisements are constructed around images of urban, middle-class, single women. As such, the "single woman" becomes an important modern social category in Indonesian society. The imperative is then to investigate further the constructions of various feminine identities among single women not only as represented by the television advertisements, but also by official and academic discourse, as well as other popular culture genres. I suggest that further investigations of the notions of femininity among single women will reveal manifold gender relations in Indonesian society and support the struggle for identity politics of Indonesian women. Bennett's book about Muslim single women in the city of Mataram, Lombok, Indonesia (2005), showing how those young women realize their "sexual autonomy" by negotiating their sexual desire vis-à-vis the social, cultural, and religious norms has broken new ground.

Obviously, this chapter discusses just a small part of the complex process of the formation of gender identity in contemporary Indonesian society. The chapter forms part of a larger study on the representations of single women in Indonesian television in the period concerned. Although it acknowledges the role of the middle classes in creating new feminine identities framed within the issues of global consumer culture, it is fully aware that not all aspects of consumer culture can be relevant to identity politics, and neither are they progressive nor libertarian. What has been discussed here consists only of a selection of a particular context with a particular aim relevant to highlighting the changing notion of femininity within contemporary Indonesian society.

Acknowledgments

This chapter is based on a chapter from my master's thesis entitled *Reframing Feminity: A Study of the Images of Women in Selected Indonesian Television Advertisements in 1998–1999*, Southeast Asian Studies Programme, National University of Singapore, Singapore, 2000. I thank the following people for their insightful suggestions on the early draft of this chapter: Goh Beng Lan, Patricia Spyer, Edwin Jurriens, and Joan Suyenaga. My thanks also go to the editors of this edition. However, responsibility for the content rests with me.

Notes

1. On September 30, 1965, six generals and a lieutenant in the army were killed in an alleged coup by the communist party. Following this incident, Suharto was granted an order known as *Supersemar* on March 11, 1966, by which he gained authority to take actions to curb the insecurity and instability caused by the abortive coup.

2. For further reference see Wieringa (2002).

3. For further discussion of the hegemonic term of *pembangunan* see Heryanto (1995).

4. The five ideals (quoted from Sen, 1998) are:
   1. Producer of nation's future generation
   2. Wife and faithful companion to her husband
   3. Mother and educator of her children
   4. Manager of household
   5. Citizen (1986, Hull, as cited in Sen, in Sen & Stivens, 1998)

5. Sandyawan Sumardi, another volunteer, a Roman Catholic priest, asserted that gang rape was systematically instigated by a group of professionals. The linkage of the army and the gang rape was one possibility (*Tempo*, 1998).

6. For a discussion on how the May rapes served the formation of a global community of diasporic Chinese see Tay (2000). Meanwhile, for a discussion on the debate over the "proof" of the May 1998 rapes through photographic visibility, see Strassler (2004).

7. TGPF was established on July 23, 1998 by the newly formed government following the fall of the New Order regime, as a joint agreement between the Minister of Defence, Minister of Justice, Interior Minister, Foreign Minister, Minister for Women's Roles, and the Attorney General. The members of TGPF come from government offices, National Human Right Commission, nongovernmental organizations, and other social groups.

8. See, for example, the circulating letter on the Internet well-known as "Vivian's Story-Indonesian Version" (Retrieved from http://www.ishipress.com/vivians.htm on February 20, 2006) and its discussion in Lochore (2000).

9. Unfortunately, despite the importance of discussing the "Othering" of Chinese descendants and Chinese women as victims of the May 1998 mass rape, doing so is beyond the scope of this chapter. For further reference see Heryanto (1998, 1999).

References

Aditjondro, G. J. (1997). *Violence by the state against women in East Timor: A report to the UN Special Rapporteur on violence against women, including its causes and consequences.* Retrieved February 20, 2006, from http://www.indonesia-house.org/archive/mei98/vaw/GJA_vio_et.htm.

Anderson, B. (1983). *Imagined communities.* London: Verso.

Atkinson, J. M. (1990). How gender makes a difference in Wana society. In J. M. Atkinson & S. Errington (Eds.), *Power and difference: Gender in Island Southeast Asia* (pp. 59–93). Stanford, CA: Stanford University Press.

Atkinson, J. M., & Errington, S. (1990). Preface. In J. M. Atkinson & S. Errington (Eds.), *Power and difference: Gender in Island Southeast Asia* (pp. vii–xi). Stanford, CA: Stanford University Press.

Bennett, L. R. (2005). *Women, Islam and modernity: Single women, sexuality and reproductive health in contemporary Indonesia*. London & New York: Routledge Curzon.

Bertelsen, E. (1998). Ads and amnesia: Black advertising in the New South Africa. In S. Nuttall & C. Coetzee (Eds.), *Negotiating the past: The making of memory in South Africa* (pp. 221–241). Cape Town: Oxford University Press.

Blackwood, E. (1995). Senior women, model mothers, and dutiful wives: Managing gender contradictions in a Minangkabau village. In A. Ong & M. G. Peletz (Eds.), *Bewitching women, pious men: Gender and body politics in southeast Asia* (pp. 124–158). Berkeley, Los Angeles, and London: University of California Press.

Brenner, S. (1999). On the public intimacy of the New Order: Images of women in the popular Indonesian print media. *Indonesia*, 67, 13–37.

Butler, J. (1990). *Gender trouble: Feminism and the subversion of identity*. New York & London: Routledge.

Errington, S. (1990). Recasting sex, gender, and power: A theoretical and regional overview. In J. M. Atkinson & S. Errington (Eds.), *Power and difference: Gender in Island Southeast Asia* (pp. 1–58). Stanford, CA: Stanford University Press.

Featherstone, M. (1991). *Consumer culture and postmodernism*. London, Newbury Park, New Delhi: Sage.

Foucault, M. (1990). *The history of sexuality: An introduction* (Vol. 1). New York: Vintage Books.

Gatra. (1998a). *Gerakan Menyapu Penimbun*, 14(IV), 63–65.

Gatra. (1998b). *Pabrik Pun Menimbun*, 15(IV), 15.

Goldman, R. (1992). *Reading ads socially*. London & New York: Routledge.

Heryanto, A. (1995). *Language of development and development of language: The case of Indonesia*. Canberra: Australian National University.

Heryanto, A. (1998). Ethnic identities and erasure: Chinese Indonesian in public culture. In J. S. Kahn (Ed.), *Southeast Asian identities: Culture and the politics of representation in Indonesia, Malaysia, Singapore and Thailand* (pp. 95–114). Singapore & London: Institute of Southeast Asian Studies.

Heryanto, A. (1999). Rape, race, and reporting. In A. Budiman, B. Hatley, & D. Kingsbury (Eds.), *Reformasi: Crisis and change in Indonesia* (pp. 299–334). Clayton: Monash Asia Institute.

Kelompok, P., Dipandi, H., & Frekuensi, K. (2006). Retrieved February 22, 2006, from http://www.geocities.com/capitolhill/4120/asiaweek3.html.

Laporan Akhir Tim Gabungan Pencari Fakta Peristiwa. (1998). Retrieved February 20, 2006, from http://id.wikisource.org/wiki/Laporan_Tim_Gabungan_Pencari_Fakta_%28TGPF%29_Peristiwa_Tanggal_13-15_Mei_1998.

Lochore, L. (2000). Virtual rape: Vivian's story. *Intersections: Gender, History and Culture in the Asian Context*, 3. Retrieved November 2, 2001, from http://wwwsshe.murdoch.edu.au/intersections/issue3/laura3.html.

McClintock, A. (1997). No longer in a future heaven: Gender, race and nationalism. In A. McClintock, A. Mufti, & E. Shohat (Eds.), *Dangerous liaisons: Gender, nation, and postcolonial perspectives* (pp. 89–112). Minneapolis & London: University of Minnesota Press.

Rosaldo, M. Z. (1974). Woman, culture and society: A theoretical overview. In M. Z. Rosaldo & L. Lamphere (Eds.), *Woman, culture, and society* (pp. 17–42). Stanford, CA: Stanford University Press.

Sen, K. (1998). Indonesian women at work: Reframing the subject. In K. Sen & M. Stivens (Eds.), *Gender and power in affluent Asia* (pp. 35–62). London & New York: Routledge.

Soemandoyo, P. (1999). *Wacana Gender dan Layar Televisi: Studi Perempuan dalam Pemberitaan Televisi Swasta*. Yogyakarta: LP3Y & Ford Foundation.

Strassler, K. (2004). Gendered visibilities and the dream of transparency: The Chinese-Indonesian rape debate in post-Suharto Indonesia. *Gender & History, 16*(2), 689–725.

Steedly, M. M. (1999). The state of culture theory in the anthropology of Southeast Asia. *Annual Reviews of Anthropology, 28*, 431–454.

Suryakusuma, J. I. (1996). The state and sexuality in New Order Indonesia. In L. J. Sears (Ed.), *Fantasizing the feminine in Indonesia* (pp. 92–119). Durham & London: Duke University Press.

Tanner, N. (1974). Matrifocality in Indonesia and Africa and among black Americans. In M. Z. Rosaldo & L. Lamphere (Eds.), *Woman, culture, and society* (pp. 129–156). Stanford, CA: Stanford University Press.

Tay, E. (2000). Global Chinese fraternity and the Indonesian riots of May 1998: The online gathering of dispersed Chinese. *Intersections: Gender, History and Culture in the Asian Context, 4*. Retrieved November 2, 2001, from http://wwwsshe.murdoch.edu.au/intersections/issue4/tay.html.

Tempo. (1998, October 6–12). *Investigasi*, pp. 56–67.

Tomagola, T. A. (1998). Ketimpangan Gender dalam Jurnalistik. In M. D. Mukhotib (Ed.), *Menggagas Jurnalisme Sensitif Gender* (pp. 37–53). Yogyakarta: PMII-INPI Pact.

Vatikiotis, M. R. J. (1998). *Indonesian politics under Suharto: The rise and fall of the New Order*. London & New York: Routledge.

Wieringa, S. (1996). *Sexual metaphors in the change from Sukarno's Old Order to Suharto's New Order in Indonesia* (Working Paper Series no. 233). The Hague: Institute of Social Science.

Wieringa, S. (2002). *Sexual politics in Indonesia*. New York: Palgrave Macmillan.

Williams, R. (1993). Advertising: The magic system. In S. During (Ed.), *The cultural studies reader* (pp. 320–336). London and New York: Routledge.

9

Television Commercials and Rural Women in India

Reaching the Unreached

Ila Patel

Since the 1990s, gender representation in television commercials in India have become more diverse than they were in the 1970s (Munshi, 1998). However, efforts are seldom made to understand the reception of television commercials by women in general, and rural women in particular. Based on an exploratory village-level study, this chapter examines the ways and extent to which rural women viewers make meaning of television commercials designed mostly for an elitist urban audience with purchasing power. It sheds light on how the gendered context of the household plays a crucial role in mediating rural women's access to television and how women's reading of television commercials is grounded in the material and ideological conditions of their social reality.

Within the context of globalization and the privatization of television broadcasting in India, television has emerged as a new medium of entertainment for which advertising has become its lifeline. Television in India captures incredibly large audiences,[1] through a wide range of entertainment programs (films and film-based programs, soap operas, music, game shows, talk shows, sports, etc.). The programs are directed primarily at upwardly mobile upper and middle classes, who serve as a captive market segment for the consumer goods being advertised.

With the improvement of average household incomes in rural areas during the post-economic reform period of the 1990s, there has been a substantial increase in the consumer base of rural India (National Council of Applied Economic Research, 2003).[2] Consequently, television has emerged as an important medium for marketers and advertisers to reach potential consumers in rural areas as well. Yet, despite the growing importance of tapping the rural consumer, advertising through conventional electronic media (radio and television) continues to be a "hit-and-miss" affair because advertisers have not yet developed effective communication strategies for engaging rural consumers (Bhatia, 2000). How can advertisements, which are designed mostly for an elitist urban audience with purchasing power, be equally successful with a rural audience? Although concerns have been expressed regarding the adverse impact of advertising on the poor (Vilaniam, 1989), systematic research on the reach and consumption of Indian television advertising among the socially and economically disadvantaged segments of the urban population or the rural audiences in India is a neglected area of communication research.

Furthermore, since the 1990s, owing to their access to income or the control over purchase decisions within their families, urban Indian women have emerged as a very important group of consumers for advertisers and marketers.[3] It is no surprise, then, that consumer advertising is increasingly being geared toward urban middle-class women. In analyzing the discourses of print advertisements and television commercials in India, Munshi (1998) showed how the construction of a "new Indian woman" fuses the ideology of femininity and feminism with that of consumerism. The advertisements provide appealing images of the "modern" and "liberated" woman in her multidimensional gender roles, and presents her as primarily responsible for the purchase of appliances, accessories, and cosmetics.

But again, the question arises: To what extent does television advertising targeted toward the urban audience touch the hearts and minds of rural women and influence their behaviors? In contrast to extensive research on gender representation in advertising in Western societies, gender and advertising is a relatively new area of communication and feminist research in India. Against this lacuna in advertising research on the female audience in general and on rural women in particular, this chapter examines the ways in which rural female viewers negotiate with television commercials designed mostly for an elitist urban audience with greater purchasing power. Based on an exploratory village-level study, within the broader context of agrarian society, and the gendered context of the household that mediates rural women's access to television, this chapter discusses how rural women TV audiences make meaning of idealized images of femininity and affluence being celebrated in Indian television commercials.

Much feminist media research critiques gender portrayals in television programs and advertising (Gallagher, 1995), and earlier media studies focused on understanding the media text as artifact through content or semiotic analyses. However, audience-based and critical analyses of media have emerged as important areas of research in feminist media studies (van Zoonen, 1991). The analytical orientation of this study is based on the tradition of reception studies that interrogates the reception or consumption of media text by female audiences (e.g., Ang, 1985; Fiske, 1987; Livingstone, 1990). This study affirms that media texts are inherently "polysemic" (Fiske, 1987) and construct diverging and sometimes conflicting articulations of femininity. However, it is also understood that female consumers actively negotiate the textual constructions and interpellations in such a way that the meanings given to the texts and the positions taken by the viewers are brought in accordance with their social and subjective experiences (Ang & Joke, 1991). Furthermore, I accept the position that female TV audiences cannot be taken as a homogeneous category; there is considerable diversity in their sociocultural and economic backgrounds and they live in specific sociocultural contexts, so reception of media is also shaped by everyday life and the gender context of the household. Thus, instead of focusing on the targeted audience of television commercials—namely, urban upper and middle-class women—this study examines the reading of television commercials by an unintended audience: rural women.

The chapter is organized in six parts. After outlining the methodological approach of an exploratory study that was conducted in Baruraj, a village in the eastern state of Bihar in India, I discuss the changing construction of femininity in Indian advertising, particularly television advertising. The next section focuses on understanding the broader context of agrarian society that shapes the reach of television to the rural audience, and the gendered context of rural households that mediates women's access to television. How rural female viewers perceived multifaceted gender roles of urban women as represented in television commercials is discussed in the fifth section, followed by a conclusion that highlights salient issues emerging from this study. Throughout this analysis, I argue that textually inscribed feminine subject positions are not uniformly and mechanically adopted by socially situated rural female viewers.

Methodological Approach

As previously mentioned, reading advertising from the perspective of rural audiences is an unexplored area of communication research in India. Hence, a qualitative research approach was considered more appropriate to develop a deeper understanding of both the context in which television and its rural audience were situated, and the consumption and reception patterns (if any) of television by rural women. The discussion of television commercials and rural women in this chapter is based on village-level fieldwork, undertaken in October and November 2000 in Baruraj, a village in the northern part of the Muzaffarpur district in the state of Bihar, India.[4]

The study used a multipronged approach for data collection. Data collection on the societal context of the village and its communication system was done with the help of students during their 2-month stay in the village through rapid rural appraisal (RRA), an interactive approach to collection of information from the local people in a semistructured way. Some of the RRA methods used in the study were social maps of the village showing locations, landholdings, and ownership of households belonging to different castes and communities; timelines of diffusion of television in the village; wealth rankings of village households to understand their relative economic status; and livelihood analyses of a few households from each caste. Media behavior of the villagers was also studied through participant observation and informal interaction with the villagers.

In order to understand rural female viewers' perceptions of television commercials, I also stayed with a family in Baruraj for 10 days. Given the caste and class divide in the agrarian society of Baruraj, and patriarchal constraints on women's mobility in the village, it was difficult to bring women together for a discussion. Therefore, I decided to interact with them in residential areas and in their homes. The principal method of data collection was focus group discussions, supplemented by participant observation, and in-depth interviews. As described in detail later, data collection was undertaken in a systematic and phased manner, beginning with the establishment of rapport between the researchers and the community.

First, five localities with high concentrations of television-owned households were selected; four were inhabited by the higher castes of *darbars* and *bhumiyars*, and one by the backward caste of *kurmi*.[5] Initially, I visited these localities and interacted with the influential community leaders of each caste. They then introduced me to the community and gave me the social sanction for the study. At the onset of my relationship with them, I did not make any deliberate attempts to interview women, but observed the general social context in which television and the rural audiences were situated.

From each chosen locality, I purposely selected two television-owned households in which women watched TV. Efforts were made to identify the households that were representative of the community, however, final decisions were made on the basis of availability of a functional television set and the willingness of women to participate in the study. Among these 10 households, 6 were from the higher castes of *darbar* and *bhumiyar* and 4 were from the backward caste of *kurmi*. Details on demographic and socioeconomic background and media exposure of these households were collected with the help of a structured questionnaire. In all the selected households, women lived in large joint families (7–10 persons) in which unmarried children and married couples of two or three generations lived together. There was no significant difference in family sizes across the households. However, social and economic status varied across the castes. Two *darbar* households and one *bhumiyar* household belonged to the upper middle class. On the other hand, three households of *bhumiyars* and all four households of *kurmis* were from the middle class. Irrespective of one's economic class, social status was determined on the basis of the caste system. In general, constraints on social mobility within the village were upheld much more rigorously among higher caste households as their social interactions were limited to their own caste and kinship groups within the same residential area. On the other hand, such restrictions were less stringent for *kurmi* women from the backward caste. In all the households, television arrived as a new symbol of social and economic status.

Before venturing into any discussions with women about television, I first established rapport with the women and their family members from the selected households. I visited their homes when they were free from domestic chores, and informally interacted with as many family members as possible. Slowly, the family members became comfortable with my presence in their homes and women started chatting with me about their family, social customs and festivals, children's education, and so on. Early visits to their homes enabled me to gain insights into their economic and social status, and observe gender relations. I also watched television with the women in their homes. During television viewing, I monitored the attention they paid to television commercials. Television viewing was followed by one focus group discussion with women viewers from each selected household. Ensuing discussions focused on general issues related to media habits and preferences, and the women's general perceptions of television commercials.

It became evident through various focus groups that the reading of television commercials differed across three groups: (a) unmarried daughters, young daughters-in-law, and mothers in their 20s and 30s; (b) middle-aged mothers in their 40s and 50s; and (c) elderly mothers and mothers-in-law (60 years and older). Each group differed in terms of its access to television within the gendered context of the household, which is discussed in detail later in this chapter. Their preferences for television programs also varied. In general, adolescents and young women enjoyed watching new Hindi films and all film-based programs (songs, talk shows, etc.), whereas middle-aged mothers liked to watch social soap operas and films. Finally, the more senior women preferred to watch religious films and serials.

To gather more information about how rural women made sense of television commercials, five women from each group were selected for in-depth interviews on the basis of their willingness and availability. Instead of asking questions related to a specific television commercial, open-ended questions were asked to gain understanding of their general perceptions about television ads. The broad questions asked included "Can you tell me something about commercials that you have seen on television?" "Why are they shown on television?" "For whom?" "What do you like/dislike about them?" "Can you describe some of your favorite television commercials?" "Why do you find them appealing?" "What are your views on the lifestyle and characters depicted in television commercials?" "What do you think about when you see women in television commercials?" "Which aspects of your behavior have been influenced by television commercials and which have not?" These questions were guided by the theoretical framework of reception studies, which examines how audiences make sense of media in everyday life. The questions were flexible and used essentially as a guideline to probe the informants. Because the women did not like to be tape-recorded, I took notes during discussions and interviews and analyzed them later.

The Changing Construction of Femininity in Television Advertising

In the vast body of literature about the representation of women on television in Western societies, advertising has received considerable attention since the 1970s. In India, there is an emerging body of feminist media studies that is also showing how television is engaged in the social construction of femininity and modernity (Krishnan & Dighe, 1990; Mankekar, 1993; McMillan, 2002). However, research on Indian advertising, particularly from a feminist perspective, is very scant (see Ahmed, 1998; Chanda, 1991; Munshi, 1998). Before examining how television commercials are received by rural women, it is important to understand how images of women have changed over time in Indian advertising, particularly on television.

In the 1970s and 1980s, women in Indian television advertising were portrayed predominantly in stereotypical and traditional gender roles.[6] However, with the onset of globalization and the advent of satellite television throughout the 1990s, India has witnessed a significant shift in the representation of women in its advertising—both print media and television.[7] Munshi (1998) examined the role of advertising discourse in the construction of a "new Indian woman," namely the multifaceted homemaker, wife, mother, and career woman. She also described how advertisers appropriated the discourses of traditional femininity and liberal feminism and wove them into the discourse of consumerism. The new Indian woman is therefore depicted as an independent and assertive woman, a successful wife and mother, who often has a career or works outside the home. She is no longer portrayed as dependent on her spouse for making decisions in the family. She is depicted as a confident young wife, mother, and a homemaker who does not seek approval of her husband or in-laws for everything. She is often shown as making important purchase decisions on her own. Munshi then argued that in constructing the new Indian woman, advertising discourse integrated a woman's "traditional" role of mother and a homemaker and "modern" role of working, independent woman without challenging patriarchal hegemony.[8] As such, advertising successfully constructs the modern Indian woman as a liberated consumer, but nonetheless perpetuates her position within dominant patriarchal ideology.

How, then, are advertisements geared toward urban Indian women mostly from the affluent strata of society, perceived by rural women who are rooted in the context of agrarian society? Divya McMillan (2002), in a pioneering study, examined the television-watching habits of female sweatshop laborers in the outskirts of Bangalore city and evaluated how exposure to television affects their behavior, lifestyle choices, and spending habits. Her study showed that television viewing encourages female Indian factory workers to buy beauty and convenience products (e.g., as skin cream), trendy clothes, packaged snacks, and instant noodles, which are all new to them. McMillan contended that purchase and consumption of these products make these women feel part of the consumer culture. At the same time, her study demonstrated that these women tended to pick and choose items that would fit their needs without disrupting the traditional patterns of the culture within which they lived.[9] Similar findings were evident in the study of rural women's perceptions about television commercials in Baruraj, as discussed later.

The Context of Television Viewing in Baruraj

We know that the consumption and reception of television commercials are shaped by the conditions in which people view television. TV viewing does not take place in isolation, but is mediated by situational factors. Hence, it is important to understand the context within which television as a medium and rural women as an audience were situated in this study.

The Village Context

The broader societal context of Baruraj conditioned access to television. There was no community television set in Baruraj, and in general, ownership of television was skewed toward socioeconomically better-off families, mostly from upper and middle castes and the Muslim community.[10] Because social relations among different castes and classes were not harmonious in Baruraj, the villagers seldom came together to watch television or films and they rarely shared privately owned television sets with others outside their kinship and caste groups. Furthermore, the lack of a regular supply of electricity was a major constraint to television viewing in the village. The number of hours a family could watch television not only depended on the availability of electricity supply at the time of viewing, but also on the availability of a rechargeable battery set, saved specifically for favorite programs in the eventuality of a power disruption. Exposure of television owners to the ever-expanding world of entertainment and information was also limited compared with urban areas by the unavailability of satellite channels and cable TV.

The Gendered Context of Households

For rural female viewers of Baruraj, television viewing was a precarious experience, shaped by the gendered context of the household and their everyday lives. On the whole, social interactions among women across various caste and class groups for television viewing were limited because of patriarchal constraints on their physical mobility in the village and the *purdah* system.[11] Many women, particularly adolescent girls and young daughters-in-law, could not even visit their neighbors or relatives on their own. Mostly, women shared television viewing with their relatives who stayed within the same residential area (*tola*).

Television viewing was also bound by household dynamics. In the conservative households of upper and middle castes, there were considerable constraints on women's mobility even within their own households. In general, female family members could easily move around in the inner courtyard and rooms, but they could not enter other parts of the house if men were around. In some households where the television set was placed in the room of the head of the household (generally, a father/father-in-law) or an elderly family member, daughters-in-law could not watch television in their presence. Thus, access to a television set by women depended on its location within the household. Also, women tended to watch television mostly in the afternoon, when the men were not around. Young daughters-in-law were the most disadvantaged within the family as far as watching television was concerned. In comparison to a daughter of the family, a daughter-in-law's physical mobility within the household was very limited. Generally, she observed *purdah* in front of all elders and men. So, even in a family where both the genders could watch television together, a young daughter-in-law would not sit with the other female family members to watch television if male relatives were around. Not surprisingly, dissatisfaction with the power structure within the family was sometimes articulated by women viewers (particularly daughters-in-law) in terms of their lack of control over when to operate a set and what would be watched.

Despite these constraints, however, television had gradually entered the lives of women from television-owned households in Baruraj. Given the lack of other forms of entertainment and social constraints on their physical mobility, television viewing had become an important leisure activity for women. None of the women with whom I spoke were employed outside the home. Their social interactions with the outside world were also limited. Hence, television for them was not merely a medium of entertainment—it was also a "window onto the world." Although women watched television during their leisure time in the afternoon or occasionally at night after dinner, they seldom did it with full concentration. It was very common for them to watch television while doing a domestic activity, for example, cutting vegetables, cleaning rice, mending clothes, knitting, nursing young children, and so on. Thus, television viewing for rural women was also structured around their domestic work.

Finally, in family viewing situations women were not always able to watch their favorite television programs, as decisions of their elders (mothers or fathers-in-law) and adult male family members (including husbands) prevailed over their preferences. Generally, women did not insist on watching their favorite programs in the presence of male family members or elderly in-laws. Rural women's access to television, then, was not only affected by lack of electricity or access to satellite and cable TV, it was also limited by the patriarchal context of the household, such as the location of a television set within the household and informal rules governing who could operate television, who could watch television with whom, and who chose the programs. Despite these constraints, women did manage to watch television within the limited social spaces provided by their families.

Making Sense of Television Advertising

Television commercials are targeted toward the urban audience—especially urban women—as potential consumers. However, with the gradual penetration of TV in rural areas, ads have also become a new form of entertainment and information for rural women as well, particularly those from better-off sections of the agrarian society. Given this context, how did rural women in Baruraj make sense of television commercials in general, and the representation of new Indian women in particular? The following sections respond to this question and are based on the focus group discussions and in-depth interviews conducted with Barurajian women.

As a whole, the reading of television advertising by rural women was contingent on what I call a commonsense approach to making sense of television commercials. Rural female viewers with limited exposure to other forms of advertising perceived television commercials as an important source of information about a variety of products. Younger women with more education were more cognizant of the fact that advertisements were produced by different companies to promote their products. On the other hand, elderly women with limited schooling viewed them more as "short programs" between television serials and films.

For rural female viewers, television was primarily a medium for entertainment and they enjoyed films and soap operas with considerable involvement. In general, women considered television commercials as interruptions to their viewing pleasure. Nonetheless, although they did not view them with as high a level of interest, they admitted to deriving some pleasure from watching them.

Rural women faced problems in decoding the visual and verbal messages of some of the commercials, which were obviously targeted at the affluent urban audience. Specifically, women with limited education and exposure to urban culture had difficulty understanding the visual symbolism, codes and conventions of westernized lifestyles of rich urban women. Moreover, despite some women being familiar with Hindi, the regional language of the state, most had difficulty comprehending the advertisements that mixed Hindi and English. Despite any unfamiliarity with the languages used both visually and verbally in TV advertising, it was evident that rural women still attempted to make sense of the world of consumerism.

What was learned from television ads varied across the different groups of women: Adolescent girls reported that they learned about the use of cosmetics and grooming products (shampoo, soap, creams, hair oil, etc.); housewives said that they came to know about various household appliances, cooking recipes and food products, washing powder, detergents, and soaps, home decorations, and so on; and mothers learned about what kind of products are suitable for children of different age groups.

Significantly, the rural women's understanding of television commercials was relatively uncritical. None of them questioned commercials as depicting unreal characters and lifestyles, the profit motive/agenda of TV ads was left unexplored, and the hegemonic role of advertisements in the construction of gender identities was seemingly irrelevant to them.

Understanding the Changing Construction of Women

Increasing exposure to television has introduced rural women to the new Indian woman in her multiple gender roles. How then do they interpret this changing construction of women?

Motherhood. In India, advertisers have long used motherhood as an icon of caring and nurturing to appeal to mothers as consumers. Rural mothers, who are generally homebound and fulltime housewives, accord considerable importance to their role as a mother and a caretaker of the family. Hence, television commercials that depicted modern mothers who use products to demonstrate their concerns for the welfare and well-being of their family were particularly salient and appealed to them in different ways.

Young mothers in their 20s perceived the archetype mother in television commercials as very knowledgeable about "modern practices" of child care and found such advertisements interesting and informative.

> I enjoy watching advertisements that show a mother taking care of her young children. She is very knowledgeable about how to take care of her children. In fact, I learned from these advertisements that special types of products (baby food, soap, bath oil, etc.) should be used for young children. (*Bhumiyar* mother, middle class, 23 years old)

> Earlier I did not even know that young children require special type of soap, oil and shampoo. I learned from the television commercials that a caring urban mother takes care of her child by using special products. (*Kurmi* mother, middle class, 26 years old)

The portrayal of modern mothers as confidently and efficiently managing the family, children, and domestic chores also appealed to some of them. Young mothers identified with the modern and efficient mother of television commercials:

> I like the way a mother in television commercials takes care of everything. She looks after her children with love and affection. She is also a good housewife, doing all household chores—cooking, cleaning, washing clothes, etc. She also pays attention to other members of her family. I wonder how she manages everything. (*Bhumiyar* mother, upper middle class, 22 years old)

> I admire the mothers shown in television commercials. They are so clever and smart that they could happily take good care of their children, house and the job. (*Bhumiyar* mother, middle class, 23 years old)

Such advertisements contributed to a desire for child-care products among young rural women and generated some discontent among them about not being able to fulfill their desires because of their lack of autonomy to make decisions in the joint family.

> I would like to use some of the products shown on television for my 1-year old son. However, as a young daughter-in-law, I don't have a say in purchase decisions of the household. (*Darbar* mother, upper middle class, 24 years old)

> I wish I had the freedom to purchase whatever I wanted for my child. In our joint family, I have to consult my mother-in-law for all the matters related to childrearing. My mother-in-law is not convinced that child-care products shown on television commercials are good for children. I cannot buy anything without her consent. (*Bhumiyar* mother, middle class, 23 years old)

The scientific discourse of advertisements explaining the nutrient properties of foods and soft drinks was beyond the comprehension of most of the young mothers because of their unfamiliarity with technical language and the concepts used in the ads. Hence, they did not question the claims made by these products, and faithfully assumed they were good for their children. Some mothers, however, particularly those with adult children or elderly mothers-in-law who valued traditional child-care practices, demonstrated scepticism toward the child-care practices being recommended by modern mothers.

> In the city, young mothers lack proper knowledge about child-care practices. So, they follow what is shown on television without questioning [anything]. I don't believe in what is suggested by television commercials. I have raised four children without using any of these products. I just used whatever was available in my home environment and followed the advice of my elders. (*Kurmi* mother, middle class, 45 years old)

> My mother-in-law believes in traditional child-care practices. She does not believe in what is shown on television. She thinks that many children in the village have grown up without using soap and shampoo as shown on television. [So,] why would one should waste money for such things? (*Bhumiyar* mother, upper middle class, 40 years old)

> Television shows mothers giving some health foods to infants and young children. Such products for children appear very attractive, but I am not sure it is healthy for them. We also give different types of homemade nutritional food to our children, but we prepare everything at home. I think our children are also healthy and strong. (*Darbar* mother-in-law, middle class, 60 years old)

They also believed that traditional child-care practices and food were better and less expensive than those shown in television commercials. Thus, despite differences in perceptions about modern child-care practices as suggested by mothers in television commercials, the portrayal of caring and nurturing mothers was appealing to rural Baruraj mothers across the various age groups.

In summary, rural women identified to some extent with the dominant construction of motherhood that emphasized their reproductive role in caring and nurturing their children and the family. Some of them also admired the way modern mothers seemed to manage their role as a caretaker. Except for a few rural mothers from well-off *darbar* families who had used some of the child-care products, most of them acknowledged their inability to purchase the products advertised. However, the young mothers admitted to wishing they could use such products, like urban women, to demonstrate their commitment to caring for their children's health and well-being. On the other hand, modern mothers and their child-care practices were not acceptable to all the rural mothers in the existing cultural context.

Homemakers. Television commercials introduced rural women to a new world of household appliances, gadgets, and home-care products. These commercials were aspirational in nature, but rooted in the social reality of modern urban households with purchasing power. Rural women found these commercials very informative as most of them had not seen such products in real life. They looked at the visual images with considerable interest, but found it difficult to fully comprehend verbal messages that frequently used English language and technical terms to describe the products. They associated consumption of such products with higher economic status, and their desire for them was grounded in their economic reality. They rationalized their desires in different ways:

> I love to watch the commercials of all the gadgets that rich women used in the kitchen. But these items are too expensive for us. Any way, blenders, ovens, refrigerators, etc., are useless here as we don't have a regular supply of electricity like in the city. (*Kurmi* housewife, middle class, 32 years old)

> I know that in big cities many educated women from good [rich] families work in schools and offices. So, they can buy many things for their home. Actually, working women need all these appliances so that they can efficiently do all their household chores like cooking, cleaning, washing, etc. (*Bhumiyar* housewife and mother, middle class, 42 years old)

Rural women were able to make some sense of the construction of new Indian women as modern homemakers, whom they perceived as affluent, educated, independent, and efficient. However, the images of such homemakers and their lifestyles were very novel to them in their cultural context. In reading these commercials, they emphasized the context surrounding these products, and not the persona of modern homemakers.

Most of the products (refrigerators, washing machines, microwaves, ovens, etc.) were considered too expensive even by women from well-off Baruraj families.

The modern homemakers of television commercials appealed to some rural women, particularly young housewives and adolescent girls because of their attractive personalities and appearances, but they could not easily identify with them because in real life they lacked the autonomy to make independent purchase decisions in the joint family, and also had limited purchasing power to buy most of the products. Mothers of adult daughters from the families of upper castes, however, wanted to purchase some of the smaller home appliances as wedding gifts for their daughters so that they could also do domestic chores quickly and easily.

A few ads for household products also showed men doing chores with the help of appliances and gadgets. Given the gender division of labor within their families, it was very difficult for most of the rural women to accept that men could do domestic work. The reaction to such commercials was divided once again across the age groups. Elderly women, who strongly identified with the existing gender division of work in the patriarchal family, found it most difficult to relate to the new gender identity of men in television commercials.

> Generally, men do not know how to cook or wash clothes and give baths to a baby. I do not think even men in the city could do domestic work. So, I am not sure that what is shown on television is "real." (*Kurmi* mother-in-law, middle class, 48 years old)

> Men should not be involved in domestic work as women know household chores better than them. I don't understand why such things are shown on television. (*Darbar* mother-in-law, upper middle class, 58 years old)

> When a husband comes home after working for the whole day, he just likes to relax. It is a duty of his wife to finish all domestic chores. (*Bhumiyar* mother-in-law, middle class, 62 years old)

On the other hand, some of the middle-aged housewives and mothers-in-law perceived such husbands in television commercials as "henpecked" and their wives as very "dominating." Younger wives, however, with some exposure to urban families, tended to more readily accept such portrayals of men in television advertisements:

> Generally, a husband is not expected to cook and clean in rural families as women stay at home and do all housework. But in urban areas, women often work full time, so their husbands are shown on television helping them in domestic work. (*Bhumiyar* wife, middle class, 33 years old)

> Men who are shown doing household work on television are very modern. They like to show that they can also use home appliances and help women in their work. (*Kurmi* wife, middle class, 26 years old)

As a whole, rural women did not identify with the textual position of modern men who did household chores. Evidently, their subjective position was shaped by their own experiences and the gendered reality of their family. Rural women were very attracted to the glamorous world of home products, however. According to them, appliances and home-care products saved time and labor for cooking, cleaning, and washing, and made routine domestic chores easy and enjoyable. Significantly—albeit not surprisingly—they did not question the tedium of daily household chores and housework as women's responsibility.

The Beautiful Women. The new Indian woman is represented in television commercials as a beautiful and sensual person, and by using attractive models, advertisers promote normative ideals of femininity to be pursued by modern Indian women. Notably, although the women depicted in ads belonged to a different social class, they still appealed to rural women, particularly adolescent girls and young women who enjoyed watching television commercials for personal grooming products (soaps, facial creams, cosmetics, shampoo, etc.). Commercials showing film actresses were most popular among the adolescent girls. It was through the consumption of some of the grooming products, endorsed by beautiful models in television commercials, that they derived some satisfaction from being part of a new consumer culture and fantasized about reaching unattainable standards of beauty and grooming.

The idealized prescription of femininity propagated by television commercials influenced the sense of self-worth and body image of rural girls and women in a subtle way. At one level, most rural women viewed themselves very far removed from the ideal of beauty as represented in television commercials and did not define themselves as "attractive."

> Women shown in television commercials are strikingly beautiful with long and silky hair, fair complexion, and a good figure. You can just fantasise about them. But in my heart I know that even if I use the same type of beauty products, I will never look half as good as them. (*Bhumiyar* unmarried girl, upper middle class, 20 years old)

> Girls in the village have also started using cosmetics, shampoo, and other things on special occasions to look attractive. But we know that they could never look as smart and attractive as the girls shown on television. (*Kurmi* mother, middle class, 40 years old)

Nonetheless, impressed by what they watched on television, the younger generation of women had become increasingly conscious of their appearance. Mothers of unmarried girls were very concerned about the way their daughters looked as potential grooms were thought to prefer "good looking and smart" wives. Some of these mothers did buy a few personal and grooming products and viewed them not as wasteful expenses, but as an investment in their daughter's future. Some young women themselves also purchased grooming products to enhance their beauty.

At another level, rural women knew that standards of beauty and grooming depicted in television commercials were beyond their reach because of their inability to purchase most of the products being advertised. As such, the younger generation of women aspired to consume several personal care and grooming products advertised on television, but their desire for the products was tempered by their economic reality:

> Every day television ads show new beauty products. It is good to know about them. One dreams about using all of them. But only a few things are within our means. (*Kurmi* mother, middle class, 24 years old)

> Through television, we learn about many new products that are used by film actresses and rich women to enhance their beauty. Even if we would like to use them, we cannot afford to buy these products. I have purchased a small sachet of the shampoo shown on television and used it few times. (*Bhumiyar* housewife, middle class, 23 years old)

> My mother has also purchased moisturising cream, scented soap, and hair oil for us from town. We cannot afford to use them regularly. Generally, we use them on special occasions like weddings and festivals. (*Darbar* unmarried girl, upper middle class, 20 years old)

There was some brand awareness among rural women, but in reality they purchased only those products and brands they could afford. "We stick to the brands that suit us" was a common statement. Because of their limited purchasing power, none had regularly started using the grooming products (e.g., shampoo, facial creams, lipstick, etc.).

Beyond the glamorous images of beautiful models, rural women did not critically view the latent messages of the ads that urged them to enhance their sex appeal or gain men's approval through the enhancement of their appearance. The routine trivialization and objectification of women in such advertisements was also not salient to them. They unquestionably "bought into" the fantasy world of beautiful models by purchasing these products or aspiring for them.

Conclusion

In general, extensive research on gender representation in television advertising has focused on understanding how gender identity is constructed. This chapter argues that although it is important to examine advertising discourses as constructed by marketers and advertisers, it is far more instructive to study consumption and reception of television commercials by female audiences from different socioeconomic backgrounds, particularly those not part of typical advertising discourse. On the basis of my exploratory village-level study in Baruraj, this chapter shows how rural women's access to television is mediated by the broader context of the village and the gendered context of household, and how these rural women make sense of the changing constructions of Indian women in television advertising.

Rural women derived considerable pleasure from watching television, particularly soap operas and entertainment programs. While watching their favorite television programs they were exposed to a new world of products and lifestyles through television commercials. For these women, watching television advertising not only involved the pleasures of escapism from the tedium of everyday life, but also the vicarious experience of participating in the consumer culture. They did not perceive television commercials as an expression of dominant culture, but viewed them as a form of learning about new products and lifestyles of the rich urban population.

The reading of television ads by rural women was not a monolithic process of interpretation. They did not uniformly and mechanically adopt the textually inscribed feminine subject positions. In fact, rural women as an audience actively negotiated with textual constructions and interpreted them in accordance with their social reality. Their interpretation of what they watched was not only contingent on the subject positions created by the text but also by a whole range of experiences they encountered in their social milieu. The way rural women made sense of the representations of modern Indian women revealed tension between real-world economic and patriarchal constraints and the possible world of fantasy. They interpreted the changing roles of women in television commercials within the boundaries of their social context and gender realities of everyday life. Women did not accept the preferred meanings proposed by advertising discourses if they were far removed from their own cultural and lived experiences. They also did not accept all aspects of the new Indian woman in her multifaceted roles, especially if they could not relate to the images because they seemed to be too unrealistic.

What was the impact of repetitive patterns of gender representation on the female audience of Baruraj? Various products and lifestyles shown in television commercials captured the attention of rural women, introduced rural women in Baruraj to the new world of consumerism and created a desire for affordable products. Also, among younger women, there was evidence of a very small shift in consumer behaviour in terms of changes in hairstyle and dress, and the use of cosmetics (talcum powder, lipstick, shampoo, hair oil, facial creams, etc.). There was, however, a sense of unease experienced by some of them as they felt that they were far removed from the idealized images of beauty as propagated by the commercials.

In conclusion, this qualitative study of how rural women make sense of television commercials, much like other reception studies about television and female audiences, has shown that advertising targeted to women is not passively received. Rather, women as audiences are actively engaged in the interpretation of them, particularly with respect to gender constructions. Significantly, women who do not belong to the same social strata as the "targeted" audience read representations in advertising in multiple ways. Furthermore, their interpretations are delineated by their social contexts and lived experiences. Many times this means an implicit acknowledgement of their own social subordination (i.e., within their family hierarchy, in terms of their purchasing power and access to disposable income, their caste, etc.). Overall, rural women read TV ads uncritically. Watching TV ads gave them vicarious pleasure in being part of urban consumer culture, but exposure to new constructions of modern Indian women did not challenge the perceptions of rural women about their gender roles in the household. Finally, most of the reception studies have focused on the targeted female audience of television and television commercials. Further ethnographic research, therefore, is required to examine how female audiences from diverse sociocultural backgrounds make sense of the ever-evolving representation of gender in advertising.

Notes

1. According to the 2006 Indian Readership Survey (IRS, Round 16), it is estimated that India had 437.8 million TV viewers in 2005 (Indiantelevision.com Team, 2006).

2. In 1985–1986, about 73.6% of rural households were in the low-income category, with only 5% constituting middle and higher income categories. Between 1992–1993 and 1998–1999, the percentage of lower income households declined from 65.5% to 57.2%. At the same time, lower middle income households increased from 22.6% to 34.8% during 1992–1999. Middle income rural households also grew at the annual rate of 7.8% during 1995–1999.

3. Notably, a 1993 survey of 10,000 women in 36 cities and towns across social classes and zones by Pathfinder-India showed that urban Indian women, working women with access to salaries, and housewives all played an important role in the purchase decisions of their families, and as such, advertisements should be targeted toward them (Pathfinder, 1993). According to another study, the National Family Health Survey (NFHS-2), which surveyed more than 90,000 women in 1998 and 1999, female television viewers increased from 32% in 1992–1993 to 46% in 1998–1999. However, only 33% of rural women, as compared with 81% among urban women in the survey had regular exposure to television (USAID-India, n.d.).

4. Fieldwork was undertaken as part of the student–faculty collaborative research project on "Commercialisation of Television in India: Perception of the Rural Audience." This research project was primarily guided by the broader concern of training postgraduate students of the Institute of Rural Management, and through village-level fieldwork.

5. In India, the caste system is a system of social stratification in which the status of the individual is determined by his or her birth and ritual purity. Caste has been defined as "small and named group of persons characterised by endogamy, hereditary membership, and a specific style of life which sometimes includes the pursuit by tradition of a particular occupation and is usually associated with more or less distinct ritual status in a hierarchical

system" (Béteille, 1996, p. 46). In Baruraj, 25% of households were from the higher castes (*brahmin, darbar* and *bhumihar*), 30% from the backward castes (*yadav, kumbhar, nai, kurmi, koiri* and *mallha*), and 15% from the scheduled castes (*harijan, tatma, paswan* and *bhat*). In each state, the government has identified several castes and communities that are socioeconomically disadvantaged in a given context, as "backward castes" for affirmative action. On the other hand, "scheduled" castes, the most socioeconomically marginalized sections of Indian society, are listed in the Constitution of India for affirmative action and social welfare. Social relations across the castes in Baruraj were not harmonious. The village community was also divided across caste lines in matters pertaining to local politics.

6. For example, in a 1986 study of gender portrayals in various types of programs on Indian television, Krishnan and Dighe (1990) examined 186 television commercials, repeated over several times during July 1986 on Doordarshan (the public broadcasting network). They found that television advertising depicted traditional and outmoded gender-role stereotypes and reinforced a two-dimensional role of women, first as caretakers of the household and the family, and second, as decorative sex objects used to sell products to both male and female consumers.

7. For example, cross-cultural analysis of print advertising in nationally circulated English magazines in the United States and India reveals that though both cultures are divergent there are striking similarities in the stereotypical depiction of women in print advertising (Ahmed, 1998; Griffin, Viswanath, & Schwartz, 1994). However, Ahmed argued that there are significant differences in the way the two divergent cultures portray women in advertising messages. Portrayal of women in Indian advertisements is more stereotypical than their U.S. counterparts, but advertising in India does not use physical exploitation of women as much as U.S. advertising.

8. For example, television commercials for washing machines regularly use scientific parlance to hook "new woman" consumers. The woman who uses such machines is portrayed as smart, intelligent, educated, and independent. The chore of washing clothes, however, still falls squarely on the woman's shoulders.

9. In another pioneering study of rural advertising (meaning commercial advertising aimed at the rural population), Bhatia (2000) showed that the representation of women in rural media and Indian-language advertising is highly diversified, and varied across media (television, radio, print, calendar, and wall paintings), ranging from sexualized portrayals to surrealist and mythical depictions. Notably, however, although he found that no single archetype of the female existed in rural advertising, his study did not provide information about the reception of rural advertising by rural women.

10. In Baruraj, agriculture is the main source of livelihoods for nearly 60% of the population, followed by agricultural wage labor (15%), government service (15%), and petty trade and business (10%). Temporary or seasonal migration of skilled and semi-skilled workers and laborers to nearby urban areas or other states is also an important aspect of the village economy in Baruraj. The village community was multiethnic, comprising 70% Hindus and 30% Muslims.

11. Physical mobility within the village was very limited for all women except women from the scheduled castes who worked in the fields as agricultural wage laborers. Women from the higher castes seldom stepped out of their homes on their own, whereas women from the middle castes generally moved around the village on social occasions. Furthermore, the traditional

Muslim and Hindu custom of *purdah* kept women secluded from the public and segregated them from men. The limits imposed by this practice, however, varied across the community. *Purdah* is strictly observed among Muslim women and involves wearing concealing clothing from head to toe, and the use of curtains and screens within the home. Married Hindu women also practice *purdah* by covering their head and face with a *sari* (traditional dress) in the presence of elderly relatives and male in-laws in the house and also when they move outside their homes. Within the household, women remained within an inner courtyard.

References

Ahmed, N. (1998). Mass-mediated stereotyping in the 1990s: A cross-cultural perspective. *Journal of Information Ethics*, 7(1), 68–78.

Ang, I. (1985). *Watching Dallas: Soap opera and the melodramatic imagination*. London: Methuen.

Ang I., & Joke, H. (1991). Gender and/in media consumption. In J. Curran & M. Gurivitch (Eds.), *Mass media and society* (pp. 307–328). London: Edward Arnold.

Béteille, A. (1996). The caste structure. In *Caste, class and power: Changing patterns of stratification in a Tanjore village* (2nd ed., pp. 45–101). Delhi: Oxford University Press.

Bhatia, T. K. (2000). *Advertising in rural India*. Tokyo: Institute for the Study of Languages and Cultures of Asia and Africa, Tokyo University of Foreign Studies.

Chanda, P. S. (1991). Birthing terrible beauties: Feminisms and 'women's magazines.' *Economic and Political Weekly*, 26(43), WS-67–WS-70.

Fiske, J. (1987). *Television culture*. London: Methuen.

Gallagher, M. (1995). *Lipstic imperialism and the new world order: Women and media at the close of the twentieth century*. A paper prepared for Division for Advancement of Women, Department for Policy Coordination and Sustainable Division, United Nations, New York.

Griffin, M., Viswanath, K., & Schwartz, D. (1994). Gender advertising in the US and India: Exporting cultural stereotypes. *Media, Culture and Society*, 16(3), 487–507.

Indiantelevision.com Team (2006). 51.2 Million C&S Homes in India: IRS 2006.

Krishnan, P., & Dighe, A. (1990). *Affirmation and denial: Construction of feminity on Indian television*. New Delhi: Sage.

Livingstone, S. M. (1990). *Making sense of television: The psychology of audience interpretations*. Oxford: Pergamon.

Mankekar, P. (1993). National texts and gendered lives: An ethnography of television viewers in a north Indian city. *American Ethnologist*, 20(33), 543–563.

McMillan, D. (2002). Ideologies of gender on television in India. *Indian Journal of Gender Studies*, 9(1), 2–26.

Munshi, S. (1998). Wife/mother/daughter-in-law: Multiple avatars of homemaker in 1990s Indian advertising. *Media, Culture and Society*, 20(4), 573–591.

National Council of Applied Economic Research. (2003). *India market demographics report 2002*. New Delhi: National Council of Applied Economic Research.

Pathfinder (1993). *P:SNAP Survey: India*.

USAID-India (n.d.). National Family Health Survey—2, 1998–99: Population Growth. http://www.usaid.gov/in/whatsnew/articles/nfhs2-popgrowth.html.

van Zoonen, L. (1991). Feminist media perspectives on the media. In J. Curran & M. Gurivitch (Eds.), *Mass media and society* (pp. 33–54). London: Edward Arnold.

Vilanilam, J. (1989). Television advertising and the Indian poor. *Media, Culture and Society*, *11*(4), 485–497.

10

Reading the "Plus-Size" Woman in *Mode* Magazine

Anita Nowak

> Reading the body involves making sense of the patterned ways that the body is represented according to broader cultural determinations and also the way the body becomes the bearer of signs and cultural meanings.
>
> —Balsamo (1997, p. 19)

Feminist scholars have long argued that many media texts offer problematic representations of women because they delimit their manifest lives by binding them to socially constructed gender roles. Winship (1987) argued, for example, that myths about women found in magazines are created to compensate for the lack of real and satisfying social identities available to them. Consequently, women's magazines provide readers with a sense of community, comfort, and pride in this mythic feminine identity, especially because the reader is situated as a friend and an equal (Bignell, 1997).

The problem with socially engineered myths, however, is that they become naturalized as ideological constructs of what it means to be a woman. And as Fiske (1990) explained, myths that are created through concrete forms, codes, and connotations, such as those found in advertising, give life to the ideology on which they rely. For example, when advertising consistently shows women happily washing clothes, the myth created is that "washing clothes makes women happy; and that using the better laundry bar makes them almost ecstatic" (Sarabia, 1995, p. 123). Goffman (1979) sardonically reiterated:

> If television commercials are to be believed, most American women go into uncontrollable ecstacies at the sight and smell of tablets and cabinets that have been lovingly caressed with long-lasting, satin-finish, lemon-scented, spray-on

furniture polish. Or they glow with rapture at the blinding whiteness of their wash—and the green-eyed envy of their neighbours. (p. 68)

The aim of this chapter is to contribute to a body of feminist scholarship that analyzes the socially constructed woman—with an inherent bias toward redress. Brunskell (1998) stated: "When feminist research is undertaken it is done so with a political commitment to the identification and *transformation* of gender relations" (p. 39). Such investigation is where political possibility lies, making feminist scholarship not just about women, but also rather *for* women (Westkoff, 1990).

Specifically, I consider the representation of "plus-size" women in print advertising. My findings stem from a larger study in which I conducted a textual analysis of advertisements from *Mode* magazine, followed by an audience study with 30 women hailing from both Canada and Singapore.[1] Given the feminist framework and epistemology of this research, I pay special attention to oppositional readings in order to investigate how ideological assumptions about "plus-size" women were and can be challenged. These moments of reading against the grain are instructive because they suggest how media literacy/education efforts and consciousness-raising/resistance strategies might be used and disseminated to ultimately empower women.

Feminist scholars have also traditionally been interested in more interpretive, reflexive, and subjective approaches to research (Levesque-Lopman, 1988) and have therefore turned to ethnography, interviews, and the analysis of personal diaries to establish how women feel and what they think about cultural products and experiences. As a result, audience studies have also become increasingly important to women's studies (Ang, 1995; Lotz, 2000). By viewing audiences as active participants in meaning-making activities, audience theorists have altered our understanding of the power relationship of media consumption, giving readers/viewers greater agency in the process:

> When a text is read, the reader interacts or negotiates with it; this negotiation involves the readers bringing their own cultural experience, their own socially located meaning systems, to bear upon the text.... The value of "negotiation," then, as an analytical concept is that it allows space to the subjectivities, identities and pleasures of audiences.... Meaning is neither imposed, nor passively imbibed, but arises out of a struggle or negotiation between competing frames of reference, motivation and experience. (Gledhill, 1992, pp. 200, 199, 195)

Gledhill also suggested that the concept of negotiation is particularly useful for feminist media analysis because it recognizes the instability of identity and the positionality of those reading the texts, as well as the unfixed meanings in the texts themselves. Significantly, the research described in this chapter is situated within the context of valuing women's voices as audience members.

Contextualizing the "Plus-Size" Female Body and *Mode* Magazine[2]

Throughout the 1950s, 1960s, and 1970s, approximately 25% of the American population was considered obese, defined as 20% above standard height and weight ratios. By the 1980s, this figure had risen to 33%—meaning roughly 38 million women and men (Etcoff, 1999). In the same period, childhood obesity also increased by 50% (Maine, 2000). The Centers for Disease Control and Prevention (CDC) reports an obesity increase among adults from 15.0% (1976–1980) to almost 33% (2003–2004). "In 2007, only one state (Colorado) had a prevalence of obesity less than 20%."[3] According to the 2004 Canadian Community Health Survey, more than 20% of Canadian adults are obese (*The Globe and Mail*, 2005). Finally, Asia is also facing a surge in obesity as a result of changes in diet and lifestyle (*The Straits Times*, 2000).

Meanwhile, as Orbach noted as far back as 1978, "we live in a culture . . . obsessed with women's body size and body shape that sees fatness and thinness as ultimate statements about people's worth rather than descriptions of the ratio of fat body tissue and lean body tissue" (p. xx).[4] Indeed, in more recent writing, a person's size and shape has come to signify and symbolize his or her emotional, moral, and spiritual state of mind (Bordo, 1993), such that fat bodies are seen as "blatantly sexual, unapologetically physical, primitive, uncultured, out of control" (Darling-Wolf, 2000, p. 287), and particularly offensive to Western ideals of attractiveness (Bartky, 1998).

Because obesity is so often thought to be self-induced, discrimination against "plus-size" people continues to be socially acceptable (Erdman, 1994). Kilbourne (1999) argued that disdain for fat people, especially fat women, is one of the few remaining socially acceptable prejudices, a point amply supported by research.[5] A "plus-size" woman who claims to be happy, despite her size, is most disturbing because she embodies (no pun intended) resistance to cultural norms (Bordo, 1993).[6] And although discrimination intensifies as weight increases, size bigotry affects even those who are only 20% above their ideal weight (Bordo, 1993).

Thus, over the last two decades, and in response to "size-ism," "plus-size" women have initiated a size-acceptance movement and technology has been put to the employ of groups intent on celebrating the "plus-size" body.[7] This includes Marilyn Wann's Web site (www.fatso.com), for example, which self-consciously proclaims on its home page that it is a space "for people who don't apologize for their size." It should come as no surprise, then, that marketers were quick to react to this new phenomenon.

Mode magazine, a high-quality women's fashion magazine targeting the "plus-size" market, hits newsstands in February 1998, positioning itself as "*The New Shape in Fashion*." Existing women's magazines such as American *Glamour*,

Cosmopolitan, *Vogue*, Canadian *Chatelaine*, and Singaporean *Her World* had all incorporated—albeit sporadically—special features addressing the concerns of "plus-size" women. *Mode*, however, was one of the first fashion magazines whose explicit mission was to do so.

The introduction and subsequent success of *Mode* occurred at a time when the average American woman stood 5'4", weighed 142 lb, and wore size 12 (Gordon, 1998). Sales of "plus-size" women's clothing in 1997 had reached US$ 22.7 billion, an increase of nearly 7% over the prior year (Gordon, 1998), and up $10 billion from 1991 (Wells, Burnett, & Moriarty, 1995). As alluded to previously, *Mode*'s launch also capitalized on the growing momentum of the anti-sizeism campaign in North America. Readers celebrated *Mode*'s arrival and wrote enthusiastic letters to the editor such as: "Thank you, thank you, thank you! I felt totally alone in a world meant for size 6 bodies, and then you arrived on the scene" (*Soledad*, December 1998 issue, p. 26).

Methodology

This study aimed to identify how women "read" the "plus-size" body in *Mode*, a magazine designed for and targeted at a "plus-size" female audience. Twelve advertisements were taken from four randomly selected issues of *Mode* magazine, namely December 1998, June 1999, July 1999, and February 2000. Criteria were established to select the 12 ads and 49 advertisements met the criteria, 12 of which were randomly selected to comprise the dataset.[8] The sample was drawn, using the technique of snowballing. Beginning with women who were part of my circle of friends and professional acquaintances, 30 participants were recruited and interviewed, 15 each from Canada and Singapore.[9] The respondents ranged in age between 18 and 34 years, with an average age of 26 years across the sample. This age group was chosen deliberately because it represents the target market for many women's fashion magazines and also constitutes the age group of women among which fashion magazine readership is highest. The respondents also ranged in terms of ethnic background, educational level, and profession.[10]

Gray (1997) viewed "the humble interview" as "an absolutely central discursive technology in the generation of experience" (p. 99) and van Zoonen (1994) sees interviewing as the ideal way in which to gain insight about the meanings circulating in society. In this study, interviews were conducted to understand the "social actor's perspective" (Lindlof, 1995, p. 166) and to uncover the "subjective side" (Marshall & Rossman, 1995, p. 100) of women's readings of "plus-size" women featured in print advertising. Notably, however, efforts were made to avoid a "romanticism" that sometimes accompanies in-depth interviewing (Miller & Glassner, 1997).

Colored copies of the 12 advertisements from *Mode* were sent through the mail to each of the 30 respondents to consider over a period of 7 to 10 days. A meeting was then scheduled with each participant for a taperecorded one-on-one interview that lasted between 45 and 75 minutes, after which I transcribed each interview.[11] At the beginning of each session, every effort was made to make each respondent as relaxed as possible. The women were reminded that there were no right or wrong answers and that all their comments would be valuable and significant to the outcome of the study.

In the interviews, each advertisement was discussed and several metaphor-elicitation exercises were carried out. These exercises were borrowed and adapted from the Zaltman Metaphor Elicitation Technique (ZMET), a method used in advertising, marketing, and consumer behavior research. This particular research tool was employed because, "for the most part, it is only through their metaphors that . . . researchers can learn more about [an audience's] thoughts and feelings" (Zaltman & Coulter, 1995, p. 38). The rationale behind employing a metaphor-elicitation technique was that metaphors are fundamental cognitive processes that govern our understanding of the world. Lakoff and Johnson (1980) explained that the essence of a metaphor is "understanding and experiencing one thing in terms of another" (p. 5) and it "thus plays a central role in defining our everyday realities" (p. 3). Thompson (1997) further elaborated: "Not only do they allow us to express opinions inventively and colorfully, but they frame how we understand issues. . . . Metaphors, then, are necessarily accompanied by value judgments . . . [and are] connect[ed] with ideology" (p. 476). Thus, to evoke personal accounts from respondents, a metaphor-based approach was deemed appropriate, innovative, and potentially very fruitful.

The ZMET was conceived to address the shortcomings of contemporary quantitative and qualitative advertising research techniques. As Zaltman and Coulter (1995) said, the ZMET is "designed to surface the mental models that drive consumer thinking and behaviour" (p. 35).[12] These mental maps are similar to schemas, which, in social psychology paralanguage, are defined as "organized sets of knowledge, beliefs, and attitudes about a given topic" (Walsh-Childers & Brown, 1993, p. 119) that are formed through experience, and once developed, "exert strong effects on many aspects of social cognition, including attention, encoding, and retrieval of social information" (Baron & Byrne, 1997, p. 108). They structure past experiences and are used as frames of reference to interpret new information and situations.

As just explained, the ZMET was originally designed to elicit metaphorical information about products, services, companies, brands, and the like, however, for the purposes of this study, parts of the ZMET were borrowed and adapted to elicit metaphorical information from participants concerning the portrayal of "plus-size" women in *Mode* magazine advertising. Table 10.1 shows the step-by-step process that was used for each interview, including the specific metaphor-elicitation exercises employed.

Table 10.1. Step-by-Step Process Used for Interviews

1. The respondents were asked to give a general impression of the women in the set of ads as if they were giving a synopsis of a book or movie.

2. The respondents were asked to describe each woman in each advertisement one at a time.

3. Responses from step 1 were read back to the respondents and each participant was then asked to pull out all the advertisements that did not adequately fit the overall description. In this way, they were left with the representative advertisements.

4. The respondents were asked to name a metaphorical symbol that best described to them the women in the representative set. They were then asked to name an opposite metaphorical symbol.

5. The respondents were told to think about the women in the "representative" set and then asked to name
   • a *scent* that they associated with those women
   • an *opposite scent* associated with those women
   • a *sound* that they associated with those women
   • an *opposite sound* associated with those women
   • a *color* that they associated with those women
   • an *opposite color* associated with those women
   • a *texture* that they associated with those women
   • an *opposite texture* associated with those women
   • a *taste* that they associated with those women
   • an *opposite taste* associated with those women
   • an *emotion* that they felt when thinking about the women in the advertisements
   • an *opposite emotion* that they felt when thinking about the women in the advertisements.

6. The respondents were asked to put the "representative" advertisements back together with the nonrepresentative ones. They were then asked to group the models into any, and as many, categories as they determined significant, however the categories had to made sense to them. The respondents were given the option of creating a "miscellaneous" category.

7. The respondents were asked to give each category a heading as well as a metaphorical symbol and opposite metaphorical symbol that best described to them the women in each of the categories that they had created.

8. The respondents were asked if they felt—generally speaking—that the portrayal of the women in the 12 advertisements was positive, negative, or neutral.

9. The respondents were asked to describe how they wished women were portrayed in advertising.

Findings and Discussion

As Walker (1985) explained, the analysis of qualitative data is a process of making sense and giving meaning and significance to findings, which can be "a highly personal activity involv[ing] processes of interpretation and creativity that are difficult and perhaps somewhat threatening to make explicit" (p. 56). Moreover, the challenge in interpreting qualitative data is not about creating interpretations but in learning how to get away from pre-established ones (Feldman, 1995, p. 64).

When asked to describe the women in the ads, responses included the following:

- "She's very soft-spoken, caring, and motherly."

- She's a "nice suburban," "modern housewife," "married to a CEO," who therefore "needs to be calm and collected."

- She is "softer," "quiet and shy," "feminine, sensitive, and vulnerable."

- She is "content," "comfortable," "confident," "looks like she's got it together," and is "super happy."

- "The quintessential woman."

- She lives in affluence "like an Ivana Trump socialite, living off her husband's salary."

- She's a "very giving woman," "a strong woman, who's kind and has a good heart . . . [who] breastfed her kids."

- She's "playful," "carefree," "energetic," "on the go," and "spirited."

- She's "comfortable with her weight" and "loves her body without a doubt."

- She's "someone who's cared for" and has "a rich father who looks after her."

- She's a "small-scale entrepreneur with a simple shop or her own business."

- She's "cheerful," "friendly," "fun and energetic," with a "positive outlook."

- "She could be a social worker" or is "someone who does some volunteering part-time."

- "She has a good family" and "could pick me up in a MPV [multipurpose vehicle] to go shopping."

- She's "somebody you wouldn't mind getting to know" because she looks "loving" and "a little submissive."

- She's a "housewife," "a mother," and "into handicrafts."

On the whole, the Singaporean respondents read "plus-size" women in these *Mode* advertisements as being older working mothers, leading happy, satisfying lives and at ease with themselves despite their larger frames. Table 10.2 shows the breakdown of descriptions used by the Singaporean respondents (note: several respondents used several different adjectives or descriptions).

Similarly, Canadians tended to view the same women as typical homemakers who also work outside the home, and despite their larger size, are still comfortable, confident, and happy. Table 10.3 shows the Canadian respondents' breakdown.

Tables 10.4 and 10.5 depict the women's response in terms of metaphorical symbols and opposite symbols used to describe the 12 women.

The metaphor-elicitation exercise (see step 5, Table 10.1) reinforced these general sentiments in that respondents found the *Mode* women to be "sweet," "emotionally expressive," and "wholesome women" who "contribute a lot to society." They were also seen as "being soft," "feminine," "confident," "bright," "cheerful," and "nurturing." In general, the women were also associated with "gentle," "pleasing," "soothing," and "natural" sounds, like waterfalls or a rainforest, rather than loud, obtrusive sounds. They were also seen as "warm," "dependable," "not high maintenance," "strong," and "resilient."

Almost half of the respondents associated fresh and natural scents (like "flowers," "lavender," "vegetables," or a "lilac tree") with the models, because "these women make me feel happy," or baking and cooking aromas because they are "mommy smells." In fact, the vast majority of respondents did not smell foul odors such as hospital smells "because they look too healthy," or alcohol because "I just couldn't see any of them as an alcoholic mom who didn't care about her kids." Finally, more than two-thirds of the respondents felt positive emotions

Table 10.2 Descriptions of *Mode* Women by Singaporean Respondents

Description	Number of Respondents
Mode women are happy, content, happy-go-lucky, and smiling	10
Mode women have larger, rounder, plumper bodies	10
Mode women as comfortable with themselves despite their size	8
Mode women as professional, working women	5
Mode women as older or middle-aged	5
Mode women as married with a family	4
Mode women as easily satisfied, happy with what they have, fulfilled, and down-to-earth	4
Mode women as confident and in possession of their own identities	4
Mode women as conservative, friendly, approachable, very real, from all walks of life, and timid	1

Table 10.3. Description of *Mode* Women by Canadian Respondents

Description	Number of Respondents
Mode women are average, typical, normal, or real women	7
Mode women are happy	7
Mode women are larger, but not that large	6
Mode women are comfortable with themselves, despite their size	6
Mode women are mothers with families	5
Mode women are confident	5
Mode women are professionals	4
Mode women are older	3
Mode women are balanced and healthy	2
Mode women are personable	1
Mode women are classy	1
Mode women are multidimensional	1
Mode women are feminine	1
Mode women are lacking self-esteem	1
Mode women are trying too hard to be sexy	1
Mode women are beautiful	1
Mode women are well done up	1
Mode women show little flesh and therefore are not objects of seduction	1

Table 10.4 Metaphorical and Opposite Symbols Used by Singaporean Respondents

Symbols	Opposite Symbols
• Fresh bread buns	• Grouchy teacher
• Smiley face	• Plain paper
• Used jeans (for comfort)	• Pretzel stick
• Middle-aged woman	• SIA flight attendant
• A boiled egg (tough and fragile)	• Fierce lion
• Silverware (for class)	• Trash (no value)
• Hairbrush (for practicality)	• Eye-catching make-up
• Big Mac (makes you happy)	• Plain bread
• Sunflower (for cheer)	• Teenager with insecurities
• Basketball (for shape)	• Snake (devious and ugly)
• Established department store	• Urban city
• Glamorous film star	• High school girl
• Ripe tomato	• Catwalk
• Butterfly (for independence)	• 16th century corset
• Butterfly (for loveliness)	• Miss Universe

Table 10.5. Metaphorical and Opposite Symbols Used by Canadian Respondents

Symbols	Opposite Symbols
• Washed-up, has-been singers	• Mask
• Sheep being herded	• Driving the speed limit
• Regular people	• Falling star (not the norm)
• A happy Buddha	• Shepherd (a leader)
• Family dinner together	• Catwalk models
• I love you just the way you are	• Runway models
• A "plus-size" woman	• Crazy, sci-fi world
• Apple tree (it evolves)	• Blank paper (no story)
• Cosy house	• Sexy women
• Flowers that turn inward	• Mid-life crisis
• Apple tree (pretty)	• Cold, sterile, art deco apt.
• A car driving too fast (trying too hard)	• Someone defiant, in control
• Field of flowers in the sun	• Someone unapproachable
• Nursing bra circus tightrope	• A stage (contrived)
	• Tight lycra dress

including "happiness," "pride," "empowerment," "more confident about myself," and even "love."

Slightly more than one-third of the respondents, however, saw the set of *Mode* women as neutral or negative. In fact, when reviewing the findings of the interviews, a discernible break became apparent between respondents who looked upon the *Mode* advertisements as positive portrayals of women, and those who did not. Although generally the "plus-size" women were regarded favorably at the level of individual advertisements, a significant minority of women made much less positive judgments, with evidence of oppositional reading clustering around several themes. To illustrate this, Table 10.6 provides some of the statements made by the respondents who read the advertisements against the grain.

These readings of "plus-size" women highlight several interesting aspects to consider in terms of an "active audience." If we accept that all media texts are constructed, then advertising is particularly adept at image manipulation and designed to have maximum appeal for most people (following Barthes, 1977). And as Messaris (1997) pointed out, "experienced creators of ads and other forms of visual persuasion are able to employ tacit conventions of the medium in such a way as to elicit relatively uniform and consistent responses from their viewers" (p. 273). This, then, explains how and why so many respondents read the advertisements in a positive light. They tended to read the preferred meanings encoded by the advertisers, illustrating the proverbial power of the text.

Table 10.6. Negative Responses to Ads

"Plus-size" women are dull

- "They come in the same flavour."
- "They are bland, like water or plain spaghetti."
- "They are bored, conformist and have settled."
- "Their clothing is blah like their personalities."
- "They are so clean and proper, there's no excitement to these women."

"Plus-size" women are docile, insecure and people-pleasers

- "They look nice, but there's nothing to them, they have no strength."
- "They simply respond to the needs of whomever they're waiting for."
- "They have husbands who don't treat them well, and they try whatever they can to please them."
- "They are nervous looking and less confident."
- "The guy is hidden behind the girl, implying that tall, thin, handsome guys don't go for gals with fuller figures."
- "They are saying, 'No matter how comfortable you are with your body, I wouldn't put you naked in a magazine.'"
- "You don't see one little piece of flesh on them except for their necks."
- "These are pretty women and the way they are dressed is what is wrong with society. These women could be wearing nice clothes, instead they advertise these tacky, old maid, Las Vegas-type of outfits."

Advertisers of "plus-size" garments do not know how to communicate with their target market

- "The advertisers are trying to make [big people] feel better, but they're doing just the opposite."
- "The advertisers are trying to convince me that it's OK to be fat."
- "Why should I 'Keep my outlook sunny?' Should I be depressed about being full-figured? It's condescending."

On the other hand, those respondents who articulated subversive meanings from the advertisements, and employed more critical reading strategies, serve to demonstrate the power of the active and engaged audience. This is not to say the oppositional readings are more correct than those more in line with the preferred readings, but it does illustrate that both the text and the reader share power in creating meaning. In this way, texts are polysemic despite a probable preferred meaning. Readers are active and do negotiate meaning from texts, but not with absolute freedom.

Because there was a tendency for the Canadian respondents to be more critical of the *Mode* advertisements, the argument that stands to be made is that social discourses (such as the North American discourse about body acceptance) also contribute to the reading strategies adopted by audience members of any historically and culturally located society. Because in Singapore there is less public discussion about "plus-size" women (most likely because to date there are less "plus-size" women and men in the local society to begin with) readers of "plus-size" advertisements in Singapore tend to read *Mode* women with less scrutiny. In Canada, on the other hand, where the acceptance discourse is more prominent, there is a greater tendency to critically consider the representation of "plus-size" women.

As already mentioned, over the last decade "plus-size" women in North America have initiated a new social discourse of size acceptance. This discourse has two fundamental aims: (a) to expose the systematic discrimination that "plus-size" people face in a society that puts enormous value on being young, slender, and beautiful; and (b) to serve as a call for emancipation, self-love and appreciation for the "plus-size" woman herself. It is difficult to really determine the success of the size-acceptance movement, because the size agenda has been hijacked in recent years by the obesity agenda, although activists such as Marilyn Wann continue to promote a "fat is beautiful" message even as Morgan Spurlock's (2004) film *Super Size Me* offers a hard critique of the political economy of weight.

Not surprisingly, *Mode* advertisers co-opted the discourse of body acceptance and anti-sizeism. It is widely accepted that the media appropriate popular images and ideas that are in circulation. This is especially the case with magazines and advertising, because "the strength of the women's magazine category rests principally . . . on the ability of this magazine group to adapt, albeit superficially, to social change" (Goldman, 1995, p. 82). For example, *Mode* advertisers were quick to appropriate the language of feminism, speaking to women as independent, free-thinking, and self-determining, while simultaneously using this discourse as a veil to cover their hidden agenda of consumerism. The celebratory and emancipatory discourse which suffuses the magazine should not be interpreted as mere altruism—*Mode* magazine is still in the business to make money after all.

As McCracken (1993) argued, "the quest for self-acceptance and non-stereotypical treatment is integrated into fashion and beauty consumerism" (p. 259), through the language of empowerment and pride for "plus-sizes." Indeed, *Mode* advertisements encourage women to find their voices, feel good about themselves, and believe in "endless possibilities" (as per the copy of 1 of the 12 ads used in this study), promising upper middle-class status, a happy, enriching lifestyle, and deeply fulfilling relationships, all in return for the purchase of clothing and accessories. In other words, the advertisements "provide a terrain on which to dream, and thus generate a desire for fulfillment (through consumption) . . . [and they also] guide the discontent of large-size women into a concept of liberation that posits consumerism as a remedy" (Storey, 1993, pp. 148, 260).

Of course, not only does a feel-good "plus-size" sensibility encourage the consumption of fashion items made for the larger figure, but the always present subtext to size acceptance (i.e. "I would accept myself more if there was a little less of me to love") means that the political economy of weight acts as both push and pull factors. Yes, buy those "plus-size" clothes but also buy that weight-reducing snack bar. As Williamson (1978) noted, "the technique of advertising is to correlate feelings, moods or attributes to tangible objects, linking possible unattainable things with those that are attainable, and thus reassuring us that the former are within reach" (p. 31). Budgeon (1994) reiterated this point when she said that advertisements for products such as clothing become meaningful because of their promise of love, happiness, and success. Significantly, however, the goods advertised in magazines never do give complete satisfaction, never do quite deliver their promises, propelling us through never-ending cycles of consumption and desire.

Thus, *Mode* advertisers do not completely encourage "plus-size" women to feel happy with whom and how they are because if women really did begin to feel good about themselves, the continuous need to purchase commodities in exchange for self-esteem or self-love would cease. "Plus-size" advertisements, like any others (especially advertising hawking products related to appearance), make "always-already" broken promises. And arguably, it is precisely women's failure to make good on those promises that feeds negative self-perception and body image, anxiety, depression, and low-self-esteem, and leads women to internalize blame (Baron & Byrne, 1997; Kilbourne, 1999), that is, "The product is great, so it must be my fault." This is how advertisers keep women running on the consumption wheel, promising, promising, promising.

Significantly, however, although *Mode* advertising contains always-already broken promises, it nonetheless presents a remarkably more realistic portrayal of women than does mainstream fashion advertising, which is obsessed with fantasy and virtually unattainable beauty. Van Zoonen (1994) and others noted that scholars have complained about the portrayals of gender in the media being unrepresentative of social reality, implying that women and men should be represented correctly. However, as she and others (see Byerly & Ross, 2006) argued, the call is not for a simple exchange of "bad" images for "good" ones, but rather for a broad diversity of representations that more accurately reflect real women's real lives.

Therefore, it was interesting, and not altogether surprising, that respondents in this current study also wanted advertisers to portray women more realistically. For example, in discussing mainstream images of women, the Singaporean respondents wanted representations of "real women," "a variety of women," and "normal women" whereby women are "truthfully and positively portrayed," and "shown with more respect" and "in less sexist ways." They also wanted "healthier women and not anorexic-looking" models. Finally, they wanted to see women who are "natural," "happy," and "down to earth." Canadian respondents also resoundingly called for mainstream portrayals of women to be "as they really are," "in diverse roles," "doing everyday activities." They wanted a "wider range of body types not just the extremes," as can be seen with "real people off the street." Finally, they wanted women to be depicted as "normal," "as a human," and "in a fair way," and wished that women were "given a voice."

To some extent, these calls for improved portrayal are attended to by *Mode*'s representation of women, but not always. This more prosaic response by *Mode*, to include archetypal fashion plates as well as the "plus-size" model, chimes with strategies used elsewhere within advertising to use attitude as a cipher for size, not to mention class. For example, Messaris (1997) described difference in facial expressions between models in high-fashion magazines and those in advertisements for lower end products: "Models who display moderately priced clothing usually smile and strike ingratiating poses. But high-fashion models are generally unsmiling and sometimes openly contemptuous" (p. 38). Thus, without necessarily consciously conspiring against "plus-size" women, *Mode* advertisers present readers with imagery that conceals the discrepant reality of being a "plus-size" woman against the fantasy realm of the desirable (read "thin") woman.

According to my respondents, *Mode* women are well adjusted, successful and contented, their happy-go-lucky demeanor supports the notion that they are not bothered by their size. Although this is a reasonably "positive" construction, given the competing (and negative) stereotypes about "plus-size" women, such advertisements nonetheless help to reinforce the idea that fat women "let themselves go" because they do not really care about their appearances. Furthermore, the fact that the *Mode* models are at the lower end of the "plus-size" range suggests that moderately "plus-size" women are tolerable, but *really* fat women, ironically, are not even good enough to sell "plus-size" clothing.

Taken as a set of indicators of femininity, the socially constructed *Mode* woman is mostly a happy, ultra-feminine, suburban homemaker and part-time working mom, reminiscent of the female images Betty Friedan (1963) analyzed in her exposé of "the problem that has no name." Seemingly innocuous, we know that "most stereotypes are not neutral; they are deeply embedded in structures of oppression and domination and become prescriptions for behavior and modes of social control" (Walters, 1999, p. 226).

Conclusion

This study aimed to identify the ways in which "plus-size" women are read by an audience of women readers in two distinct cultural contexts, namely Canada and Singapore. The readings were framed within a research problematic that asked women to "read" a series of advertisements in relation to normative constructions of femininity and in relation to their own lived realities. Given my respondents' readings, I have shown that advertising in *Mode*, despite being in a magazine aimed at a "plus-size" female readership, constructs "plus-size" women using conventional renditions of femininity including the archetypal figure of the mother. Such stereotypical representations provide comfort and enjoyment to some women readers—even as others challenge the stereotypicality embodied therein at the level of the individual advertisement. Thus, although it was possible to discern the polysemy of advertising texts that "allowed" readers to offer different interpretations, taken as a discrete set of images, there was considerable similarity of view amongst all the respondents, despite their very different cultural viewing contexts. Respondents *generally* considered women in *Mode* to be happy, comfortable, suburban homemakers who possibly worked part-time outside the home. Notably, these findings are consistent with those of the textual analysis that was also conducted as part of the larger research project but not discussed in this chapter.

This finding suggests an interplay, rather than a dichotomy, between the "power of the text" and the "power of the audience." As such, I contend that audience meaning-making is simultaneously—and to varying degrees—dependent on three factors: the relative openness of the text, the positionality of the reader, and the cultural constructs and discourses circulating within any given social context. It is precisely the combination of these elements that determines, in the end, the extent to which the text or the audience exerts the most power. I wish, indeed, that the audience held more.

Notes

1. This chapter is an edited version of my master's thesis, "Reading the "Plus-Size" Woman in Print Advertising," written at the School of Communication and Information Studies at Nanyang Technological University (Singapore), in 2002. I would like to acknowledge the important contributions made by several individuals to the original piece of work: Karen Ross (external examiner); Ong, Siow Heng (internal examiner); Lee Hong Hwee, Michael (colleague); Li Zhan (colleague); and in particular Gan, Su-lin (thesis supervisor). I also remain indebted to the 30 women who participated in the study.

2. "*Plus-size*" refers to any human body that, according to contemporary social norms, carries excessive weight. We put the term in quote marks to highlight both the problematic nature of this commonsense description, as well as the irony that "plus-size" in North America has now become the norm.

3. Source: NHANES Data on the Prevalence of Overweight and Obesity Among Adults: United States, 2003–2004. (CDC Web site: http://www.cdc.gov/nccdphp/dnpa/obesity/trend/maps/index.htm; retrieved January 2009.)

4. Orbach (1978) was instrumental in theorizing that being fat is "a response to the inequality of the sexes" (p. 6). Others, including Kilbourne (1999) have also noted that the "obsession with thinness is most deeply about cutting girls and women down to size. It is only a symbol, albeit a very powerful and destructive one, of tremendous fear of female power" (p. 137).

5. For example, according to a 1998 study carried out at The University of Michigan, which analyzed data collected with more than 7,000 men and women, obese women earn 60% less than "normal" weight women, after adjusting statistically for factors such as age, education, professional status, marital status, and health (*The Economist*, 2000). Another study conducted in 2000 at London's Guildhall University involving 33,000 workers of equal qualifications and of the same age, found that women and men who are more attractive, taller and slimmer earn up to 30% more than their larger and less attractive counterparts (*The Straits Times*, 2000). Other studies have found that overweight women are 20% less likely to get married than normal weight women, and astoundingly, college students would prefer to marry an embezzler, drug user, shoplifter, or blind person than someone who is fat (Maine, 2000). Indeed, more than half of females between the ages of 18 and 25 would rather be run over by a truck than be fat, and two-thirds would choose to be mean or stupid than fat. Another study revealed that 11% of people would abort an unborn child if it had a predisposition to obesity (Poulton, 1996). A survey conducted in 2000 with 2,000 British women, showed that 80% of respondents thought big was definitely unattractive (*The Straits Times*, 2001), and a 1988 report found that girls as young as 7 believe thin is beautiful (Kalin, 1990). Yet another study concluded that 81% of 10-year-olds are even afraid of being fat (Maine, 2000).

6. For an excellent collection of short essays on the politics of "fat" see *Feminist Media Studies* (vol. 5, issue 1, 2005).

7. As McCracken (1993) explained, "arguing that common prejudices exaggerate the importance of outward appearance, newly formed groups of 'plus-size' women insist that they are valuable people whatever their size" (p. 258). In fact, formal organizations now exist to fight against sizeism, including the Canadian Association for Size Acceptance, and NAAFA, which according to their Web site (www.naafa.org), "is a non-profit human rights organization dedicated to improving the quality of life for fat people . . . [aiming] to eliminate discrimination based on body size and provide fat people with tools for self-empowerment through public education, advocacy and member support."

8. The criteria were as follows: Each advertisement must present a woman as a central subject and do so by showing her face and at least a partial body shot (to avoid pure body shots and depictions without facial expressions); each advertisement must be for clothing or fashion accessories (to consider advertisements in the same product category); and each advertisement must contain at least one caption (to help in considering the rhetorical elements of each advertisement).

9. Choosing to interview women from Singapore and Canada was a specific strategy I used in order to overcome the predominance of studies that only take account of Western audiences. The choice of Canada and Singapore, however, was based on a convenience sample as I was temporarily studying and working in Singapore and returned home to Canada during the research period.

10. From the Singaporean set, women were of Chinese, Malay, and Indian descent, and from the Canadian set, women were of British, French, Italian, Israeli, German, Caribbean, Native Canadian, African-Canadian, etc., descent. In terms of education, most of the respondents held a bachelor's degree. However, the areas of study varied widely from sociology, to microbiology and commerce. Finally, with respect to their professional career, the group of respondents was comprised of attorneys, students, a filmmaker, a nurse, and a music instructor, among others. While it is acknowledged that a small sample of 30 respon-

dents is not generalizable, I felt it was nonetheless important to have as wide a variety of women participating in the study as possible.

11. All the interviews with Canadian respondents took place in February 2000 and all those with Singaporean participants took place in October 2000.

12. Zaltman and Coulter explain that several interrelated premises about cognitive thinking and metaphors are what theoretically ground the ZMET. They include most communication is nonverbal; thoughts occur as nonverbal images; metaphors are essential units of thought and are the key windows/mechanisms for viewing consumer thoughts and feelings and for understanding behavior; sensory images provide metaphors; and consumers have "mental models" that represent their knowledge and behavior.

References

Ang, I. (1995). The nature of the audience. In J. Downing, A. Mohammadi, & A. Sreberny-Mohammadi (Eds.), *Questioning the media: A critical introduction* (pp. 207–220). Thousand Oaks, CA: Sage.

Balsamo, A. (1997). *Technologies of the gendered bodies: Reading cyborg women.* Durham, NC: Duke University Press.

Baron, D., & Byrne, R. A. (1997). *Social psychology.* Needham Heights: Allyn & Bacon.

Barthes, R. (1977). The rhetoric of the image. In *Image, music, text* (pp. 32–51). Glasgow: Fontana.

Bartky, S. L. (1998). Foucault, femininity, and the modernization of patriarchal power. In R. Weitz (Ed.), *The politics of women's bodies: Sexuality, appearance and behavior* (pp. 25–45). New York: Oxford University Press.

Bignell, J. (1997). *Media semiotics: An introduction.* New York: Manchester University Press.

Bordo, S. (1993). Feminism, Foucault and the politics of the body. In C. Ramazanoglu (Ed.), *Up against Foucault: Explorations of some tensions between Foucault and feminism* (pp. 179–202). London: Routledge.

Brunskell, H. (1998). Feminist methodology. In C. Seale (Ed.), *Researching society and culture* (pp. 37–47). London: SAFE.

Budgeon, S. (1994). Fashion magazine advertising: Constructing femininity in the "post-feminist" era. In A. Manca & L. Manca (Eds.), *Gender utopias in advertising: A critical reader* (pp. 55–70). Syracuse, NY: Procopian Press.

Byerly, C. M., & Ross, K. (2006). *Women and media: Critical issues.* Blackwell.

Darling-Wolf, F. (2000). From airbrushing to liposuction: The technological reconstruction of the female body. In B. Miedema, J. Stoppard, & V. Anderson (Eds.), *Women's bodies/women's lives: Health, well-being and body image* (pp. 277–293). Toronto: Sumach Press.

Erdman, C. K. (1994). Nothing to lose: A naturalistic study of size acceptance in fat women. In K. A. Callaghan (Ed.), *Ideals of feminine beauty: Philosophical, social and cultural dimensions* (pp. 161–173). Westport, CT: Greenwood Press.

Etcoff, N. (1999). *Survival of the prettiest: The science of beauty.* New York: Doubleday.

Feldman, M. S. (1995). *Strategies for interpreting qualitative data.* Thousand Oaks, CA: Sage.

Fiske, J. (1990). Women and quiz shows: Consumerism, patriarchy and resisting pleasures. In M. E. Brown (Ed.), *Television and women's culture: The politics of the popular* (pp. 134–143). London: Sage.

Frieden, B. (1963). *The feminine mystique*. Middlesex: Penguin Books.

Gledhill, C. (1992). Pleasurable negotiations. In F. Bonner, L. Goodman, R. Allen, L. Janes, & C. King (Eds.), *Imagining women: Cultural representations and gender* (pp. 193–209). Cambridge: The Open University Press.

Goffman, E. (1979). *Gender advertisements*. Cambridge, MA: Harvard University Press.

Goldman, R. (1995). Constructing and addressing the audience as commodity. In G. Dines & J. M. Humez (Eds.), *Gender, race and class in media: A text-reader* (pp. 88–92). Thousand Oaks, CA: Sage.

Gordon, J. (1998, October 19). A larger dose of reality. *Forbes,* p. 47.

Gray, A. (1997). Learning from experience: Cultural studies and feminism. In J. McGuigan (Ed.), *Cultural methodologies* (pp. 87–105). London: Sage.

Kalin, R. (1990). *The manufacture of beauty*. Boston: Brandon.

Kilbourne, J. (1999). *Deadly persuasion: Why women and girls must fight the addictive power of advertising*. New York: The Free Press.

Lakoff, G., & Johnson, M. (1980). *Metaphors we live by*. Chicago: The University of Chicago Press.

Levesque-Lopman, L. (1988). *Claiming reality: Phenomenology and women's experience*. Totowa, NJ: Rowman & Littlefield.

Lindlof, T. (1995). *Qualitative communication research methods*. Thousand Oaks, CA: Sage.

Lotz, A. D. (2000). Assessing qualitative television audience research: Incorporating feminist and anthropological theoretical innovation. *Communication Theory, 10*(4), 447–467.

Maine, M. (2000). *Body wars: Making peace with women's bodies*. Carlsbad: Gurze Books.

Marshall, C., & Rossman, G. B. (1995). *Designing qualitative research*. Thousand Oaks, CA: Sage.

McCracken, E. (1993). *Decoding women's magazines: From "Mademoiselle" to "Ms."* New York: MacMillan Press.

Messaris, P. (1997). *Visual persuasion: The role of images in advertising*. Thousand Oaks, CA: Sage.

Miller, J., & Glassner, B. (1997). The "inside" and the "outside": Finding realities in interviews. In D. Silverman (Ed.), *Qualitative research: Theory, method and practice* (pp. 99–112). London: Sage.

Orbach, S. (1978). *Fat is a feminist issue*. New York: Paddington Press.

Poulton, T. (1996). *No fat chicks: How women are brainwashed to hate their bodies and spend their money*. Toronto: Key Porter Books Ltd.

Sarabia, A. L. (1995). Notes for a framework for the analysis of women, media and violence. In B. Tankha (Ed.), *Communication and democracy: Ensuring plurality* (pp. 119–129). Penang: Southbound Sdn. Bhd.

Storey, J. (1993). *An introductory guide to cultural theory and popular culture*. Athens: University of Georgia Press.

Thompson, G. (1997). *Rhetoric through media*. Boston: Allyn & Bacon.

van Zoonen, L. (1994). *Feminist media studies*. London: Sage.

van Zoonen, L. (1995). Gender, representation and the media. In J. Downing, A. Moham-madi, & A. Sreberny-Mohammadi (Eds.), *Questioning the media: A critical introduction* (pp. 311–328). Thousand Oaks, CA: Sage.

Walker, R. (1985). *Applied qualitative research*. Brookfield, VT: Gower.

Walsh-Childers, K., & Brown, J. D. (1993). Adolescents' acceptance of sex-role stereotypes and television viewing. In B. S. Greenberg, J. D. Brown, & N. Buerkel-Rothfuss (Eds.), *Media, sex and the adolescent* (pp. 117–133). Cresskill, NJ: Hampton Press.

Walters, S. D. (1999). Sex, text, and context. In M. M. Ferree, J. Lorber, & B. B. Hess (Eds.), *Between feminism and cultural studies* (pp. 222–260). Thousaand Oaks, CA: Sage.

Wells, W., Burnett, J., & Moriarty, S. (1995). *Advertising: Principles and practice*. Englewood Cliff, NJ: Prentice-Hall.

Westkoff, M. (1990). Feminist criticism of the social sciences. In J. McCarl Nielson (Ed.), *Feminist research methods: Exemplary readings in the social sciences* (pp. 58–68). Boulder, CO: Westview Press.

Williamson, J. (1978). *Decoding advertisements*. London: Marion Boyars.

Winship, J. (1987). *Inside women's magazines*. Pandora Press: London.

Zaltman, G., & Coulter, R. H. (1995). Seeing the voice of the customer: Metaphor-based advertising research. *Journal of Advertising Research*, 35–51.

11

Kellogg's and Virginia Slims Offer Only a "Wink" to Women While New Advertising Campaigns Dare to Enter the Sign of Feminism

Vickie Rutledge Shields and Dawn Heinecken

These ads make me angry. This is an ad that is typical of a lot of advertising where women are shown in these passive positions, eyes closed, head drawn back or bowed. So I wasn't angry when I saw this ad. I've seen so many of these ads. They also make me laugh. They are so stereotypical. I don't think these are very realistic of the way most woman act: lips pouted out, head drawn back . . . the man is never shown this submissive. So, I think it is unfair. And I wouldn't agree that anyone should be submissive, so in either case I wouldn't like the submission or the power that is shown.

—Ginger (aged 25)

That's not the meaning of life, to look good. What about my personality, my mind? People forget about that . . . [A]s long as we buy magazines like [*Cosmo*] then we'll always have the sexy girl mentality and the perfect man mentality. We'll never become ourselves.

—Jamie (aged 22)

Embedded in these comments by female participants in a larger reception study[1] of idealized gender images in advertising is the desire to find images of women that project qualities of independence and subjectivity (see Shields, 1999; Shields

201

& Heinecken, 2002). Many ads today address this desire. In the past 15 years or so marketers have made a concerted effort to develop ad campaigns that seem to speak directly to female experience. Advertisers have tried also to capitalize on the fact that after 30 years of second-wave feminist rhetoric infusing U.S. popular culture, women seem more conscious than ever that full-time body work may not be the most productive use of their time and resources, while at the same time the cultural media traps (women's magazines, commercial television, print advertising) that suggest women should devote their time to body work are as persuasive as ever. Real women find themselves pulled between these competing discourses (see Shields & Heinecken, 2002). It is at this particular juncture that advertisers for products such as Special K cereal, for example, have exploited this rhetorical schizophrenia. Advertisers have also picked up on the fact that women are tired of the size 4 body being presented as "every woman" across media. However, most of these ad campaigns offer a "wink" toward women's desire for empowering images and not a viable alternative to traditional "sex sells" campaigns.

Advertising scholar Daniel Nicholson (1997) described the wink—or self-referentiality—within an ad: when advertisers want the reader to recognize that "we know you know what we're trying to do, but because we're letting you know we know, it makes it okay—because we're so hip to your hipness. Get it?" (pp. 182-183). The wink is one way that advertisers have co-opted the images and ideologies of social movements and used them to sell products. Nicholson, for example, wrote that ads that wink have

> appropriated the resistant, anti-establishment attitudes of Generation X and commodified them for the purpose of selling resistant, antiestablishment identities in order to make money. They rely on the frustration, or *weltschmerz*, of their target market and offer an outlet for expressing this discontentment, and in doing so, circumvent the affective agency of the individuals who compose the antiestablishment group. Social activism is replaced by fashion and resistance is contained within the marketplace. (p. 194)

The wink can also be construed as a post-feminist attitude (Dow, 1996), a covert acknowledgment that social equality for women has been achieved and the only politics worth pursuing are the micro-politics of one's own life. Gender politics play out at the individual level, political correctness is no longer necessary, and shows like U.S. cable channel Comedy Central's *The Man Show* are not criticized as backlash, but received as *satire*.[2] The problem with this style of presentation is that it suggests the world is really changing or has significantly changed, while maintaining the status quo in gender representation.

This is not surprising. It is important to remember that ads exist to make money for groups who have a vested interest in maintaining current power relations. Stuart Hall and Sut Jhally in their writings, but more explicitly in the Media Education Foundation videos, *Representation and the Media* (Hall, 1996) and

Dreamworlds II (Jhally, 1997), theorized that media censorship is the norm. Corporate media now dominate the globe and control the production and distribution of media texts. We are only seeing those texts that tend to reflect their interests. Ads that provide liberatory messages for any disempowered social group may threaten these interests. For example, if a woman was to feel good about herself, she would have little reason to purchase the latest in diet products.

Most attempts to radically change media representation for those groups who have traditionally been "symbolically annihilated"[3] have come from those who are outside the dominant media system. Alternative media has an important place in activism and disruption to traditional media systems in the form of exposing viewers to alternatives. However, access by mainstream audiences to alternative media is not always guaranteed. Although the leftist academic agenda has concentrated its creative energies primarily on alternative interventions, the stifling codes and conventions of White, male, heterosexist media flourished in the end of the 20th century and into the new millennium. Thus, it is important to examine mainstream texts that follow dominant conventions of production but also have the potential to challenge and disrupt dominant forms of representation.

This chapter provides close readings of selected media texts targeted to women that adopt a more progressive and "feminist" rhetoric either overtly or covertly. We examined ads from sources that could be expected to offer a range of images because of their different positions relative to the dominant media industry. Ads from the first 6 months of 2000 were drawn from *Cosmopolitan*, a major mainstream fashion magazine that could be expected to offer dominant imagery, as well as *Mode*, a fashion magazine that negotiated with dominant imagery in that it glorified plus-size women while maintaining an emphasis on beauty. Finally, we selected radio and television ads from the National Abortion and Reproductive Rights Action League (NARAL) because of the organization's explicit political agenda as well as its connection to feminist movements. These ads were broadcast in the United States on commercial radio stations and the four major commercial television networks as part of NARAL's 1998–1999 national campaign and were airing nationally at the time of this study.

The objective of this chapter is to provide a theoretical mapping of the differentiation between mainstream mediated messages that propose to advance the cause of feminism in their verbal and visual rhetoric and those that contain specific criticisms of women's social experiences and thereby can be described as more progressive forms of gender representation. The following analysis outlines examples of the wink in action, demonstrating how these ads suggest change but actually work to reconfirm the status quo by co-opting feminist signifiers and reattaching them to regressive, patriarchal codes. The analysis then moves to two specific media texts that are attempting to implode cultural expectations from within the aesthetics and conventions of well-established and popular media forms: the women's magazine and the commercial radio and TV ad.

The Wink

A series of recent *Special K*[4] ads highlight the way the wink functions. For example, a television ad campaign in the mid-1990s suggested that women should not be taken in by the prescriptions they see in the media, but rather, they should accept themselves. This particular campaign does not linger visually on any female body, but features a woman, probably in her 40s, moving to light music as if in a yoga class. She is shot in soft focus, no full body shots are revealed and no body fetishes are lingered over. The irony of this message of self-acceptance is that it was *Special K* commercials in the first place that got American women to obsess in the 1970s about whether they could "Pinch an inch." *Special K's* ad campaign was more of a prescription than an ad slogan and tapped directly into a culture of thin-obsessed girls and women who were willing to take advice on how to achieve thinness from almost anywhere, even a cereal commercial. Years later, around the same time they were suggesting that women just relax and accept their bodies and themselves, a print ad in women's magazines featured a small floral bikini simply lying against a white background. The caption reads "It's not doing any good in your drawer." Again, *Special K* could not resist tapping into one of U.S. women's phobias—being seen in a bathing suit. Therefore, it would seem that over three decades, the marketers of *Special K* suffer from a type of schizophrenia.

Subsequent ads for *Special K* seem to be one of the biggest winks toward women yet. The television ads feature supermodel Cindy Crawford first making fun of her/our participation in fashion trends and then suggesting it is just as silly to participate in eating fads, finally suggesting that *Special K* has always been and remains a sensible dietary food choice; positioned somehow outside of diet trends. A very natural looking and unglamorous Crawford is metaphorically winking at us. She is saying, "I know that you know I've probably done as much as anybody to make you feel paranoid about your body through two decades of modeling, but when we are all in our jeans and t-shirts we are just the same—responsible grown-ups who can live both in and outside of diet trends and fads—Right?"

Another *Special K* ad that can be seen as reflecting a "feminist" aesthetic is a TV commercial, shot in black and white, featuring a group of middle-aged men sitting around a bar, complaining about their bodies (Kilbourne, 1999). "I have my mother's thighs" one man sighs, "I just have to accept that." The copy seemingly asks female viewers: "Why do we worry?" because it is ludicrous for women to worry about things like their weight. But notice how real-life differences are being erased here: The ad ignores the fact that women's concern over appearance and weight is not a choice made freely; women are obsessed with body image because the culture demands it of them. The ad is thus making fun of women for reacting and responding to the demands of the sexist culture in which we live (aren't we silly?) It also suggests that *Special K* is the solution to our unreasonable neuroses:

we can adopt a "healthy" attitude toward food and our bodies if we choose to eat the cereal. Once again, *Special K* is asking us to ignore its role in creating women's body obsession.

The wink toward women in ads is now a popular, if not commonplace technique. However, several recent examples suggest that there are media texts that, using the conventions of dominant production, have at least the potential to present positive images of women. While traditionally, advertising images have constructed women as passive objects of a sexualized gaze and as a commodity, positive images of women would include images of active, empowered women who possess sexual agency and who are valued for more than their appearance (Goffman, 1979; Kilbourne, 1999). Ads contained within such media texts are encoded with feminist signs of gender equality and representation. Indeed, what is so interesting about these ads is the way *they* have co-opted dominant imagery from mainstream texts. Although these ads certainly exist to sell products they nonetheless simultaneously offer images that may empower women.

Mode

One example of a media text with the potential to empower is *Mode* magazine. *Mode* received much publicity for its stated intent to provide attractive images of women that reflect the diversity of women, both size-wise and racially. *Mode* began as a quarterly publication in 1997 with a US circulation of 250,000, rising to 615,000 by 2001. Late in 2001, *Mode* had an estimated readership of 3.5 million.[5] However, the pro-plus-sized publication went out of business that same year. It is unclear at this point which factors led to *Mode*'s demise: unsound business practices, too little market share, or the magazine's inability to break into "point-of-purchase"[6] shelf space. However, unlike *Big, Bold and Beautiful*, another U.S. magazine that caters to larger women, *Mode*'s stated goal was to promote a positive self-image for women of all sizes. Reflecting the unwillingness to label by size, until January 2000 the cover of *Mode* used to read "*Mode: 12, 14, 16 . . .*" In its last 2 years, the cover simply read "*Mode: The New Shape in Fashion.*" As such, it presented itself as not only anti-fat oppression, but anti-sizeism. For example, in the February 2000 issue under the regular feature "Mode Matters" a story titled, "Can't Lick It!" addresses how sizeism affects all women, thick or thin:

> Size discrimination in Hollywood has taken a new turn. Lara Flynn Boyle, Jennifer Aniston, Calista Flockhart, and others are being referred to as "The Lollipop Girls" (big heads, stick bodies). After our initial snicker, we realized that it's still size discrimination. We believe no one should look to anyone for validation. Give your body what it needs to live a happy life. Oh, and of course, read *Mode* for real inspiration. (Day, 2000, p. 32)

The slightly knowing, "in with the joke" tone in the last sentence of "Lollipop Girls" cues us into another quality of *Mode*. It presumed and played on a high-level of media literacy and the fact that its readers were cognizant of the pressures found in mainstream advertising. In other words, its readers were already presumed to be negotiating or resistant readers. This is clearly evidenced in the letters to the editor section, which offered much more interesting and often critical responses to the content of *Mode* than are found in other magazines. For example, in the February 2000 edition, MH wrote:

> Regarding your recent query about *Mode* men, please don't go there!!! Virtually every other women's magazine on the market has scores of article on men, sex, dating, etc. The very thing that keeps me hooked on *Mode* is that it helps me (at size 14-16) look the best *I* can. I don't need any more advice on relationships or men or anything else. Please keep your wonderful magazine in its original, fresh, relevant, and helpful state. (p. 21)

MH worried that *Mode* would become too much like other magazines with an insistence on compulsory heterosexuality. However, it is clear from many reader and editorial comments, as well as advertising imagery, that part of the appeal of *Mode* was based on how it took images that are currently outside the dominant frame and attempted to normalize them. Letters to the editor consistently expressed the relief (and inherently the past pain) experienced by many women at finally recognizing themselves in ads. Part of the appeal of *Mode* was that it made women feel like they belonged, that they, and their size, were "normal," even beautiful, and that they too could indulge in the pleasures of other women, like fashion magazines and style.

"Magic in Manila" wrote:

> Oh my. It was the first time I'd ever seen a glossy magazine that delighted and inspired me! The models on your pages actually have tummies. They are shaped just like me! I've always been full-figured, and my whole life has been a struggle for acceptance. Your magazine has boosted my self-esteem to such a high level that I feel great about my body. Even the Just My Size ad (the one that goes "I am not 100 pounds...") brings tears to my eyes. (p. 21)

> When looking in *Mode*, I realized something; that you don't have to be thin to be beautiful and sexy! When flipping through your January issue, I saw something that changed my life—a photo of one of your models. I stared at that beautiful woman for a long time with my mouth open. My first thought was, "She is beautiful!" Then I thought, "I am beautiful!" Never in my life have I had these feelings about myself. I could not have asked for a better Christmas gift than this. (AP, Bloomington, IN, March 2000, p. 44)

Unlike *Ms.*, *Mode* did not take a "feminist" perspective per se and was not presented as an alternative magazine. *Mode*'s glossy paper was like that of any mainstream fashion magazine. The advertisements reflected traditional advertising aesthetics, but also offered more images of "normal"-sized women. Indeed, the content, format, and style of *Mode* were much like any other fashion magazine. The articles dealt with dating tips, new seasonal styles, a health and fitness section, make-up tips, and bridal pages. The products offered inside its covers were primarily clothing and make-up, with an occasional car ad or other product featured. *Mode* stressed the fact that all women want to be and can be stylish. The similarity of *Mode* to other fashion magazines meant that women could read *Mode* without feeling ostracized from other women. The magazine was not positioned as alternative or other, but as addressing the same concerns other women's magazines have—with the exception of representing greater diversity of size.

Nonetheless, it is noteworthy that although the rhetoric of anti-sizeism was clear and there was a repeated editorial insistence on the dangers of labeling, *Mode* actually did quite a bit of size labeling. Many letters to the editor, feature profiles on notable women, and blurbs on the magazine models featured some kind of reference to their size, framed usually within a clothing size (14-16 or 22). While on one hand this reinforced the idea of size as a label, it also projected and spoke what is usually unspoken for women of normal and heavier weights and/or sizes. By speaking and naming the size as 22 or 18, those sizes were rendered more acceptable. Yet this also reinforced the idea of women fitting into precategorized shapes. This is particularly interesting because the meaning of a "size 14" varies from designer to designer.

It is important to note, however, that the actual number of women of different shapes, sizes, and ethnicity may be less important to readers than the fact that *Mode* offered *any* differing images. Given the impassioned reaction by readers, it is worthwhile to examine the codes at play within ads that break with traditional imagery. What is it that caused these ads to stand out and be read in such a positive light?

It is interesting that there was so little difference between *Mode*'s ads and other mainstream fashion ads. In the ads more than in any other part of the magazine *Mode* seemed to resort more to winking at women than offering interventions in dominant ideology. This makes sense, because the content of the ads was not produced by the editorial staff of the magazine. *Mode*'s ads may have shifted the size of the model used, but otherwise the ads remained much the same. When standard advertisements are placed in progressive publications there is a dampening effect first identified by Gloria Steinem in 1990, the critical date when *Ms.* adopted a no-ad policy. According to Steinem (1990), "what became more and more clear is how few media are able to give consumers facts that may displease advertisers" (p. 17). In *Mode*, the different sizes and shapes of its models remained contextualized within a traditional discourse of individuality and choice and the products advertised were primarily for cosmetics, fashion, and cigarettes.

An example of this traditional rhetoric can be found in a *Virginia Slims* ad appearing in the March 2000 issue of *Mode*. It is a two-page spread featuring an older, but thin and noticeably blonde woman with short-cropped hair and piercingly blue eyes, staring aggressively out at the reader. The copy, placed on the left-hand page, reads: "I look temptation right in the eye and then I make my own decision. *Virginia Slims*. Find Your Voice." This ad is typical of its kind in that it has co-opted the language of feminism, for example, using the feminist image of "voice" as a term of empowerment to sell cigarettes. This woman is so strong that she refuses to run away from her own desires (to smoke), as she looks "temptation" in the eye. She isn't controlled by others (like the medical community or the boring status quo) but makes her own decisions. She doesn't smoke just because it is cool or socially acceptable—she is a rugged individual who is "empowered" enough to *choose* to smoke. Smoking is a sign of her rebellion against those who would silence "her voice," her articulation of her individuality and personal perspective.

The *Virginia Slims* ad is notable because of the ironic promotion of the use of an addictive drug as a means to achieve female empowerment. However, its rhetoric of individuality and choice is fairly typical of advertising and, when not contextualized against the selling of cigarettes, seems to connect more easily with a "feminist" sensibility (Kellner, 1990). *Mode* ran ads with similar discourses of individuality and choice associated with the "new woman" rhetoric, using standard ideas of femininity, but combining them with alternative body sizes to create a new discourse of body acceptance. Many of the ads focused on transformation and on freedom as meaning not only freedom from others but of freedom from negative opinions about the self.

Just My Size pantyhose has created a series of ads that are quite successful in this tactic, titled "Just My Opinion" that consistently run in *Mode* magazine. In one ad, the left-hand bottom shows a color picture of an African-American woman partially reclining against some pillows with one leg stretched in the air and her hand caressing her leg. She wears a black bra, white pearls, a wedding band on her finger, and a pair of pantyhose. She is smiling and looking out at the spectator. Although part of her stomach is hidden by her arm and leg, we can see the fleshy creases around her lower belly, and her legs and partially exposed bottom appear thick. Her skin has a rich brown sheen. Her eyes sparkle. She looks like she is glowing. Partially printed across this image are the words "I am the product of a lifetime of learning." The image works against the grain of the anti-age aesthetic by stressing the "lifetime of learning"; weight is somehow being associated with knowledge and experiences. That experience, as suggested by the wedding ring, includes a man. Her pearls signify economic stability.

The woman in this ad is clearly posed in a way that is sexual. Half dressed, she reclines on what appears to be a couch, but there is a blanket that is half pulled off. Obviously the sight of a large-sized woman being shown in *dishabille* and posed sexually is new, even for the pages of *Mode*. The idea of "looseness" that the ad urges goes against most traditional ideas of advertising. Most ads urge for control over "loose" bodies that threaten to go out of control. This *Just My Size* ad clearly equates a large, lived-in body with sexuality, a romantic life and comfort.

The power of this image, particularly for those who have not seen their images represented as attractive or sexual, should not be overlooked. The psycho-sexual rejection of many fat women, the exclusion from "normalcy," is powerful in its negativity. Exclusion means that not only is one different—but in an odd way one is almost inhuman. Goldman (1992) explained that the power of the gaze in advertisements is invoked more by what ads conceal than what they make visible:

> These ads conceal diverse forms of terror experienced by women who objectify themselves. There is the mundane psychic terror associated with not receiving "looks" of admiration—i.e., of not having others validate one's appearance. A similar sense of terror involves the fear of "losing one's looks"—the quite reasonable fear that aging will deplete one's value and social power. A related source of anxiety involves fears about "losing control" over body weight and appearance. The neurotic obsession with body and food has become the scourge of young women (p. 123).

A fat woman loses her right to sexuality—the very thing that defines her as a woman (supposedly). Unlike most ads, it does not associate fat bodies with negativity or low self-esteem, but high self-esteem. There appears to be a contradiction here. Feminist scholars generally argue against the objectification of woman. Why then might it be desirable to objectify large women anymore than thin women? The difference is in the right to be seen as a sexual object. Ads gain their meaning from context—from their relationship to other ads as well as their relationship to the larger world. As Sut Jhally (1990) observed, there is nothing inherently bad about visual objectification. It is part of human nature to objectify and to want to be objectified at times. The evaluation of that objectification as positive or negative comes from the image's relationship to other images in a system. In a sign system in which female sexuality and objectification is a sign of female success, the absence of objectified heavy women as sexual means that they are symbolically annihilated from being seen as sexual beings. In U.S. culture, an advertising standard continually urges women to take up less space and control their desires. These *Just My Size* pantyhose ads are radical in that they present the large woman as being not only normal, but refined.

Signs of Feminism: NARAL Ads

Another series of ads work as feminist, not by distancing themselves from the concepts of individuality utilized by most advertisers, but, curiously, by co-opting them; reframing messages of individuality, placing them in a new context in a way that does work for feminist goals. These advertising campaigns may be read as interventions in that they consciously deal with the female body as a contested terrain over which political and ideological battles are fought (Shields, 2003).

In the mainstream media, we often see the female body being depicted as a sexualized object. As an object, of course, female bodies lose subjectivity and individuality. The attitude that fosters this dehumanization of the female body is accompanied by and linked to attitudes in which the female becomes separated from her body. Depicting women as dehumanized objects removes their subjectivity. If the female body is an object to be enjoyed and controlled by others, then the female herself has no right to her body: no right to control her body against the advances of others, no right to sexual pleasure in her own body, and no right to control her reproductive choices.

Obviously, there is a give-and-take relationship between cultural attitudes toward women's right to control their own bodies and their media presentations. Recent pro-choice ads have chosen a very interesting approach by which to transmit their message. The NARAL "Choice for America" campaign co-opts the rhetoric and discourses of the right-wing and anti-choice factions. These ads frame reproductive rights as being intrinsically linked to "American" values of individuality and freedom—the foundation of subjectivity. They also co-opt the language of faith and responsibility frequently used in pro-life rhetoric. In using these tactics, NARAL promotes female subjectivity at the same time that the body is presented for examination. Yet because the female body is repositioned amidst images of individuality and choice, the viewer is asked to reconsider the meaning of gazing at the female body.

NARAL strategically uses imagery that presents America as made up of a group of individuals from all walks of life. For example, one radio ad features a "monologue" in which each line is delivered by a different voice, suggesting a range of speakers of different races and genders. It features both male and female voices.

> We the people. We the people. We the people. Live in the land of the free. We live in a country founded on freedom. Freedom of speech. Freedom to vote. Freedom to choose my faith. Freedom to choose what's right for me. My family. My life. My body. We the people. Have fought for this freedom. To make sure that every pregnancy is wanted. And every woman is blessed with health and reproductive freedom. We will protect this freedom against violence, harassment and intimidation. It's not always easy. But we live in the home of the brave. Understand and protect your right to choose. . . . The choice is yours to decide. The choice is yours to keep.

NARAL ads play with themes of individuality and concepts of individual freedom as an essential "American" quality. They also explicitly reference the battles that Americans have fought, equating the pro-choice position with protection against the "invasion" of foreign forces. This is typically a right-wing rhetoric used against the perceived threat of forces that would "invade" and take over the "American" way of life—such as the Soviets during the Cold War and most recently the terrorism of Islamic extremists. The ad appeals to the history of the American military by evoking images of battle and bravery and America as a nation of fighters.

The use of the word *blessed* is telling. It presents freedom as a "natural" gift and also suggests that NARAL is articulating a religious view. In contrast to those who would argue that abortion is a godless act, the ad suggests that not only does God exist, but that God sanctions choice and NARAL is the correct interpreter of God's wishes. The appeal to the pro-life ideal of protecting life is altered as the ad references social responsibility as including concern for the well-being of woman and child.

Much of the ad presents images of basic American beliefs that most people would agree with such as free speech and religion. The use of multiple voices evokes inclusion, plurality and the idea of the melting pot. It recalls the fact that the United States is made up of immigrants who came to America to have freedom, religious as well as economic. The inclusion of male voices separates abortion from being a "woman's" issue to one that is intrinsically connected with every American's right to individual civil liberties and our unspoken but ubiquitous notions of citizenship. It is only at the end of the ad, by now thoroughly framed within the context of this traditional rhetoric, that a pro-choice statement is revealed.

Of course, radio is a medium in which sound, not sight, is the primary means of communication. The acoustic nature of radio helps divorce abstract issues like freedom and independence from the body. By removing the messy, problematic body from sight, the groundedness of the battle, the fact that it has to do with flesh and blood bodies (both of the woman and the fetus) is diminished. The issue becomes abstracted. Rhetoric, language, assumes primary importance, while the sign of women's subjugation (the reproductive, sexual, objectified body) becomes absent from this discourse. How, then, does NARAL deal with the medium of television, in which the hiding of the body, given its visual basis, becomes impossible?

Several ads highlight the techniques used by NARAL to circumnavigate the traditional signification of women's bodies. For example, one recent NARAL ad features a montage of women of different races and ages and in different activities. Images of women in action, families, and close-ups of women's faces are juxtaposed against a sound track of the song "America" and a voice-over monologue delivered by a young to middle-aged woman. A shot by shot analysis of how this ad constructs its message is worthwhile here.

The voice-over states:

I believe there's a reason we were born with free will. And I have a strong will to decide what's best for my body. My mind. And my life. I believe in myself. In my intelligence. In my integrity, my judgment. And I accept full responsibility for the decisions I make. I believe in my right to choose. Without interrogations, without indignities, without violence. I believe that's one of the founding principles of our country. And I believe that right is being threatened. The greatest of human freedoms is choice. And I believe that no one has the right to take that freedom away.

Visually, the ad starts with a long shot of a family, against the background of the desert. They are in the lower right-hand corner of the screen framed by landscape. The landscape, gray and expansive, dominates the screen. The effect of the powerful majesty of nature is enhanced by the rolling clouds, which move swiftly overhead. They are filmed with time-elapse photography, a technique that emphasizes the tumultuous power of the clouds at the same time as it contrasts them to the stillness of the family and the landscape. The visual effect is one of timelessness, that despite the constant changes and progress of time, two constants remain: the rugged, unspoiled wilderness and the American family.

Again, this ad plays with several ideas that draw on traditional right-wing rhetoric and imagery. First, the ad plays with notions of individuality and American freedom. The notion of 'free will' recalls typical Protestant religious sensibilities and the founding of the United States as based on religious freedom as well as the desire for self-government. In contrast to the notion of women who get abortions as being "irresponsible" and uncaring about the welfare of others, the voiceover states that responsibility occurs in the act of *choosing*, rather than in the final decision.

In a counter-intuitive moment, female bodies are fetishized in this ad. But it is done in a way that works to emphasize their unique, singular, impervious, individuality—much like the figure of the western cowboy hero in Zane Grey Westerns.[7] The ad consistently juxtaposes close-ups of female and male faces with scenes of bodies in motion and bodies placed against a landscape.

As in the radio ad, there is a connotation of plurality. The wide variety of faces creates a sense of a melting pot, as well as a shared subjectivity. Although many of the faces are of women, several male faces are included. Once again, the issue of freedom is not a "woman's" issue, but is one that concerns men as well. Additionally, the close-ups of faces are always shot from a low angle. The viewer is put into a slightly inferior position to the person being viewed. The women are often slightly out of frame, caught turning toward the viewer. This breaks with the static position of woman as object. By placing the woman slightly out of the frame, her body is extending beyond the frame of the camera—she continues on, out into space beyond the viewer's gaze. Thus, although we see her in close-up, she resists being pinned by the gaze. Similarly, the turning body conveys a sense of moving out into space. The women in these close ups are often looking at the viewer, returning the gaze, a move which in music videos is said to refute the male gaze (Kaplan, 1989).

Other women in the ad are shown in motion—engaged in activities such as hiking, swimming, or playing with children. Their physicality breaks against traditional representations of women as passive. The two girls hiking are shown on a mountain pinnacle. Again, we see them from below. Their positioning recalls imagery of triumphant explorers, who have conquered nature and physical hardships and climbed the top of Everest. It recalls the statue of the Battle of Iwo Jima with the soldiers struggling to a peak to raise their flag.[8]

Scenes featuring a mother releasing her daughter into the adult world project an all-American image of nurturing. They call upon the commonplace imagery of Americans doing battle for freedom, not only for themselves, but for the protection of future generations. This again connects to military imagery in which soldiers died in the past to protect the rights of others. Similarly, the sacrifices made by past Americans to ensure the future are referenced by the elderly couple seated in front of the flag. The presence of the flag waving at full mast in many of these scenes similarly reinforces imagery of "America" that is tied to battles.

The close up of the mother's hand—importantly the only body part on these women besides their faces that is fragmented—shows the hand in the act of release. Another NARAL ad extends upon the imagery of the mother and daughter in this previous ad. Once again filmed in slow motion, the mother launches the daughter on her bike. The mother watches in joy as her daughter rides her bike straight off into the camera.

> I want every good thing in the world for you. I want you to know, right down to your toes, that all of life's choices are open to you. Sure, you'll skin your knees along the way. But you'll learn. That it's your body, your life and your responsibility. Never give up the freedom to choose. Your dreams are tied to it.

This ad co-opts ideas of nurturing motherhood as the basis for American values and society—a bedrock of American mythology that is tied to the idea of America as a place where dreams for the future come true. In order to achieve the American dream, daughters will need choice. In this way, the act of letting go is shown to be a nurturing, protective move. It calls upon the idea of not only letting one's children grow up to be responsible, productive citizens who are self-reliant and able to make their own choices, but also the idea that relinquishing control over others is a caring, nurturing act.

There is an interesting play with images of time occurring in the NARAL ads. The ads are filmed in such a way that the sense of imminence, of being in the moment, is extended, even fetishized, thus connecting to a sense of timelessness, of infinity. This timeless quality is further enhanced by the use of muted colors and the overexposed quality of many of the images. The ads' gritty, overexposed appearance is not realistic, but instead seems hyper-realistic at the same time it signals a break with reality. John Berger (1972) talked about the difference between nude and naked. The naked is a representation of a naked body, whereas the nude is a stylized version, a particular way of seeing in which the naked body is transformed into being more than it is, invested with meaning outside of itself, a symbol. Likewise, color in these ads moves beyond a realistic representation in order to heighten the visual importance of what we are seeing.

In these two ads, the visual fetishization of the moment, through camera work, slow-motion, and time-elapse techniques and color, does something else. It *heightens* the importance of the body at the same time it strengthens the female body. Presenting the body as an object is not necessarily an act of oppression. Men, after all, are regularly photographed without losing their subjectivity. The different interpretations of these images are informed not only by the differing cultural connotations in which they are received but by the *way* in which their bodies are filmed. Male bodies, even when filmed in a slightly fetishistic manner, as they are in action movies and westerns (Tasker, 1995; Tompkins, 1992), inspire different cultural connotations about their owners relative power and penetrability than do images of women (Bordo, 1999). One reason that male subjectivity is reinforced is that they are always *more* than their bodies.

This imagery has been carefully crafted to appeal to people from all political positions. Although most U.S. Republicans may be against many progressive social reforms, many would agree that women have the right to work and be independent. The NARAL ads are quite clever, co-opting the language of imagery of its adversaries. The rhetoric of motherly love as both protective and encouraging of self-reliance is one that appeals to all sides of the political spectrum, as does the American mythology of the successful individual. The ads also work to create a sense of timelessness—that the values NARAL supports are natural, blessed by God, and are eternal.

Conclusion

In recent years, advertisers seem to have recognized that women are tired of being presented with uniform, unrealistic visions of the "ideal" woman. As a result, they have created campaigns that on one hand seem to address women's concerns, while on the other hand offer only a wink toward women. The wink is a way of addressing the audience, suggesting that social equality for women has already been achieved. However, closer examination reveals that the wink is one way that traditionally conservative ideals are recycled into a more palatable "feminist" or progressive framework, while in fact achieving no real significant change in how women are represented.

Nonetheless, there are the isolated incidents of media forms examined here that seem to be seriously trying to present more "positive" images of women. *Mode* magazine provides a useful case study here in that the magazine presented itself as an anti-sizest fashion magazine. Although *Mode* often failed to present the progressive images it purported to embrace, it was nonetheless somewhat successful in normalizing some images, such as those of large-size women who have previously been outside the dominant frame. The success of such ads can at least partly be measured by letters to *Mode*'s editor that consistently expressed the joy readers felt at finally recognizing themselves in ads and in magazine articles. The *Just My* Size pantyhose ad works to correct two kinds of symbolic annihilation at once, that of the self-possessed Black woman and that of the large woman.

However, it is important to note that *Mode*'s ads share more in common with mainstream magazine ads than depart from them. The different sizes and shapes of *Mode*'s models, no matter how revolutionary, remained contextualized within a traditional discourse of consumption, individuality and choice and divorced from any collective political agenda aimed at social change.

Rhetoric of individuality and choice, however, has been co-opted by at least one ad campaign that is revolutionary and progressive, consciously dealing with the female body as a site where political and ideological battles are fought. NARAL's ad campaign reinforces notions of individuality. However, its use of camera work, slow motion, and color does this in a way that emphasizes the body's unique, singular, and seemingly impervious qualities. Recalling the way that men's bodies have been glorified in western and action films, the women of the NARAL ads always seem to be *more* than their bodies, imbued with an over-determination of meaning connected to individuality. In this way, NARAL ads move from presenting the female body as object, to presenting the body as a sign of subjectivity. Unlike *Special K*'s mythology of the individual women's new-found body acceptance as a means to sell cereal, NARAL ads tie their imagery to a legitimate feminist goal.

What are criteria that distinguish those ads that merely wink versus those that offer genuine interventions? One distinction can clearly be made based on the commodity that is being sold and whether or not the commodity has liberatory potential for consumers. In public service announcements, the product being "sold" is an ideology. Ideology "becomes commodified and [is] the direct object of consumption" (Montes-Armenteros, 1997, p. 148). NARAL ads are quite clearly selling a political position. Despite their co-optation of the discourse and their appropriation of images from the political right, NARAL ads present a clear counter-hegemonic ideology. "Buying into" the message of these ads means that you acknowledge the ad's political position.

In contrast, ads that wink work to erase political awareness. In this way, the wink is part of the postmodern trend in popular media in which the meaning of differences are flattened and erased—differences like race, class, gender that people *live* and experience in very concrete ways. As signs and meanings are re-appropriated and re-framed, dislocated from their original context, they increasing become seen as equivalent. "Instead of distinctions, endless *differences* reign—an undifferentiated pastiche of differences, a grab bag in which no items are assigned any more importance or centrality than any others" (Bordo, 1999,

p. 258). Bordo exemplified this in her example of audience readings of an ad featuring a black model wearing blue contact lenses as merely fashion. Audiences see the adoption of blue eyes as an individual choice and ignore the racist cultural context in which such a *choice* is made.

The result of making all differences the same is to create an equivalency between political positions. Such postmodern ads seem to present a view from nowhere, but in fact, every position is a view from somewhere. The self-reflexive nature of ads that wink work similarly to erase the difference between producer and audience—they suggest that the viewer and the producer are on the same page, that they understand each other, and that this is a joke shared by both. Thus, the producer cannot be read as manipulating audience viewpoints. But what is hidden is the position from which the producer is really speaking. For example, the wink in *Special K* ads continues to reflect sexist ideologies as well as the desire for profit. The ad in which the men complain about their bodies suggests that men could be paranoid about their bodies but choose not to—a suggestion that ignores the relative positions of men and women in society. For many women, "choosing" to ignore their appearance can result in real-world negative repercussions and is thus no choice at all.

What sets the *Mode* and NARAL ads apart from other contemporary advertising is that these ads speak *from* and *to* specific positions—they are, on the surface, political. It is important to note that hegemony means that we believe that it is common sense that things work the way they do, and the ideologies and practices that keep culture the way it is are fairly transparent. Hegemony is also "leaky" (Hall, 1997), allowing for counter-hegemonic moments to occur. *Mode* magazine can be considered an earnest attempt at creating a counter-hegemonic moment in the production, distribution, and consumption of women's magazines. It encouraged readers to question at least *some* facets of dominant culture. Even though *Mode* urged its readers to conform to other conventional standards of femininity, and stressed individuality and "agency" based on consumption, the fact that different body sizes and colors were presented at all, along with an explicit anti-sizest discourse, separate *Mode* from texts like *Special K* ads. Although *Special K* ads ultimately reinforce the same old message—"Be thin, have the proper attitude, buy this"—*Mode*'s message asked, "Why be thin? You *have* the proper attitude, buy this."

Many *Mode* ads, in effect, function as consciousness-raising tools. Not only do they directly speak to viewers' knowledge and awareness of the unfair focus on women's looks, but in doing so, they *validate* this personal knowledge, encouraging a conscious recognition of the arbitrariness of beauty norms. As reader letters reveal, by showing women that they too can be beautiful these ads open up space for readers to begin to question what is and what is not really beautiful—to question the status quo—a small step, but one that is nonetheless counter-hegemonic. They also serve to show that the messages of female "independence," bodily integrity and individuality coded in the ads find an eager audience in females. This is good news since the promise of individuality and subjectivity for women continues to be a feminist goal.

Although the advertising campaigns discussed here shed some positive light on how advertising can be made more woman-friendly, it is necessary to examine the advertising tactics that stress individuality, since this rhetoric is often employed at the expense of social concerns and community ethics. Only the public service announcement by NARAL can stand alone as counter-hegemonic, because in the end the social political agenda is the product and in all other advertising conditions the profit motive inherent in ads must water down the progressive political potential of those ads. No matter how positive *Mode*'s ads were and how effectively they affected women's positive self-esteem, the irony remains that when women buy into a progressive idea put forth through advertising, they also buy into the products and support major corporations whose business practices may be less than praiseworthy.

Acknowledgment

Versions of the arguments in this chapter appear in Shields with Heinecken (2002).

Notes

1. For Measuring Up: How Advertising Affects Self-Image, the pool of in-depth interview participants total 73. The core sample is a group of 15 women and 15 men who were interviewed during a 3-month period in late Fall and early Spring 1993. The remaining 43 men and women are from two other studies. The first was conducted as part of a gender and communication class at a major mid-western research university. The 73 men and women represent a fairly culturally diverse group, although not representative of the larger population. Their ages ranged from 18 to 45. The sample included six African-American women and two Hispanic women. The sample also included three gay men and five lesbians. At least 50% of the men and women in the sample were not full-time students at the time of the interviews, but working in such self-reported positions as receptionists, psychologists, house painters, artists, and "between gigs."

2. Described as "a sort of frat brother to South Park" by David Wild (1999), *The Man Show* is a cable comedy series aimed at male viewers between the ages of 18 to 34. A regular section of the series features scantily clad women bouncing on trampolines.

3. In media theory, a conspicuous and serious under-representation of certain social groups has been coined *symbolic annihilation* (Gerbner & Gross, 1976; Gross, 1991; Tuchman, Daniels, & Benet, 1978).

4. Special K is a trademark breakfast cereal manufactured by Kellogg Co. USA, a multinational corporation with headquarters in Michigan.

5. Start up circulation figures were reported in "Magazine Mode to Fit," Lexington Herald-Leader 2 April (1998) Final ed. Pg. 6. Final circulation figures reported in "Mode magazine to stop publishing" *The Write New* 24 September (2001). Writenews.com/2001/092401_mode_magazine_cease.htm

6. A point-of-purchase display refers to the prime spaces in a store where consumers make split-decision purchasing choices. These points of purchase cost advertisers more money than regular shelf space. One example is the pyramid of beer accompanied by a life-size cutout of a supermodel that stands in front of the shelf for beer. For magazines the prime point-of-purchase is at the checkout line. Most purchases of non-subscription magazines occur at the checkout. Magazines that only appear on the shelf in the store are ineligible for this last-minute impulse buy.

7. Zane Grey, the pen name for Pearl Grey, was a prolific American writer. Grey pioneered the literary genre of the western in the early 20th Century.

8. The Marine Corps War Memorial, Washington DC, is a 62-ft. bronze statue fashioned after the Pulitzer Prize winning photograph of soldiers raising the American flag after the bloody Battle of Iwo Jima in World War II.

References

Berger, J. (1972). *Ways of seeing.* London: BFI.

Bordo, S. (1999). *The male body: A new look at men in public and private.* New York: Farrar, Straus & Giroux.

Day, H. (2000, February). Can't lick it. *Mode,* p. 32.

Dow, B. J. (1996). *Prime-time feminism: Television, media culture, and the women's movement since 1970.* Philadelphia: University of Pennsylvania Press.

Gerbner, G., & Gross, L. (1976). Living with television: The violence profile. *Journal of Communication, 26*(2), 172–199.

Goffman, E. (1979). *Gender advertisements.* Cambridge, MA: Harvard University Press.

Goldman, R. (1992). *Reading ads socially.* London: Routledge.

Gross, L. (1991). Out of the mainstream: Sexual minorities and the mass media. In M. A. Wolf & A. P. Kielwasser (Eds.), *Gay people, sex and the media* (pp. 19–46). Binghamton, NY: Harryton Park/Haworth Press.

Hall S. (1996). *Representation and the media* [Video]. Amherst, MA: Media Education Foundation.

Hall, S. (1997). *Representation: Cultural representation and signifying practices.* Thousand Oaks, CA: Sage.

Jhally, S. (1990). *Dreamworlds* [Video]. Amherst, MA: Media Education Foundation.

Jhally, S. (1997). *Dreamworlds II* [Video]. Amherst, MA: Media Education Foundation.

Kaplan, E. A. (1989). *Rocking around the clock: Music, TV, postmodernism, and consumer culture.* New York: Routledge.

Kellner, D. (1990). Advertising and consumer culture. In J. Downing, A. Mohammadi, & A. Sreberny-Mohammadi (Eds.), *Questioning the media: A critical introduction* (pp. 242–254). Newbury Park, CA: Sage.

Kilbourne, J. (1999). *Deadly persuasion: Why women and girls must fight the addictive power of advertising.* New York: The Free Press.

Montes-Armenteros, C. (1997). Ideology in public service announcements. In K. Frith (Ed.), *Undressing the ad: Reading culture in advertising* (pp. 132–148). New York: Peter Lang.

Nicholson, D. (1997). The Diesel jeans and workwear advertising campaign and the commodification of resistance. In K. Frith (Ed.), *Undressing the ad: Reading culture in advertising* (pp. 175–196). New York: Peter Lang.

Shields, V. R. (1999). Advertising to the gendered audience: Using sense-making to illuminate how audiences decode advertisements of idealized female bodies. *The Electronic Journal of Communication / La Revue Electronique de Communication, 9*(3).

Shields, V. R. (2003). The less space we take, the more powerful we'll be: How advertising uses gender to invert signs of empowerment and social equality. In A. Valdivia (Ed.), *Blackwell companion to media studies* (pp. 247–271). Malden, MA: Blackwell.

Shields, V. R. with Heinecken, D. (2002). *Measuring up: How advertising affects self-image.* Philadelphia: University of Pennsylvania Press.

Steinem, G. (1990). Sex, lies and advertising. *Ms. 1*(1), 1–20.

Tasker, Y. (1995). *Spectacular bodies: Gender, genre and the action cinema.* New York: Routledge.

Tompkins, J. (1992). *West of everything. The inner life of westerns.* New York: Oxford University Press.

Tuchman, G., Daniels, A. K., & Benet, J. (Eds.) (1978). *Hearth and home: Images of women in the mass media.* New York: Oxford University Press.

Wild, D. (1999, June 24). Television. *Rolling Stone,* p. 73.

12

"Ladies Night"

Bar Flyers as a Technology of Heteronormative Construction of Gender

Aurélie Lebrun

The use of flyers[1] to advertise nocturnal events was first popularized by the European rave scene of the 1980s (Jordan, 2000; McCall, 2001; Thornton, 1995). Long considered an artistic means to promote underground culture, today, flyers are a tool of mass marketing, especially for special events, and are produced and distributed by the thousands, oftentimes by professional promotional agencies. There is enormous variety in the content and quality of flyers, ranging from handwritten photocopies to collectible works of art. Circulated strategically in spaces and places around clubs and other nightlife venues and targeting a large, young, urban audience, they are strewn on sidewalks, adorn windshields, and obscure storefronts. Now mainstream, flyers are part of any major city's landscape, including Montreal, the Canadian city from which the flyers analyzed in this chapter originate.

Arguably, nightlife, like any other commercial activity, needs to promote itself to encourage and sustain consumption of its product, and this has necessitated a constant reinvention, or a commodification of the nightlife experience. With flyers, then, clubs endorse more than just schedules, programs, openings, or special events. Rather, by using the imagery of airports and desert scenes for example, they offer the experience of "going out" for consumption—much like a voyage, an adventure, or a dream.

One type of flyer in particular, however, focuses exclusively on the representation of women's bodies in highly suggestive and sexualized ways. Women are depicted in bikinis and high heels, and some are topless, reclining, tied up, or simulating sexual acts. Furthermore, to reinforce the sexual possibilities that these flyers imply, sexually suggestive names are given to special events such as "Kamasutra Saturdays," "Sexxxy Night," "Soirée Clito-Alterno." I have collected flyers from Paris, London, Barcelona, Amsterdam, Tokyo, Toronto, New York, and Montreal, and despite cultural differences that might exist between these cities or the disparity in their respective municipal laws, there is nonetheless a common theme: The bar scene flyer aesthetic is strikingly similar to that of advertising for escort agencies and erotic boutiques. Why is this the case?

Generally speaking, women do not play a major part in the bar industry business, they are absent from the bar industry as owners, managers, or in the promotion of nightlife (McCall, 2001; McRobbie, 1994; Pini, 1997). However, women's attendance in bars and clubs is considered vital to their success (McRobbie, 2000; Pini, 1997; Thornton, 1995; Thomas, 1993), explaining why bar owners encourage female patronage by offering incentives such as free drinks and lower cover charges under the guise of "Ladies Night." But if bar owners are attempting to encourage women's presence in their clubs through advertising, why do they choose such overtly sexualized images of women on their flyers to do so? How does one reconcile this marketing phenomenon, whereby women are portrayed in sexually suggestive postures to sell a woman's night out? Don't these images contradict the whole concept of Ladies Night as originally conceived in North America?

In the Canadian province of Quebec, for example, Ladies Night first emerged as signs on tavern doors in the 1970s, declaring: *Bienvenue aux Dames* ("Women Welcome"). This was in response to feminist demands for "women-only" spaces—both discursive and real. Ironically, however, whereas "women welcome" signs made it possible for women to enter these male bastions, I contend that Ladies Nights have been usurped and re-appropriated by heteronormative culture. Indeed, as others have shown, official and unofficial regulation of leisure spaces and entertainment continues to be mainly organized and defined around masculine values (Campbell, 2000; Demczuck & Remiggi, 1998; Hey, 1986; Morton, 1998). Montreal is no exception; "The Village" and the Red Light District tell us what to expect, what is appropriate, what is desirable, and what is not (England, 1993; Lévesque, 1989, 1995; Myers, 1996; Podmore, 1999). Likewise, as my analysis shows, "ladies night" in Montreal is a means of production of heteronormative night spaces.

The heteronormalization of night space refers to a process by which masculine domination is perpetuated by the sexual objectification of women. Because these flyers sell the experience of "going out" by relying on and reinforcing the male gaze on the female form, much as with prostitutes and erotic dancers, these flyers allow men to consume women as passive sexual objects. These flyers also appropriate feminist scripts in their promotion of Ladies Night, thus creating the illusion of women's agency and pleasure in being sexual objects. As I argue in this chapter, the night scene sees no contradiction between the co-optation of slogans that herald women's empowerment in male spaces and the sexually explicit images of women—imagery that is associated with the devaluation and denigration of women's bodies and identities.

The Heteronormative Construction of Gender

To contextualize this analysis of bar flyers as a medium of heteronormative production, it would help to first consider the social construction of gender (i.e., the construction of women's and men's identities as objects of regulatory discourse; Richardson, 1996). First, gender is relative and in a perpetual state of construction and reconstruction; it is a tool, a technology, "a primary way of signifying relationships of power" (Scott, 1988, cited in Lorber, 1994, p. 5). Thus, the production of gender identities and spaces is never absolute. As De Lauretis (1987) stated:

> The construction of gender goes on today through the various technologies of gender (e.g. cinema) and institutional discourses (e.g. theory) with power to control the field of social meaning and these produce, promote, and "implant" representations of gender. (p. 18)

Furthermore, there are no generic men and women, only "gendered men" and "gendered women" (Harding, 1992, p. 339) and "women" and "men" as categories and products of normative discourses should be considered "artifices" (Irigaray, 1974) or fictions (De Lauretis, 1984).

Second, "gender has to be theorised as a construction of heterosexuality" (Richardson, 1996, p. 47). As Butler (1990, 1993) argued, although heterosexuality is far from "natural," it is always in the process of being produced through repeated performances that imitate its own idealizations and norms, and thereby produce the effects of being natural. Heterosexuality qualifies as normative then, because it is systemic and imposed on society through institutional and cultural arrangements that privilege people for being or appearing to be heterosexual (Rich, 1980). Significantly, however, not only does "the normative status of heterosexuality . . . render any alternative sexualities 'other' and marginal" (Jackson, 1999, p. 163), it is also a discourse "of gender inequality and female subordination, in which androcentric constructions of femininity and masculinity remain dominant" (Bondi, 1992, pp. 166–167).

Given that gender hierarchies regulate female–male relationships as well as female–female and male–male relationships, Ladies Night flyers can be seen as a technology of heteronormativity that uses specific scripts and discourses to produce normative identities. As demonstrated here, heteronormative identities are constructed on these flyers through the *mise-en-scène* of women's bodies and the mimicry of sexual acts.

Ladies Night in Montreal: Women Enter the Night

Montreal is described as a city of pleasure and sexual freedom—*une ville ouverte* (Charpentier, 1999; Gilmore, 1988; Weintraub, 1996) and is perceived by Anglo-

Canadians and Americans as particularly permissive (Dumas, 2001), a city with a Latin flavor, even 'the Orient of North America' (see Said, 1978). Every weekend hundreds of (sex) tourists sweep through the streets to enjoy lap dances in strip clubs or the services of escorts and prostitutes. And the *Québécoises* are perceived as young, promiscuous, and sexually available. This wasn't always the case, however.

Women in Montreal were traditionally under the sway of the church and strongly advised to stay at home except to attend mass (Bellefleur, 1983; Lemieux & Mercier, 1989). Married women were virtually imprisoned in their homes by the pace of childbearing and their domestic responsibilities (Dumont-Johnson, 1982; Lavigne & Pinard, 1977). In the 1940s, however, a growing number of emancipated women, lesbians in particular, but also single working-class women (Weintraub, 1996), began patronizing women's locales at night on a regular basis (Demczuck and Remiggi, 1998). As such, when the full force of the women's liberation hit Québec in the late 1960s, most *Québécoises* were fully ready to take equal ownership of the night by protesting in front of taverns where they were still excluded by law. By 1971, *Bienvenue aux Dames* signs began to appear, marking the beginning of the transformation of the male-centric heterosexual night landscape.

Since then, the presence of women has evolved to include many graphic representations of the female body on storefront signage in Montreal, albeit concentrated primarily along St. Catherine's Street, the principal shopping and entertainment artery in the downtown core. Thus, some would argue that women's liberation and the sexual revolution essentially served to facilitate the resulting commodification of Ladies Nights. On the other hand, many third-wave feminists would adamantly disagree. In fact, the "New Girl Order" challenges what they identify as "the sexual orthodoxies of their Second Wave feminist mothers' narrow and humourless attitudes toward women's and men's sexuality" (Pearce, 1999, p. 271). Moreover, contrary to the insights of the earlier sexual revolution, they perceive sexuality as liberatory in itself and not as a means of liberation. As such, proponents of "Pussy power" argue that everything that has been perceived and defined as oppressive and exploitative by previous feminist movements and theories can be reappropriated as powerful tools. They argue that prostitutes and porn actresses are the truly liberated women, and "pussy," "cunt," and so on, are words of empowerment. Finally, they contend that in clubs, as in consumer culture, women's power is "the ability to attract" (Andersen, 2002, p. 231). To tease out the issues surrounding the representation of women in nightlife flyers, given these two diametrically opposed viewpoints, it is useful to consider them through the lens of heterosexual politics. In other words, what are the social and political implications of women's bodies being used so copiously to promote nightlife in Montreal?

Analyzing Ladies Night Flyers

Between 2000 and 2002, I collected 100 flyers throughout metropolitan Montreal that were intended for a heterosexual audience. They advertised venues of different sizes (from 50 to 2,000 in capacity), that were for the most part well established in the city's mainstream nighttime landscape. Of the 100 flyers collected, 60 were what I would describe as graphically and visually "neutral" because they did not depict human bodies. The remaining 40 portrayed women along a spectrum of sexual explicitness. Among these, I have analyzed flyers that promote Ladies Nights.

As we all know, advertising is composed of both images and copy and both are usually used to nudge consumers toward a preferred reading of ads. As such, the Ladies Night slogans direct us toward a particular reading that will help us to better understand the meaning of Ladies Nights flyers. To do this, I turn to semiotic methodology as it allows for the synthesizing of the information about the text, the viewers/readers' responses, and the cultural context.

Within a feminist framework, I conduct an informal semiotic analysis: I am attentive to clothes, postures, positioning and poses, camera angles, camera as voyeur technical codes such as the framing of the image, and so on. I then look at how these techniques contribute to sexual objectification and commodification of women. By sexual objectification and commodification, I refer to a *mise-en scène* of women's bodies that put "the emphasis on being desirable, not on experiencing desire" (Kilbourne, 1999, p. 148).

The Always-Already Sexually Available Woman

Women shown on Montreal bar flyers give the impression they are always-already welcome to a sexual encounter. Most of them are shown naked in wait, as with the *Angel's* flyer, which shows a topless woman lying on her side smiling seductively. Her eyes are missing from the shot, but her nipples are clearly visible above the copy. Another flyer for *Bed Room* has a woman sitting on a bed, wearing just her underwear and a pair of high heels. The general theme of these flyers is a provocatively dressed woman waiting for a man to join her, and the implication is that she is the prize at the end of the night. These flyers blur the line between fantasy and reality, and in doing so, the act of going out becomes synonymous with sexual conquest.

To support the impression that these sexual encounters are likely, some flyers also multiply the images thus creating the illusion of an unlimited and infinite number of ready young women. On a *Publix* Ladies Night flyer the same woman with hair blowing in the wind is represented identically three times. On yet other flyers, we see the silhouettes or shadows of countless young women.

226 ◆ Chapter 12

Powerful Seductress

Another popular representation of women on Montreal bar flyers is that of the self-confident woman, sexually promiscuous by choice, aware and empowered by her sexual prowess. For example, on a flyer for a chic club called *Bubbles*—"the only bar to serve 14 different kinds of champagne"—a woman stares back intensely, assertively, without a smile. Her face takes up the whole frame and blends with the self-focus background in order to emphasize her steadfast stare and full lips. The caption beside her eyes reads: "Ladies, let yourselves be spoiled." The flyer suggests that at *Bubbles*, independent and liberated women can take a break from their responsibilities and be pampered for a change.

More often, however, self-confident, assertive women are shown as mere body parts—an eye, a full red mouth, cleavage, and so on. The femme fatale has therefore been rendered to a body part to be looked at:

> The sleek, smooth tight butt is a badge, a medal asserting that anal compulsive-ness is an unalloyed virtue. Perfect thighs . . . are achievements to be admired and envied. They signify that the woman has made something of herself, that she has character and class, that she is master of her body, and, thus of her fate. (Douglas, 1988, p. 11)

This is what Goldman (1992) referred to as "feminism tailored to the demands of the commodity forms" (p. 130). Goldman explained that by the late 1980s, advertisers had no choice but to respond to women's condemnation toward representations of themselves in the mass media. As such, marketers created a "feminist version of femininity" by "dissecting the female body into zones of consumption" and assembling "signs which connote independence, participation in the work force, individual freedom and self-control" (Goldman, 1992, p. 132). One example is on a flyer for the bar *Karina*, which features a woman whose torso and face are completely obscured. Only her disproportionately long legs are visible. She wears an evening gown and high heels and her hair is elegantly coiffed. A rose lies at her feet. She appears mature and sophisticated, reminiscent of a 1940s-style glamour, and her posture, stance, and style ooze control and confidence.

Infantilizing and Sexualizing Young Women

On the other hand, as with mainstream advertising, Ladies Night flyers use very young women as models—many of whom are virtual replicas of famous female singers such as Britney Spears. They are dressed almost in uniform, wearing the same sexy short skirts and barely-there halter tops. Notably, this phenomenon has extended beyond just the models and starlets, as staff at nightclubs must now also conform to this dress code and desired image.[2]

Ladies Night flyers also depict women as innocent creatures, naked almost by mistake. Promoting an open bar for women, a flyer for *The Living* portrays a very slender woman with a childish look, her hair loose and messy. She is on her knees, her legs slightly spread apart, and her head is inclined looking up at the camera from the bottom of the frame. She hides her bare breasts with her hands. The entire photo is tinted a hot pink hue and the leopard curtains in the back match her skimpy leopard panties. The flyer epitomizes the infantilisation and sexualisation of young women commonly seen in advertising.

Porn-Chic

As with the "Lolita-tization" of young women in public spaces in general, and on flyers in particular, we also notice a mainstreaming of pornography that has been called "porn-chic" (McNair, 2002). The pornophication of public space is also manifest on bar flyers in the postures, clothing and imaginary scenarios being played out by the female models. A good example of this can be seen on a *Sona* flyer, with its computer-drawn depiction of a woman's genitalia ornamented by water droplets. Apparently, women at *Sona* are already wet with pleasure, ready to be consumed, perpetuating the myth of the eternally sexually available woman.

I have just described how, in a multitude of ways, the representation and sexual objectification of women on bar flyers in Montreal helps to construct heteronormative identities through the powerful male gaze. Now the question remains: Does a female gaze also exist? And if so, would a female gaze produce a passive and eroticised man? To answer this question, I consider the only flyers that feature images of men. The first is for Montreal's only male strip joint—a venue that promotes a Ladies Night truly intended for women! The second is a flyer for *The Living*, which depicts the naked backside of a man. Not surprisingly, it too is advertising a performance by male strippers.

According to Peterson and Dressel (1982), male strip clubs require us to question feminine stereotypes such as sexual passivity and affirm that women "can exhibit an aggressiveness usually associated with the societal stereotype of men" (p. 110). Aggressiveness here means the ability to gaze, the ability to perceive men's bodies as passive erotic sites. But the sexualisation of men's bodies has arisen from the mainstreaming of gay culture and male stripper imagery continues to be influenced by gay aesthetic (Rohlinger, 2002). So, unlike the heterosexual male gaze that consumes the representation of women, the female gaze is met by gay men as objects of sexual desire. Thus, although women can certainly look, they have little space for imagining the male body in a heterosexual situation. Women, therefore, when looking at Ladies Nights flyers are essentially encouraged to consume the woman's body to secure their heteronormative identities.

The illusive so-called power and ownership that women have through expressing their sexuality and gaze is more obvious when one looks at flyers advertising swingers' clubs. These flyers are not (yet) found on sidewalks, but do appear in free newspapers (*Voir, Hour, Ici, Mirror*). Their message is that it is okay to swing, the era of sexual repression has passed and it is time to enjoy safe sex[3] with multiple partners, regardless of their marital status. Furthermore, the "couples-only" rule is no longer hard and fast. Women and men can arrive solo as well: women for free, and men for a variable price between $50 and $80.

A flyer for the swingers' club *L'Orage* depicts the naked torso of a woman reclining. The photo is cropped so that her head is not shown and the emphasis is on her breasts and erect nipples. Again, she is an objectified, sexualized body, fully aroused. The photo looks like a negative, suggesting a mysterious, dark underground atmosphere evocative of the lighting in the club itself. There are no couples represented, so we are left to ask: Who are these flyers actually targeting?

Significantly, Ladies Nights also exist at swingers' clubs[4] and their promotional flyers use strikingly similar aesthetics to those of "regular" bars: they depict sexually objectified models to target *women*. Indeed, rather than encourage women to swing with men, these evenings are actually intended to teach women to engage in lesbian sexual relations. Apparently, although female patrons do not have difficulty swinging with men, many need coaching to swing with other women, and seemingly these Ladies Nights are more like preparatory courses for eventual swinging activities than nights for women's own real pleasure.

Again, the heteronormative construction of sexuality occurs when women are encouraged to desire other women not as a subject of their own sexual orientation—as would be the case with authentic lesbian sexuality—but rather for the pleasure of males. Thus, *L'Orage* makes explicit what is implicit in the majority of bar flyers: "Women are presented as sexual objects whose primary importance is wish fulfillment for men, and men's ideas and men's perceptions of what sex should be like constitute the status quo" (Reichert, Maly, & Zavoina, 1999, p. 129). Ultimately, then, these flyers can also be considered an efficient technology of heteronormative identity formation.

Conclusion

In this chapter, I argued that Montreal bar flyers serve as a technology that produces both a heteronormative night landscape—where going out equates to having sex—and heteronormative identities. Women are represented as sexual objects to be looked at and consumed, men are the invisible actors and voyeurs, and this whole process is sold as empowering to women. This "illusion of feminism," however, is a sham because the apparent gratification derived from being an object of desire actually comes with strong constraints for women. As Andersen (2002) argued, "power and pleasure are so closely fused in advertising that pleasure is assumed from the promise of power and control, not allusions of sexual gratification" (p.

233). Thus, on the Ladies Night flyers I have analyzed, women may appear in charge of their sexuality and open to sexual encounters, but they have no real power. On the contrary, Ladies Night flyers reaffirm men's dominance and control over night spaces through the ongoing sexual objectification of women's bodies. To maintain heteronormativity, women are indeed welcome, provided their sexual identity conforms to the heteronorms and as long as they are passive and sexually available to men.

Notes

1. A flyer is an advertisement usually printed as a leaflet intended for wide distribution.
2. In the free Montreal *Nightlife* magazine (*nl*), three to four pages are dedicated to the fashion-wear of bar and nightclub staff.
3. "Notably, single women need to be prudent before meeting strangers for intimate relations" see http://www.orageclub.com/index2eng.htm
4. A similar "Men's Night" at the time of writing did not exist.

References

Andersen, R. (2002). The thrill is gone: Advertising, gender representation, and the loss of desire. In E. R. Meehan & E. Riordan (Eds.), *Sex and money. Feminism and political economy in the media* (pp. 223–239) Minneapolis & London: University of Minnesota Press.

Bellefleur, M. (1983). Loisir et pouvoir clérical au Québec, 1930–1960. *Loisir et Société/Society and Leisure*, 6(1), 141–165.

Bondi, L. (1992). Gender symbols and urban landscapes. *Progress in Human Geography*, 16(2), 157–170.

Butler, J. (1990). *Gender trouble: Feminism and the subversion of identity.* London & New York: Routledge.

Butler, J. (1993). *Bodies that matter: On the discursive limits of "sex."* New York: Routledge.

Campbell, R. A. (2000). *Sit down and drink your beer. Regulating Vancouver's beer parlours, 1925–1954.* Toronto: University of Toronto Press.

Charpentier, M. (1999). *Broadway north: Musical theatre in Montreal in the 1920s.* Unpublished thesis. Department of History, McGill University, Montréal.

De Lauretis, T. (1984). *Alice doesn't: Feminism, semiotics, cinema.* London: Macmillan.

De Lauretis, T. (1987). *Technologies of gender: Essays on theory, film and fiction.* Bloomington: Indiana University Press.

Demczuck, I., & Remiggi, F. W. (Eds.). (1998). *Sortir de l'ombre. Histoires des communautés lesbienne et gaie de Montréal.* Montréal: Vlb Éditeur.

Douglas, S. (1988). Flex appeal, buns of steel and the body in question. *In these Times, 19,* 7–13.

Dumas, H. (2001). Montréal, la ville préférée des magazines. *La Presse*, 24 août.

Dumont-Johnson, M., & Collectif Clio. (1982). *L'histoire des femmes au Québec depuis quatre siècles*. Montréal: Les Quinze.

England, K. (1993). Suburban pink collar ghettos: The spatial entrapment of women? *Annals of the Association of American Geographers, 83*, 225–242.

Gilmore, J. (1988). *The story of jazz in Montreal*. Montréal: Vehicule Press.

Goldman, R. (1992). *Reading ads socially*. New York: Routledge.

Harding, S. (1992). The instability of the analytical categories of feminist theory. In H. Crowley & S. Himmelheit (Eds.), *Knowing women. Feminism as knowledge* (pp. 338–354). Cambridge: Polity Press.

Hey, V. (1986). *Patriarchy and pub culture*. London: Tavistock.

Irigaray, L. (1974). *Spéculum de l'autre femme*. Paris: Editions de Minuit.

Jackson, S. (1999). *Heterosexuality in question*. London: Sage.

Jordan, J. T. (2000). *Searching for the perfect beat: Flyer designs of the American rave scene*. New York: Earth Program Ltd.

Kilbourne, J. (1999). *Can't buy my love: How advertising changes the way we think and feel*. New York: Simon & Schuster.

Lavigne, M., & Pinard, Y. (1977). *Les femmes dans la société québécoise*. Montréal: Boréal Express.

Lemieux, D., & Mercier, L. (1989). *Les femmes au tournant du siècle 1880–1940. Les âges de la vie, maternité et quotidien*. Montréal: I.Q.R.S.

Lévesque, A. (1989). *La norme et les déviantes: Des femmes du Québec pendant l'entre-deux guerres*. Montréal: Éditions du Remue-Ménage.

Lévesque, A. (1995). *Résistance et transgression études en histoire des femmes du Québec*. Montréal: Éditions du Remue-Ménage.

Lorber, J. (1994). *Paradoxes of gender*. New Haven, CT: Yale University Press.

McCall, T. (2001). *This is not a rave. In the shadow of a subculture*. Toronto: Insomniac Press.

McNair, B. (2002). *Striptease culture: Sex, media and the democratization of desire*. London: Routledge.

McRobbie, A. (1994). *Postmodernism and popular culture*. London: Routledge.

McRobbie, A. (2000). *Feminism and youth culture*. New York: Routledge. (Original work published 1991).

Meehan, E. R., & Riordan, E. (Eds.). (2002). *Sex and money: Feminism and political economy in the media*. Minneapolis-London: University of Minnesota Press.

Morton, S. (1998). A man's city: Montreal, gambling and male space in the 1940s. In T. Myers, K. Boyer, M. A. Poutanen, & S. Watt (Eds.), *Power, place and identity. Historical studies of social regulation in Quebec* (pp. 169–182). Montréal: Montréal History Group.

Myers, T. (1996). *Criminal women and bad girls: Regulation and punishment in Montréal: 1890–1930*. Unpublished thesis, Department of History, McGill University, Montréal.

Pearce, K. C. (1999). Third wave feminism and cybersexuality: The cultural backlash of the new girl order. In M. G. Carstaphen & S. C. Zavoina (Eds.), *Sexual rethoric. Media perspectives on sexuality, gender, and identity* (pp. 271–282). Westport, CT: Greenwood.

Petersen, P., & Dressel, P. L. (1987). Equal time for women: Social notes on the male strip show. In E. D. Salamon & B. W. Robinson (Eds.), *Gender roles. Doing what comes naturally?* (pp. 105–118). Toronto: Methuen. (Original work published 1982)

Pini, M. (1997). Women and the early British rave scene. In A. McRobbie (Ed.), *Back to reality? Social experience and cultural studies* (pp. 152–169). Manchester: Manchester University Press.

Podmore, J. (1999). *St. Lawrence Blvd. as third city: Place, gender, and difference along Montreal's "Main."* Unpublished thesis. Department of Geography, McGill University, Montréal.

Reichert, T., Maly, K. R., & Zavoina, S. C. (1999). Designed for (male) pleasure: The myth of lesbian chic in mainstream advertising. In M. G Carstaphen & S. C. Zavoina (Eds.), *Sexual rethoric. Media perspectives on sexuality, gender, and identity* (pp. 123–133). Wesport, CT: Greenwood.

Rich, A. (1980). Compulsory heterosexuality and lesbian existence. *Signs, 5*(4), 631–660.

Richardson, D. (1996). *Theorising heterosexuality. Telling it straight.* Buckingham & Philadelphia: Open University Press.

Rohlinger, D. R. (2002). Eroticizing men: Cultural influences on advertising and male objectification. *Sex Role, 46,* 61–74.

Said, E. (1978). *Orientalism.* New York: Pantheon Books

Scott, J. (1988). *Gender and the politics of history.* New York: Columbia University Press.

Thornton, S. (1995). *Club cultures. Music, media and subcultural capital* (pp. 69–73). Cambridge: Polity Press.

Thomas, H. (1993). An-other voice: Young women dancing and talking. In H. Thomas (Ed.), *Dance, gender, and culture.* Basingstoke: Macmillan.

Weintraub, W. (1996). *City unique. Montreal days and nights in the 1940s and '50s.* Toronto: M&S.

Contributors

Sue Abel is a Senior Lecturer in the Department of Film, Television and Media Studies and the Department of Māori Studies at the University of Auckland, New Zealand. Her research interests are in the areas of race, indigeneity and the media, journalism studies, advertising and consumer culture. Her PhD "'It's Girls being Girls': Young Women Reading Gender in Advertising" explored postfeminism and its implications.

Jane Caputi is a professor of Womens Studies at Florida Atlantic University in Boca Raton. She is the author of *The Age of Sex Crime* (Bowling Green University Popular Press, 1987), *Gossips, Gorgons and Crones: The Fates of the Earth* (Bear & Co., 1993), and *Goddesses and Monsters: Women, Myth, Power and Popular Culture* (Popular Press, 2004). She also collaborated on *Webster's First New Intergalactic Wickedary of the English Language* (Beacon Press, 1987) with Mary Daly. Most recently, she completed an educational documentary, *The Pornography of Everyday Life*, distributed by Berkeley Media, www.berkeleymedia.com.

Fabienne Darling-Wolf is Associate Professor of Journalism in the School of the Journalism and Theater at Temple University in Philadelphia. She also teaches and supervises graduate students in the school's Mass Media and Communication Doctoral Program. Dr. Darling-Wolf's research focuses on processes of mediated cultural influence and negotiation in a global context, paying particular attention to how such processes intersect with gendered, racial and ethnic identity formation.

Marjan de Bruin is Director and Senior Lecturer at the Caribbean Institute of Media and Communication (CARIMAC) at the University of the West Indies, Mona, Jamaica. Her research areas are: communication for social and behaviour change; gender and journalism; media violence and its effects on children. In recent years she has been co-chair of the section Gender and Communication of the International Association of Media and Communication Research (IAMCR) of which she has also been a vice-president.

Dawn Heinecken is Associate Professor of Women's and Gender Studies at the University of Louisville and is the author of *The Warrior Women of Television: A Feminist Cultural Analysis of the New Female Body in Popular Media* (Peter Lang, 2003) and, with Vickie Shields, a co-writer of *Measuring Up: How Advertising Affects Self-Image* (University of Pennsylvania Press, 2002). Her publications have focused on critical cultural analysis of gender and body image representations in popular culture, including professional wrestling, romance novels, fan fiction, and the marketing of "adult home novelty" products to women.

Todd Holden is Professor of Mediated Sociology at Tohoku University, in Sendai, Japan. His writings embrace Japanese society, social theory, semiology, advertising, sports, gender, identity, nationalism, and political communication. His most recent book was *medi@sia: media/tion in and out of context* (Routledge, 2006). Recent chapters have addressed: Japanese digital youth; Japanese Internet dating; conceptions of heroes in Japanese culture; and masculinities in Japanese TV food shows. His current work centers on Japan's sport globalization, and also the engineering of emotions and cultural identity on Japanese TV. He publishes a regular column on Japanese popular culture as well as a Travelblog for the e-zine PopMatters.

Damla Isik is Assistant Professor of Anthropology at Western Connecticut State University. She holds a PhD in Anthropology from The University of Arizona (2007) with a Graduate Certificate in Women's Studies. Her teaching and research interests include gender, globalization and labor politics in Turkey and the Middle East; NGO organizing and poverty alleviation; transnational feminisms; rhetoric, representation, and media studies. She is currently doing research on the gendered ethics of poverty alleviation projects in NGOs in Turkey and working on a manuscript titled, "Woven Assemblages: Informal Economy and Women's Labor Politics in Turkey."

Aurélie Lebrun is a feminist and has worked on gender in clubs and bars since her first years of University. Her research focuses on the social construction of gender and the norms of heterosexuality. Her PhD thesis in social geography looks at strategies of resistance and conformity to normative heterosexuality by single patrons of cruising bars. Since 2003, she has worked on prostitution and trafficking in women. She is a founding member of la CLES (Concertation des luttes contre l'exploitation sexuelle) and of CATHII (Comité d'action contre la traite interne et internationale).

Anita T. Nowak has been pursuing her PhD in Education at McGill University, Canada. She earned her MA in Communication Studies at Nanying Technological University in Singapore, where she analysed magazine representations of plus-sized women. She is a co-editor of *Rethinking Media Education: Critical Pedagogy and Identity Politics* (Hampton Press, 2007).

Ila Patel is a Professor at the Institute of Rural Management, Anand (IRMA), India. She holds a PhD in International Development Education and MA in Communication from Stanford University (U.S.A.). She teaches courses on Development and Rural Communication and Gender and Development at the graduate level. Her academic specializations are adult literacy and basic education, broadcast media in development, and gender and development, which she examines from the perspective of political economy and sociology. She has published widely in several Indian and international academic journals, and written several monographs and reports on various projects in education and development communication in India.

Birgit Pretzsch is currently teaching English Literature at the Johann-Wolfgang-Goethe University Frankfurt, Germany. She holds a Master's degree in Women's Studies (Trinity College, Dublin) and is in the process of finishing her PhD dissertation on "Feminisms, Bodies and Cyberpunk: Theories of Embodiment and Subjectivity in Bruce Sterling's Novel Holy Fire."

Vickie Rutledge Shields, PhD, is the Dean of the College of Social and Behavioral Sciences and a Professor of Communication Studies at Eastern Washington University in Cheney, Washington, USA. She researches in the areas of cultural and critical approaches to the study of media and popular culture; gendered images and audiences of film, television and advertising and the relationship between media images and women's body discipline. She is the author of *Measuring Up: How Advertising Affects Self-Image* with Dawn Heinecken. Dr. Shields' recent research appears in the *Journal of Visual Literacy, Text and Performance Quarterly*, the *Electronic Journal of Communication* and the *European Journal of Cultural Studies*.

Wiwik Sushartami is a graduate student at the Anthropology Department, Leiden University, the Netherlands. Her present research concerns media, women and cultural studies in Post-Suharto Indonesia. She has been part of the Indonesia in Transition Project, a collaborative project between the Royal Netherlands Academy of Arts and Social Sciences (KNAW) and Social Science Faculties in several Indonesian Universities (2001–20005). The piece that she contributes in this collection is based on her MA thesis written during her years as a master student at the National University of Singapore, Singapore (1998–2000).

Isabelle Loring Wallace is Associate Professor of Contemporary Art at the Lamar Dodd School of Art at the University of Georgia in Athens. Her research attends to broad philosophical questions about the nature of representation and subjectivity in the West, and her publications have covered a wide range of artists and objects in an effort to address these issues: Edouard Manet, Marcel Duchamp, Jenny Saville, the Chapman Brothers, Paul Pfeiffer and, most intensively, Jasper Johns, the subject of her book-in-progress. Professor Wallace is also co-editing, with Jennie Hirsh, an anthology entitled *Contemporary Art and Classical Myth*.

Author Index

Subject Index

pornography *(continued)*
  worldview, 66
  worldview challenge, 43–60
Pornography of Everyday Life, 66
Positionality, 18
Postmodern notions, 5
Post-World War II middle-class American
    women, 19
Potency, 5
Power, 3–4, 19, 46–47
  enhancement, 103
P-Poppin (Ludicris), 43
Pre-history, 34
Primordial era, 34
Prison, 52, 56, 56f, 57f
Promotional flyers, 4
Prügl, Elisabeth, 131
Psycho, 51
Psychoanalysis, 53
Psychological abuse, 64
PT Indonesia Satellite Corporation
    (Indosat), 153
Public-domestic dichotomy, 146–147
Public service announcements, 7
Publix Ladies Night flyer, 225
Purchasing, 16
Purdah system, 167–168, 179
Pure and dirty, 59–61
Puritanical worldview, 45
Purity
  distorted notions, 61
Pussy
  abuse, 43
  name calling, 52
  power, 224

Racism, 58
Rader, Dennis, 58
Radical feminist perspective, 4
Ranking, 19
Ranma 1/2, 105
Rape, 51
  East Timor, 150
  gang, 49f
  mass, 150

myth, 12
Nature, 62
pornography, 49
silence, 50
silent victims, 50
Rapid rural appraisal (RRA), 163
Reality control, 64
Reality theory, 86
Relative size, 93
Release, 96
Religion, 62
Representation, 11–28, 85–86
  definition, 17
  unleashing meaning, 18
Representation and the Media, 202
Reproduction, 7, 203, 216–217
  a-sexual, 34
  liberation, 36
  rights, 210
Resistance-domination dichotomy, 116
Rethinking single women, 156–157
Ridgeway, Gary L., 51–52
Ritual
  degradation, 44f
  gender behavioral practices, 19
  subordination, 19, 93
Roadshow magazine, 118
Roberts, Charles C., 67
RRA. *See* Rapid rural appraisal (RRA)
Rumsfeld, Donald, 56

Said, Edward, 129
Saint Paul, 50
Salary man, 106
Sameness, 4, 29–42
Science of signs, 3
Screen magazine, 118
Seat, 77–78
Second Sex (de Beauvoir), 13
Seductress, 226
Self-determination, 16
Self-doubt, 17
Self-empowerment, 16
Self-image, 114
Self-objectification, 16

Breinigsville, PA USA
25 October 2009

226423BV00002B/28/P